E. PAULINE JOHNSON, TEKAHIONWAKE

Collected Poems and Selected Prose

E. Pauline Johnson (Tekahionwake) was a Native advocate of part-Mohawk ancestry, an independent woman during the period of first-wave feminism, a Canadian nationalist who also advocated strengthening the link to imperial England, a popular and versatile prose writer, and one of modern Canada's best-selling poets. Johnson longed to see the publication of a complete collection of her verse, but that wish remained unfulfilled during her life. Nine decades after her death, the first complete collection of all of Pauline Johnson's known poems, many painstakingly culled from newspapers, magazines, and archives, is now available.

In response to the current recognition of Johnson's historical position as an immensely popular and influential figure of the late nineteenth and early twentieth centuries, this volume also presents a representative selection of her prose, including fiction about Native-settler relations, journalism about women and recreation, and discussions of gender roles and racial stereotypes.

Edited by Carole Gerson and Veronica Strong-Boag, authors of the enthusiastically received *Paddling Her Own Canoe: Times and Texts of E. Pauline Johnson (Tekahionwake)*, this collection exhibits the same impeccable scholarship and is essential to a full understanding of Johnson as a major Canadian writer and cultural figure.

CAROLE GERSON is a professor of English at Simon Fraser University.

VERONICA STRONG-BOAG is a professor of Women's Studies and Educational Studies at the University of British Columbia.

E. Pauline Johnson, Tekahionwake

Collected Poems and Selected Prose

INTRODUCED AND EDITED BY
Carole Gerson and Veronica Strong-Boag

UNIVERSITY OF TORONTO PRESS
Toronto Buffalo London

© University of Toronto Press Incorporated 2002
Toronto Buffalo London
Printed in Canada

ISBN 0-8020-3670-8 (cloth)
ISBN 0-8020-8497-4 (paper)

Printed on acid-free paper

National Library of Canada Cataloguing in Publication Data

Johnson, E. Pauline (Emily Pauline), 1861–1913.
E. Pauline Johnson (Tekahionwake) : collected poems and selected prose

Includes bibliographical references and index.
ISBN 0-8020-3670-8 (bound)   ISBN 0-8020-8497-4 (pbk.)

I. Gerson, Carole   II. Strong-Boag, Veronica Jane, 1947–.   III. Title.

PS8469.O283A17 2002   C811'.4   C2001-903606-X
PR9199.2.J64A17 2002

University of Toronto Press acknowledges the financial assistance to its
publishing program of the Canada Council for the Arts and the Ontario
Arts Council.

This book has been published with the help of a grant from the Humanities
and Social Sciences Federation of Canada, using funds provided by the Social
Sciences and Humanities Research Council of Canada.

University of Toronto Press acknowledges the financial support for its pub-
lishing activities of the Government of Canada through the Book Publishing
Industry Development Program (BPIDP).

Contents

II. The Prolific Years: 1889–1898

III. Later Years: 1899–1913

IV. Anonymous and Pseudonymous Poems

PROSE

Illustrations follow page xxxii

Acknowledgments

The acknowledgments to *Paddling Her Own Canoe*, our critical and historical study of Pauline Johnson that preceded this edition of her poetry and collected prose, thank a multitude of friends, colleagues, e-mail acquaintances, librarians, archivists, and students for their assistance and support. This volume is indebted to a similar 'Pauline Patrol,' who answered questions, hunted down references, and assisted with preparation of the manuscript. We remain grateful to everyone who helped with *Paddling* (which represents the research underpinning this book). The receipt of the Raymond Klibansky award for *Paddling* both recognizes the collaborative nature of our project, and pays tribute to Pauline herself.

We hope we have remembered everyone who contributed in some way to this volume. We have enjoyed participating in a community of Johnson researchers that includes Sheila Johnston, whose *Buckskin and Broadcloth* pioneered the recovery of Johnson's uncollected writing, Charlotte Grey, whose biographical research has uncovered new resources, and two authors of recent dissertations on Johnson – Christine Marshall and Erika Aigner-Varoz. For enabling our access to holdings that concern Johnson we again thank Anne Goddard and staff at the National Archives of Canada, Bernadine Dodge and staff at Trent University Archives, and Ann Carroll at the City of Vancouver Archives. We are especially grateful to Paula Whitlow at Chiefswood Historical Site and Tom Hill and Judy Harris at the Woodland Cultural Centre for giving us access to Johnson's scrapbook. The ongoing cooperation and support of Carl Spadoni and Renu Barrett greatly facilitated our use of the Johnson Collection at McMaster University. We also thank Don Stewart, of McLeod's Books in Vancouver, for allowing us to see books and documents in his possession, and Ralph Stanton for adding these Johnson materials to the Special Collections holdings of the Simon Fraser University Library. Assistance from the inter-library loans division of the SFU Library was essential throughout this project. We are very pleased that John B. Wilkes gave us permission to publish the manuscript poem that Pauline Johnson wrote to Gerald Wilkes, the little boy who later became his father.

Over the years, we received help with the multitude of preliminary and subsequent tasks involved in preparing the manuscript – typing, scanning, proof-reading, indexing, computer assistance, and miscellaneous library errands – from Kim Doucette, Nancy Earle, Sandra Even, Janet Friskney, Jo Hinchliffe, Marie Howton, Wendy Plain, Alison Rukavina, Jenn Suratos, Kristin Schop, and Sandra Walker. Katrina Harrack's attentive final proofreading caught many elusive typographical errors. At the University of Toronto Press, we are grateful to Jill McConkey, Siobhan McMenemy, Frances Mundy, and our copy-editor, Diane Mew, for their responsiveness, hard work, and consistent good humour.

For various references to Pauline Johnson that might otherwise have escaped our attention, we are grateful to Gwendolyn Davies, Paul Delany, Janet Friskney, Jenny Litster, Holly Pike, and Mary Rubio. For conversation and advice, we thank Sandra Alston, Jean Barman, Gillian Creese, Jo Fiske, Martin Gerson, Sneja Gunew, Jack Little, Michael Marker, Angus McLaren, Arlene Tigar McLaren, Larissa Petrillo, Chris Ross, Blanca Schorcht, Daphne Strong-Boag, and Tom Vincent.

Our initial research on Pauline Johnson was supported by grants from SSHRC and the Hampton Place Fund at the University of British Columbia. This volume was completed with additional aid from the SSHRC Institutional Grants program at Simon Fraser University.

Introduction:
'The Firm Handiwork of Will'

From the 1880s, when her poems first began to appear in Ontario news-papers and magazines, until her spectacular funeral in Vancouver on 10 March 1913, Pauline Johnson captivated English-speaking Canada. A charismatic performer and beloved author, she self-consciously drew on her part-Mohawk heritage to create a public image that fostered her role as spokesperson for Native concerns; in the words of a close friend, 'her unique position as the one Canadian of mixed white and Indian blood articulate in English verse was a source of inexhaustible interest to her own mind.'[1] Our earlier volume, *Paddling Her Own Canoe: The Times and Texts of E. Pauline Johnson (Tekahionwake)*, examines the compli-cated issues of race and gender that inform Johnson's life and work. In establishing her historical and cultural significance, we argue in that book that her poetry and prose have been unjustly neglected. This vol-ume of her collected poems and selected prose, more complete than any yet available, offers readers the opportunity to reconsider one of Canada's most significant writers. Johnson's verse, fiction, and non-fic-tion are ultimately the abiding legacy of a Mohawk-Canadian woman who tested the boundaries of what it meant to be Mixed-race and female in the imperial and patriarchal world of Europe and North America during the decades after the creation of the new Dominion of Canada in 1867.

Johnson's lifetime of 1861 to 1913 spans the period from Confedera-tion to the eve of the Great War. This critical era in Canada's history saw change and conflict as the country evolved from a collection of separate colonies to full-fledged nationhood. Although author L.M. Montgom-ery was later to fantasize that 'a man or woman who was born about 1830 and died in 1913 would have lived his whole life in what was the happiest period of the world's entire history to date,'[2] such nostalgia overlooks how Canada was swept not only by the major international movements of the age, but also by unique local upheavals. Crises wrought by the continuing dispossession of the Métis and First Nations, as well as by urbanization, immigration, and industrialization in general, mobilized the native-born and immigrants in petitions, associations, strikes, and even the occasional pitched battle. Political consensus on crucial national issues was in short supply as women denounced governments and laws that ignored their interests, Aboriginal peoples protested the denial of their rights, workers insisted that the rich reaped unfair advantage, and individual provinces reconsidered Confederation. As political elites cobbled together problematic solutions, optimistic patriots sought to create unifying visions of the new nation.

After Confederation, nationalist myth-makers of every sort set about claiming Canada, in the process often highlighting the United Empire Loyalists, the War of 1812, Laura Secord, the 'true North,' and British fair play in the treatment of natives. The popular anthems 'O Canada' (first sung in English in 1901) and 'The Maple Leaf Forever' invoked a romantic sense of patriotism to rally Canadians to an emerging identity. While most efforts to imagine the new nationality affirmed racial stereotypes and elevated some groups over others, there were always currents of opinion that posited a nationality more inclusive of all social classes, of women as well as men, and of a variety of Europeans and Aboriginals. From such a perspective Canada, as the influential historian W.L. Morton would later claim, promised to become a 'unity under the Crown admitting of a thousand diversities,'[3] in contrast to the monolithic melting-pot chosen as the prevailing emblem by the rebellious republic to the south. For Pauline Johnson and some members of her generation, who grew to adulthood in a climate of idealism, the age appeared one of unparalleled opportunity. Perhaps the twentieth century, to paraphrase Sir Wilfrid Laurier, would indeed belong to an unprecedented range of Canadians.

Johnson's Life and Career

Emily Pauline Johnson was born on 10 March 1861 at Chiefswood, the substantial family home on the Six Nations Reserve outside the town of Brantford, in Canada West, now southern Ontario. She was the youngest of the four children of George Henry Martin Johnson (1816–84) and Emily Howells Johnson (1824–98). Her father, a traditional chief, was the son of an elite Mohawk family which had long resisted European sovereignty. Her English-born mother also counted dissenters among her kin – Quaker abolitionists who emigrated to the United States to join the American struggle against slavery. The couple met when Emily joined her elder sister, Eliza Howells, the wife of Reverend Adam Elliot, the Anglican missionary at Six Nations. George, a handsome young man fluent in several Six Nations languages, was working as the church translator. Their marriage in 1853 attracted considerable attention, only slowly overcoming family disapproval on both sides. While such matches were not unknown on the reserve or elsewhere, most Mixed-race unions involved Native women and White men. The reverse, together with the distinguished genealogy of both wife and husband, sparked particular curiosity in an increasingly race-conscious society.

While Emily Howells Johnson ensured that her Mixed-race household would survive its inevitable notoriety by schooling her children in English middle-class culture and manners, respect for their Native heritage, also part of their training, was reinforced by Mohawk kin, notably Pauline's paternal grandfather, the distinguished chief Sakayenwaraton, or John Smoke Johnson (1792–1885). During the second half of the nineteenth century, the Six Nations community itself was vibrant but divided about how to address mounting pressure from Anglo-Canadian society. Confident Mohawks such as George and John Smoke Johnson led Christians who anticipated finding an advantageous accommodation with the Euro-Canadian power structure. Others, notably traditionalists among the Onondaga, viewed such Mohawk intermediaries and the surrounding settlers with considerable suspicion.[4] Such divisions meant that Emily and her children were never fully incorporated within the Iroquois community. On the reserve itself they lived apart at Chiefswood, a stately home on the eastern bank of the Grand River, set on a two-hundred-acre estate purchased by George at the time of his marriage. A telling indicator of these cultural tensions is that none of the Johnson children would remain at Six Nations after their relatively protected life abruptly ended in 1884 with the death of their father, following a beating by the White liquor traders he had opposed.

After the subsequent loss of Chiefswood, twenty-two-year-old Pauline moved into a modest Brantford dwelling with her mother and elder sister Evelyn. While the independent-minded Evelyn took various office jobs, Pauline followed the common practice of impoverished gentlewomen in the nineteenth century, and picked up her pen. From 1884 through to December 1891, while enjoying an active social life (presumably waiting for marriage), winning recognition for her canoeing skills, and cultivating a reputation as a bohemian free spirit, she published some sixty poems in various North American serials. The majority appeared in *Saturday Night* and *The Week*, the dominion's leading magazines, based in Toronto. By 1890 she had branched out into prose, with stories and sketches in the *Brantford Courier*, the *Brantford Expositor*, *Saturday Night*, the *Dominion Illustrated* (Montreal), *Outing Magazine* (New York), and the *Weekly Detroit Free Press*. With the exception of her first few poems and sketches, all her work, including the two poems selected by W.D. Lighthall for inclusion in his important 1889 anthology, *Songs of the Great Dominion*, appeared under the name 'E. Pauline Johnson.' While effectively eliding her Native heritage for all but the knowledgeable, this signature boldly announced her female identity.

Writing to a friend in 1890, Johnson specified her ambitions:

> I am willing to consent to anything legitimate, that will mean success in the end. Not that I ever expect that success to mean Fame. I have not the ability ever to command a wreath of bays, but I have a double motive in all my work and all my strivings – one is to upset the Indian Extermination and noneducation theory – in fact to stand by my blood and my race. The other is that I am not a millionairess – aye, I am as the proverbial Church Mouse. Someday I hope to see something of the great world – to travel in the Holy Land – the old world – the Rockies – the far west, and to do this one must work.[5]

By the end of her relatively short life she had achieved most of her goals: she was famous, she had countered prevailing negative views of the Indian, and she had travelled widely, although she was never to reach the Holy Land.

In January 1892 Johnson's career took a decisive turn in response to an invitation from Frank Yeigh, a leading cultural nationalist, to participate in a Canadian Literary Evening organized by the Young Liberal Club of Toronto. Already attuned to the stage as a performer in occasional amateur theatricals, Johnson proved the star of the event with her recitation of 'A Cry from an Indian Wife.' This poem, first published in 1885 in *The Week*, served as a dramatic indictment of the mistreatment of the prairie tribes during the second Northwest rebellion. Yeigh and Johnson quickly capitalized on enthusiasm for an attractive performer and liberal guilt about the repression of the First Nations. Within a few short weeks she was launched on a performing career in which she dramatized her writings, and which would see her celebrated variously as a Canadian Boadicea and a Mohawk Princess.[6] While not a public supporter of woman suffrage (so far as we yet know), she nonetheless was later to remind her English readers, in 'The Lodge of the Law-makers' (reprinted here for the first time), that women wielded considerable power in the Iroquois Confederacy. Pauline Johnson can now be seen as one of Canada's turn-of-the-century bright New Women, part of the generation of her sex who pursued independent lives as they contested the boundaries of respectable femininity.

The autumn of 1892 found Johnson busily designing a costume for the stage. Her asymmetrical buckskin dress, short enough to reveal ankles chastely enclosed in leggings, was embellished with visible symbols of Native culture, including fur pelts, Iroquois silver medallions, wampum belts, and her father's hunting knife. From Ernest Thompson Seton, the well-known naturalist, she later acquired a necklace of bear claws; one photograph shows her with a feather in her hair and a necklace of elks' teeth. In 1895 she obtained a scalp from a chief of the Blackfoot.[7] According to her sister Evelyn, the original buckskin fringe serving as the right sleeve came from the Northwest, and the 'rest of her Indian costume and silver brooches were copied from a picture which we had of Minnehaha,' Longfellow's fictional companion to Hiawatha. Johnson became well known for wearing her Indian dress for the first half of her concerts and an elegant evening gown for the second. This provocative performance of the hybrid inheritance of Canada and the British Empire, our understanding of which has been enhanced by recent work on gender theory,[8] took Johnson far from Ontario, to Canada's east and west coasts and beyond, to the United States and England.

In her first season in small-town Ontario, Johnson shared the program with various local musicians and elocutionists. During the fall of 1892 she teamed up with Owen Smily, the first of her male performance partners, touring the northeastern United States and arriving in London, England in the spring of 1894. Here, in addition to entertaining British audiences and journalists, she furthered relations with influential patrons, including the Duke of Connaught, Queen Victoria's son and adopted chief of the Six Nations, and Theodore Watts-Dunton, the powerful literary critic. Most importantly, while in London she arranged for the publication of her first book, *The White Wampum*, its very title invoking peace between Europeans and Iroquois. Dedicating the volume to both her parents, Johnson linked her two cultures through their most sanctified modes of communication:

> As wampum is to the Redman, so to the Poet are his songs; chiselled alike from that which is the purest of his possessions, woven alike with meaning into belt and book, fraught alike with the corresponding message of peace, the breathing of tradition, the value of more than coin, and the seal of ownership.

This elegant volume of verse was issued in 1895 by the avant-garde British publisher John Lane, whose list included Oscar Wilde, Aubrey Beardsley, and the *Yellow Book*. In the English metropolis the young colonial learned to polish her display of the exotic insider, not unlike other imperial half-castes described by Antoinette Burton and Judith Walkowitz in their studies of British relations with the Indian subcontinent.[9] Like many Canadians of her time, she also began to refine her own nationalist sensibilities. In line with the imperialist components of Canadian nationalism analysed by Carl Berger in *Sense of Power*, Johnson should be understood as a patriot who regarded the dominion as the rightful heir of a powerful empire. Her ideal Canada and Britain were high-minded and fair dealing, forming an inclusive international community that valued both Natives and Europeans. As a woman who carried letters of introduction from Canada's vice-regal couple, Lord and Lady Aberdeen (herself a leading international feminist of the day), Johnson had travelled a long way from her modest beginnings on small-town Ontario stages. While she would never abandon her fascination with empire, she later acknowledged many of its failures. Her romantic idealism held both imperial Britain and its offspring dominion to high standards.

Upon her return to Canada, Johnson extended her compass to include Vancouver in September 1894 and the Maritime provinces in 1900. After the demise of her well-publicized engagement to Charles Drayton of Winnipeg in 1898–9, she settled into her enduring stage partnership with Walter McRaye, many years her junior. This light-weight but genial entertainer specialized in the poems of William Henry Drummond, whose popular anecdotes, given in an accented dialect, were once regarded as an affectionate portrayal of French-Canadian speech.[10] The two friends worked together until her retirement from touring in 1909 and remained close for the remainder of her life. McRaye subsequently served as her champion until his own death in 1946.

Johnson's travels introduced her to Native communities across the country, deepening the pan-Indian feelings revealed in her earlier work. Equally significant was her acquaintance with a generation of pioneering women journalists and activists, such as Nellie McClung, the prominent suffragist. Such relationships helped sustain a performer who brought her advocacy of Natives and New Women to potentially unfriendly audiences in North America and England. Her travels across the prairies and to the Pacific coast, which included visits to Indian residential schools and contact with the region's Mixed-race families, helped transform the eastern-bred entertainer into a western enthusiast. Like her friend McClung, Johnson believed she saw the basis of a more inclusive nationality in the lands annexed to Canada after Confederation. In 1903 she issued her second book of poems, *Canadian Born*, with a preface that makes explicit her vision of an egalitarian nation:

Let him who is Canadian born regard these poems as written to himself – whether he be my paleface compatriot who has given to me his right hand of good fellowship, in the years I have appealed to him by pen and platform, or whether he be that dear Red brother of whatsoever tribe or Province, it matters not – White Race and Red are one if they are but Canadian born.

However, the appearance of this new volume did not signal sustained literary activity. In fact, her writing of poetry had abruptly declined in the mid-1890s, and virtually ceased by the turn of the century. The verses which appeared sporadically during the last phase of Johnson's career lack the passion of her love poetry, the advocacy of her Indian poetry, and the vigour of her nature lyrics. Despite the prevailing elevation of poetry above other genres during her lifetime and afterwards, a hierarchy which she professed to accept,[11] Johnson's image as a 'poetess' is difficult to sustain in view of the diminution of her output after 1895. The extensive and generally positive reception of *The White Wampum* did not inspire outpourings from her pen. Indeed, the reverse seems true: by 1895, two-thirds of her lifetime output of about 165 poems had appeared in print, the majority in newspapers and magazines. In the years between *The White Wampum* and *Canadian Born*, she wrote or published only thirty new poems, many quite light or occasional. Just twenty poems date from her final decade (1904–13).

After the century turned, a taxing performing schedule and the struggle to construct a life of single independence impeded substantial publication until 1906–7. Johnson's meeting with Su-á-pu-luck (Joe Capilano) and other British Columbia chiefs in London, as they presented their land claims to King Edward in 1906, helped shift her attention from Ontario and the prairies to the Pacific coast. By the time she settled in Vancouver in 1909, Johnson was welcomed by the Squamish as a sympathetic celebrity. During these last years she renewed her writing life and her finances as a contributor of prose to three major serials: the *Boys' World* and the *Mother's Magazine*, both issued by the David Cook Publishing Company of Elgin, Illinois, and later, the *Vancouver Province Magazine.*

A bustling young metropolis, Vancouver was enlivened by a vigorous and congenial community of writers and activists, busy clubwomen, and a determined Native presence. For a Mixed-race New Woman, the combination was inspirational. Until morphine could no longer dull the pain of inoperable breast cancer, Johnson's pen raced. Before she died on 7 March 1913, three days before her fifty-second birthday, Pauline was sustained financially and emotionally by a so-called friendship plot hatched by the city's feminist and press elite.[12] A selection of her Native legends from the *Province Magazine* was published in 1911 as *Legends of Vancouver*, to raise money for her support. Similarly, some of her poems were collected in *Flint and Feather*, later misleadingly subtitled her 'Complete Poems.' In 1913, shortly after her death, friends ensured that her outstanding debts were paid by the profits from two volumes of her periodical stories, *The Moccasin Maker* and *The Shagganappi.*

Johnson's Publishing History

A brief account of Johnson's publishing history enhances understanding of both the production and reception of her work. British critic Theodore Watts-Dunton, who wrote for *The Athenaeum*, an important London periodical, initiated imperial critics' preoccupation with her exotic parentage in his influential review of W.D. Lighthall's *Songs of the Great Dominion*, which gave disproportionate emphasis to Johnson's lineage as a source of interest.[13] She would never escape this stereotype of the colonial Other. The arrangement and design of her first book, with its exoticized Native imagery, suggest that British editors bear significant responsibility for the subsequent construction of the poet by audiences and by Johnson herself. When *The White Wampum* appeared, the distinguished American anthropologist Horatio Hale, himself a good friend of the Johnson family, shrewdly observed that 'The first inclination of the reader will be to look in her poems for some distinctive Indian traits, and to be disappointed if these are not strikingly apparent. Her compositions will be judged as those of a "wild Indian girl," and not those of a well-bred and accomplished young Canadian lady with a dash of Indian blood, such as she really is.'[14]

Of the approximately one hundred poems Johnson had written before the end of 1894, only a dozen refer to First Nations topics. Eight of these are among the thirty-six selected by her publisher, John Lane. More importantly, seven Indian poems are placed at the beginning of *The White Wampum*, thus casting a Native aura over the subsequent verses. This volume marks Johnson's first significant use of 'Tekahionwake,' the only word to appear on the book's front cover. Here, a sense of the primitive is visually enhanced by both colour and image: the dark red-brown cloth (the colour of dried blood) is decorated with a large black stamped image of a tomahawk draped with a wampum belt, enclosed in a broad border whose oblique geometric lines and angles suggest traditional Iroquois art. In contrast, the spine shows the title stamped in gold, above the name E. Pauline Johnson. While the exterior of the book thus separates Johnson's two names, the title page unites them, surrounded with an elegant art nouveau frame illustration whose authenticity is as specious as Johnson's buckskin costume. Teepees of Plains Indians are improbably pitched in a dense coniferous forest, against a background of lofty western mountains, behind which extend the rays of the setting sun.

Such images bear even less relevance to Johnson's Georgian-style home at Chiefswood and the longhouses of her Mohawk ancestors than does a costume derived from an artist's rendition of Minnehaha, who at least shared some imaginary connection with Johnson's Iroquois forebears. Both designed by the same artist, E.H. New, the illustrations on the cover and the title page are complementary, a significant feature of Bodley Head publications. While no details have survived concerning Lane's co-publishing arrangements with Copp Clark in Toronto and the small literary house of Lamson, Wolffe in Boston, we can infer that the crossed tomahawks placed above the names of the three firms on the title page – reiterating the single tomahawk on the cover – were chosen as a potent image that promised readers on both sides of the Atlantic the thrill of encountering savagery within the comfort of an aesthetically familiar format.

In contrast to the lavish artwork which dramatizes Johnson's first book, the visual appearance of her second seems decidedly demure. Issued by Morang in Toronto without international co-publishers, *Canadian Born* sports an undecorated title page. Copies survive in two different cloth bindings – pale blue or white – the latter probably higher priced. The front cover bears the title and the author's full name – E. Pauline Johnson (Tekahionwake) – stamped in graceful gold letters, enhanced with one small maple leaf. Unlike the dark colours and strong images of *The White Wampum*, the delicate colours and lettering of *Canadian Born* convey restraint, and perhaps femininity. The subtlety of the design highlights the impact of the book's frontispiece photograph of the author in her Native costume, an introductory image that was to reappear in many subsequent editions of her work. Like New's design of *The White Wampum*, these photographs shaped readers' understanding of Pauline Johnson's poetry and prose.

The White Wampum and *Canadian Born* were never reprinted after their original editions, because their contents were later incorporated into *Flint and Feather*. While the copious reprinting of Johnson's later books during the decades after her death attests to her continuing appeal, this same enthusiasm renders it difficult to discern the particulars of their publishing history. *Flint and Feather* and *Legends of Vancouver* were frequently reissued, but the sparse documentation of such matters as editorial decisions, print runs, illustrations, bindings, and prices means that the record has to be reconstructed largely from the books themselves. As publishers have used the terms 'edition,' 'impression' and 'printing' inconsistently, and often don't differentiate between the year of copyright and the year of production, we offer a general summary.

The production history of *Legends of Vancouver* is probably the most complex. The volume began as a Vancouver initiative, organized by the Pauline Johnson Trust Fund to raise money to support the dying poet, who personally autographed many hundreds of copies. Between 1911 and 1913 the book was issued by several different Vancouver booksellers and printers at least eight times. One edition, from Thomson Stationery, entered into competition with the official version produced by G.S. Forsyth by adding three more of Johnson's stories from the *Vancouver Province Magazine* to the original selection of fifteen. Numbering of subsequent editions by both Forsyth and Thomson suggests that this expanded volume was viewed as the third edition. Dated 1912, it runs to 167 pages, with the additional stories of 'The Legend of the Seven Swans,' 'The Story of Lillooet Falls,' and 'The Legend of the Ice Babies.'

The eighth edition (to use the terminology of the printer, Saturday Sunset Presses) appeared in 1913 after Johnson's death, with the biographical sketch from earlier editions now supplemented with several final paragraphs advising readers of her decease. This is likely the edition being promoted by Forsyth in the photograph of his shop, reproduced elsewhere in this volume.

It is difficult to estimate the number of books produced in these first eight editions, many of which would now more properly be described as impressions. One source claims that ten thousand copies sold before Johnson's death. We do know that the first edition of one thousand copies was quickly exhausted.[15] An undated publicity brochure from the Trust Fund claims that 'Over 2000 copies of this book have been sold in Vancouver alone to date,' and offers autographed copies for two dollars each. However, the book first sold at half that price, reaching the local shops just before Christmas. On Monday, 8 December 1911, an elated Pauline wrote to her sister, cheerfully addressed as 'Dear old Ev':

My book went out in the book stalls on Saturday at noon hour, & by Wednesday, not a single copy was left in the publishing house. Spencers (who is like Eatons in Toronto) sold 100 of them last Friday. There never has been such a rush on a holiday book here. Brantford telegraphed for 100 to be sent there, but Mr. Makovski could not let them have *one single copy*. The entire edition is sold out, is it not glorious? I am so tired with people coming here with 4 & 5 books for me to autograph day in & day out. The books sell at one dollar, & the reviews have been magnificent, all the papers seem to think that I have done great things for the city by unearthing its surrounding romance.[16]

While a 1912 letter from the printer, describing an agreement to publish 'an additional 1000 copies,'[17] does not indicate how many were previously produced, all evidence proclaims that the book was clearly a Canadian bestseller by the time it was taken over by the established Toronto publishing house of McClelland, Goodchild, and Stewart in 1914. As McClelland and Stewart, this firm continued to issue the book for many more decades. Most copious was its production of a new edition in 1922 with a cover and title page by the noted painter and designer J.E.H. Macdonald. By 1949 this edition had reached its ninth printing. In 1961 a new edition appeared from the same publisher for the centenary of Johnson's birth – the only edition to omit Johnson's own foreword, paying tribute to her 'honoured friend,' Chief Joe Capilano. In 1997 the book returned to a Vancouver publisher in a fresh edition from Douglas and McIntyre.

Flint and Feather, in contrast, was always published in Canada by the same Toronto press, Musson, and co-published in England (and later Canada) by Hodder and Stoughton. The second edition of 1912 added four poems to the original selection; the third edition of 1914 added one final poem, '"And He Said, Fight On,"' thus allowing the publisher to present this volume as a 'Revised and Enlarged Edition / Including Poem Written During Her Final Illness.' While the first four editions (1912–16) are subtitled 'Collected Poems,' Musson changed this description in the fifth edition (1917) to 'The Complete Poems of Pauline Johnson.' It has misleadingly remained so ever since. In 1920 Musson brought out the sixth edition, which introduced misarrangement of the lines of the opening stanza of 'The Songster,' an error which remained uncorrected in all subsequent editions. This text of 166 pages was the standard edition until the 1950s. While we don't know the size of each run, we do know that *Flint and Feather* was reprinted at least six times during the 1920s, four times during the 1930s, and again during the 1940s. During the 1960s Musson joined forces with the Toronto office of Hodder and Stoughton to issue a new edition; its 1967 imprint claimed to be the twenty-sixth printing of *Flint and Feather* since 1912. Taken over by PaperJacks in 1972, this edition was reprinted many times, its last known appearance dated 1987 (both this and the 1981 volume claim to be the '3rd printing'). Whatever the exact numbers of printings and books, *Flint and Feather* has indubitably been one of the most frequently issued volumes of Canadian poetry, supporting a popularity which, as we noted in *Paddling Her Own Canoe*, has irritated a number of Canadian literary critics.

In the 1920s, before modernist assessors began to dismiss Johnson's writing, the reprinting of *The Shagganappi* and *The Moccasin Maker* documented her continuing appeal. The two volumes were originally issued in Toronto late in 1913, after Johnson's death, by William Briggs, Book Steward of the Methodist Book and Publishing House. Records for *The Moccasin Maker* reveal that nearly half the first edition of three thousand copies, listed at $1.25, had sold within the first six months.[18] After the publisher was renamed the Ryerson Press, both books were reissued in undated second editions from new plates, with some updated photographic illustrations. We can now date these volumes as 1927, when Ryerson placed a full-page advertisement in the August issue of the *Canadian Bookman* headed 'Do You Know Pauline Johnson's Stories?'

Romantically but erroneously, the ad described the source of Johnson's stories as 'manuscripts left lying dormant for a long time.'[19] In fact, the present volume is the first to bring previously unpublished material to public attention.

This Edition

In preparing a volume of her poetry that is as complete as possible, we have implemented Johnson's own wishes. In January 1910 the Musson Book Company approached her about bringing out a reprint of *The White Wampum*. She responded quickly:

> I am ... just compiling a book of my complete writings in verse. I am anxious to place my entire poetical work in one volume before the Canadian public ... I have a large amount of fugitive work, published recently in different periodicals. I wish to combine 'The White Wampum,' 'Canadian Born' and this fugitive work (this latter is of course my best work as it is more matured) in one complete collection ... I can have it in your hands immediately ... The demand for my complete works I find constantly growing, but the public does not appear to care for a 'selected' edition. They want one big volume of all I have written.[20]

Whether or not such a manuscript actually existed, or whether some poems have disappeared, the book that subsequently emerged towards the end of 1912 was considerably less than the 'one big volume' Johnson had desired. The first edition of *Flint and Feather*, prepared by members of the Johnson Trust, added only fourteen separate poems to the contents of her first two volumes, plus the nine brief poems in the suite 'Autumn's Orchestra.' These appear in a final section titled 'Miscellaneous Poems,' described as 'all of later date,' but actually including at least six that were first published before 1903. The second edition of 1913 added four more titles; the third edition, of 1914, incorporated one final poem, '"And He Said, Fight On."' In total, little more than half of Johnson's poems (eighty-seven) appear in the final edition of *Flint and Feather*. The rest have largely been lost to both general readers and academic critics.[21]

In 1962 renewed interest in Johnson, following celebrations of the centennial of her birth, generated discussion between Richard Pilant, of the Institute of Iroquoian Studies, and publisher Jack McClelland, regarding the production of a 'portable Pauline Johnson' which would include a selection of her best poetry and prose. The project was further supported by Marcus Van Steen, author of the introduction to McClelland and Stewart's 1961 edition of *Legends of Vancouver*, who noted that 'the IODE women who put together "Flint and Feather" while Pauline was lying near death in Vancouver discarded many love lyrics as being "too personal."' Despite Pilant's argument that 'Flint and Feather has sold 75,000 copies in fifty years, 2000 copies last year,'[22] the project fizzled. While the archive yields no explanation for its failure, a clue may lie in Jack McClelland's allegiance to the literary values of two of his authors, Mordecai Richler and Earle Birney, who had publicly derided Johnson in the Vancouver press.[23] Undeterred, Van Steen turned to another publisher with a history of interest in Johnson. In 1965 the Toronto office of Hodder and Stoughton issued his selection of Johnson's writings as *Pauline Johnson: Her Life and Work*, followed by a reprint in 1968.

The absence of original manuscripts and the presence of few significant differences in the published versions of individual poems mean that the preparation of Johnson's entire opus of poetry poses few editorial challenges. The book now in your hands is a practical edition, a format described by Peter Shillingsburg as a 'carefully edited and annotated' text, often intended for the classroom, which occupies the 'middle ground between full-scale editions and mere reprints.'[24] Following this model, our goal is to present a reliable version of all Johnson's verse, in chronological order, with notes that identify each poem's copy-text (the editors' source text) as well as relevant contextual information. Substantive variants are described when Johnson herself made significant changes. The selection of copy-texts is fairly straightforward, according to the principle of following the author's final intention. This is easy to discern with the poems that appeared in *Flint and Feather*. Because Johnson issued a list of corrections for the first edition, the second edition can be followed, for the most part. She missed a few typographical errors that we have corrected, such as restoring the appropriate spelling of 'Cypress' (rather than 'Cyprus') in reference to the Cypress Hills in 'The Quill Worker,' and changing 'sweep' back to the original 'weep' in line 23 of 'Workworn,' so that 'eyes' now 'weep / Through desolation.' Poems omitted from *Flint and Feather* also pose surprisingly few problems. Johnson clipped most of her early verses from the newspapers and magazines in which they appeared, and pasted them into a scrapbook preserved at Chiefswood, making alterations and corrections which we have respected.[25] With these uncollected poems, we have again silently corrected obvious errors: for example, in 'The Death-

Cry,' the barking cog is now a dog. In two cases where a poem exists in two distinct, undated versions, rather than choose between them we have reproduced both texts. Hence this volume includes both 'Temptation' and 'Misguided,' and both 'To C.H.W.' and 'Heidleburgh.'

As editors, we have necessarily made a few other decisions. In Johnson's volumes of poetry, certain spelling patterns were altered from those that prevailed in earlier newspaper and magazine versions: for example, 'altho' ' became 'although,' 'thro' ' became 'through.' As well, American spellings of 'favor,' 'honor' and other words ending with 'or' were Anglicized to end in 'our.' In this edition, in the interest of consistency, we have applied these same principles to all Johnson's work, both poetry and prose. With Johnson's prose that was published only in newspapers or magazines, the texts have been adapted to book format, by adjusting conventions of periodical publication such as internal titles and short paragraphs. Other than correcting obvious typographical errors, this edition usually retains her original punctuation and capitalization, even when her usage departs from current practice. Thus we have not eliminated the hyphen in words like 'to-day' or italicized the titles of books and names of magazines and newspapers.

Canada's historical celebration of poetry, which elevated Johnson from a work-a-day journalist to a drawing-room poet, has seriously detracted from her production of prose, the range and extent of which remain unappreciated. Her uncollected oeuvre includes dozens of travel and sporting sketches. In the early 1890s she produced a series of recreation articles for the Canadian and American press which established her image as an ardent canoeist and bohemian spirit. She also presented herself as an adventurous New Woman who advocated strenuous outdoor exercise for the well-being of her sex, whose consequently improved health would in turn enhance that of the nation. Two examples are selected for this volume: 'Forty-Five Miles on the Grand,' which appeared in the *Brantford Expositor* in 1892, and the first of her columns on 'Outdoor Pastimes for Women,' a series published in New York in *Outing Magazine* (1892–4). All such articles appeared under the name of E. Pauline Johnson, and although none outrightly identify the author as Native, some do contain clues for the alert reader. In the same period she wrote several articles about the Six Nations in which the narrator, while arguing for justice, assumes different positions in relation to her own ethnicity. A notable and unfortunately unrepeated foray into literary criticism produced 'A Strong Race Opinion on the Indian Girl in Modern Fiction,' an extraordinary condemnation of racism which seems to have met with silence from readers of the Toronto *Sunday Globe*, where it appeared in 1892. Perhaps it was this resistance, as well as her need to make a living, that subsequently inclined her to choose less confrontational ways to deliver her message, as in her celebration of the progress of Native women in 'The Iroquois Women of Canada.' This article, first circulated in newspapers in 1895, was reprinted in *Women of Canada*, a special volume issued by the National Council of Women of Canada for the 1900 World's Fair in Paris.

The 1890s saw Johnson increasingly turning her hand to fiction as she attempted to enlarge the market for her talents. Despite her enthusiasm for the British Empire, she sold the great majority of her stories to Canadian and American publications. While she experimented with different styles of short stories, a number, including 'A Red Girl's Reasoning,' continued to highlight the humanity of First Nations. Her production of prose, as of poetry, dropped dramatically around the turn of the century, only to pick up after her London visits of 1906 and 1907. After she settled in Vancouver, local friends and admirers offered Johnson a unique opportunity to place her views in the *Vancouver Province*, which had long been distinguished by its racism towards the First Nations. A series that began in 1910 in the Saturday *Province Magazine*, edited by Lionel Maskovksi, formed the basis for *Legends of Vancouver*, published the following year. During the same period, North American readers of the *Mother's Magazine* and the *Boys' World* grew accustomed to encountering her polite but firm reminders of the value of women and of Natives. Two selections for this volume are boys' stories that present radically partisan defences of traditional Native practices: the White Dog Feast of the Onondaga in 'We-hro's Sacrifice,' and the West Coast potlatch in 'The Potlatch.' By the time she died, Pauline Johnson was known for her prose as well as her poetry, a reputation enhanced by the posthumous publication of *The Shagganappi* and *The Moccasin Maker*.

The existing collections of Johnson's prose are, however, ultimately inadequate. The standard edition of *Legends of Vancouver* omits a number of the stories she received from her friends Su-á-pu-luck and Líxwelut (Joe and Mary Capilano). *The Shagganappi*, while noteworthy for its inclusion of the previously unpublished title story, collects only a sample of her scores of contributions to *Boys' World*. Likewise, *The Moccasin Maker* selects a mere dozen of her pieces for adult readers from the many more stories and articles written for the *Dominion Illustrated, Saturday Night, London Daily Express*, and *Mother's Magazine*.

To reprint all this material would fill many thick volumes, and is therefore not possible here. The full chronology of Johnson's writings, which appears as an appendix to *Paddling Her Own Canoe*, documents the quantity and range of her work. We regret that we have had to be highly selective, aiming at a balance of the obviously excellent and the clearly representative, while reflecting our own sensibilities as feminists, one of us a literary critic and the other a historian. Some prose remains untraceable, despite hints in newspaper reports or private letters. We continue to hope that more will turn up. We are aware that some writing, such as the contents of the regularly reprinted *Legends of Vancouver* and the occasionally reissued *Moccasin Maker*, is quite accessible. While we include a few selections from these volumes, notably 'A Pagan in St Paul's Cathedral,' which Johnson reportedly described as one of her own favourite pieces, we have preferred to use this occasion to present samples of her prose that are more obscure. Hence we reprint for the first time her lesser-known autobiographical memoir, 'From the Child's Viewpoint,' rather than 'My Mother,' which is available in *The Moccasin Maker*. We also want to highlight selections from Pauline Johnson's fiction and non-fiction which take up questions about the survival of Native and Mixed-race peoples in an imperial world, and the role of women in patriarchy. Hence we have included not only previously published but hitherto uncollected pieces that knit together these themes, such as 'A Strong Race Opinion on the Indian Girl in Modern Fiction' and 'Mothers of a Great Red Race,' but also an essay that remained unpublished, 'The Stings of Civilization.' We are sorry not to be able to reprint more of Johnson's travel and canoeing pieces, where the eye of a Mixed-race woman seems to complicate significantly what Mary Louise Pratt has identified as the imperial gaze of the nineteenth-century lady traveler.[26] We also recommend more attention to Johnson's articles on Mohawk silver work, represented here by one brief selection. Her descriptions of these artifacts offer particular insights into First Nations life and values, as do the legends we necessarily omit in the interest of space. Such restrictions notwithstanding, the prose reprinted in this volume adds significantly to our understanding of an author who was ultimately a great deal more than a poet.

Reading Pauline Johnson Today

It is unusual for authors to have an opportunity to revisit their earlier books. We addressed certain implications of Johnson's work at length in *Paddling Her Own Canoe*, and have integrated some of that commentary into this introduction. We would now like to expand our earlier discussion to encompass several additional topics. To begin with, we want to enhance our earlier consideration of oral culture by drawing attention to the significance of storytelling in Johnson's work. In contrast to a well-known 1936 elegiac essay by the German critic Walter Benjamin, who ascribes the decline of storytelling in modern European culture to a detachment from experience,[27] recent work by anthropologist Julie Cruikshank has alerted us to First Nations' use of narrative form to 'subvert official orthodoxies' and to 'challenge conventional ways of thinking.' Historians such as Ian McKay are also suggesting that, while traditional orality within European settler communities became a subject of modern study because it was believed in decline, storytelling was in fact alive and well.[28] A revival of storytelling in the 1980s and 1990s has resulted in a thriving network of Canadian storytellers who interweave the oral cultures of many ethnic communities. Johnson's work regularly recalls the persistence of such traditions as well as her own platform career, in that from the beginning she developed a writing style that both echoed and suited oral performance. Many of her stories and poems originated in tales that were recounted to her orally, beginning with her grandfather, and continuing in her exchanges with friends and travellers.

Indeed, the majority of her poems, whether lyric or narrative, are related in the first person, thus suggesting the presence of listeners. Sometimes the narrator directly addresses a desired, albeit often absent, hearer, such as the 'Belovèd one' of 'Wave-won,' or 'dear Christ' of 'Brier.' Other poems reach to a wider audience, such as the 'you' of the story-poem 'Dawendine,' in the reiteration that 'You can hear' the ghostly voices of the lovers whose legend is being recounted. The role of Su-á-pu-luck, Líxwelut, and other narrators is foregrounded in *Legends of Vancouver*; perhaps less evident is the emergence of Native interpreters of traditions that might bridge the worlds of Aboriginals and settlers in boys' stories such as 'The Scarlet Eye' and 'The King Georgeman.' In the poem 'Wolverine,' in contrast, it is a trapper for the Hudson's Bay Company who corrects a misinformed settler concerning the unhappy fate of an Indian whose generosity has been rewarded with starvation and death. The respectful listening required of audiences in general and by potential storytellers in particular is similarly invoked in tales of maternal heroism such as 'Hoolool of the Totem Poles' (reprinted here) and 'The Tenas Klootchman.' Elsewhere, human messages are communicated by spiritual voices in the aural landscapes of several narrative poems, such as 'The Legend of the Qu'Appelle Valley,' 'Dawend-ine,' and 'The Pilot of the Plains.'

Johnson's storytellers, like those among the First Nations today, regularly confront White ignorance and arrogance. As the trapper friend of Wolverine insists, his authenticity corroborated by the representation of his voice in dialect, '"You won't believe it, sir, but what I'm tellin' you is true."' He doggedly counters prejudice with '"No, sir, you're wrong, they ain't no 'dogs.' I'm not through tellin' yet;/You'll take that name right back again, or else jest out you get!"' The power of the truth is reiterated: '"You'll take that name right back when you hear all this yarn, I bet."' Such narrators, much like Cruikshank's collaborators and subjects, establish 'connections – between past and future, between people and place, among people whose opinions diverge.'[29] In other words, Johnson's regular invocation of orality, with its assumption of a community of speakers and listeners, suggests that two-way conversations may permit overdue truths to be told.

The issue of naming raised by Johnson's Hudson's Bay Company trapper also increasingly interests us. Most obviously this topic arises with the writer herself. Her choice to assume Tekahionwake, the particular Mohawk name of her great-grandfather, Jacob Johnson, asserted paternal lineage. This insistence upon a name that belonged to a 'pure blood' effectively denied not only her English mother but also her Mixed-race paternal grandmother, Helen Martin. In a paradoxical affirmation of membership in a matrilineal society, Johnson erased not only a central part of her own family's and community's history but the genealogy of imperial contact itself. On another occasion, renaming symbolically assimilates or captures one leader of the former imperial foe, transforming him into an ally. In one of her infrequent depictions of Six Nations, Johnson celebrates the adoption of Prince Arthur, son of Queen Victoria, as Kavakoudge the Mohawk.[30] Self-consciously, we believe, she engineered a reversal of this pattern in the names chosen for two important fictional characters in stories reprinted here: Christine ('A Red Girl's Reasoning') and Esther ('As It Was in the Beginning') recall and appropriate for Native and Mixed-race peoples the Judaeo-Christian iconography of sacrifice and courage. Similarly, in her story 'The Deep Waters,' Johnson reminds readers that Mount Baker is 'the Mount Ararat of the Pacific Coast people.'[31] The arrogance of ignorant imperialists attempting to cast the landscape in their own image is highlighted again when Johnson records the land's pre-contact names. In 'The Two Sisters' she points out that twin mountain peaks north of

Vancouver were sisters long before English settlers rechristened them lions after the Landseer monument in Trafalgar Square. On another occasion, she reminds us that Point Grey, named by George Vancouver in tribute to a fellow naval officer, was originally the 'Battle Ground of the West Wind.'[32] Her conferral of nicknames also seems significant, just as it was at Six Nations and within her own family. The promising son of a remarkable mother is hailed as 'little "North-West,"' while another high-minded Anglo-Canadian boy hero is given the name 'Can,' a far from subtle allusion to Canada.[33] On a different occasion, the name of a boy sent to Canada from London by Dr Barnardo's Homes for poor children is changed from Buckney, suggestively rhyming with Cockney, to Buck, with its own reminder of Native youth.[34] Mixed-race youth, such as the title characters Little Wolf-willow and Shagganappi, invoke another battle when each insists upon preserving his Native name.[35]

Moreover, Johnson examines the extent to which women have a voice in the power nexus of language. As she reminds her readers on several occasions, there are fifty chief matrons of Iroquois clans who wield the indisputable right to 'nominate the succeeding chief when death leaves the chair empty in the council house,' and 'to speak in the assembled council of the Six Great Nations of the Iroquois.'[36] In contrast, in 'The Lodge of the Law-makers' she points out the more limited political and verbal power of European women. Another story, 'Her Dominion – A Story of 1867, and Canada's Confederation,' subtly uses White women's lack of linguistic authority to highlight their subordination. While the character Mrs Fairleigh, an invaluable and under-valued mother, coins the description of the new country of Canada as a confederation, with its echo of the Six Nations' confederacy, it is her son who later receives public credit for the term.[37] There is an ironic justice in the fact that Johnson generated a reversal of the usual colonial paradigm when the popularity of her poem 'The Lost Lagoon' led to public renaming of the small body of water in Vancouver's Stanley Park that was previously and more prosaically known as Coal Harbour.

Just as naming represents power, its loss represents defeat. Shortly before her death, Johnson was forced to accept the title *Legends of Vancouver* for the book that she wanted to call 'Legends of the Capilano.'[38] This change effectively erased the prominence of the Capilano, whom she had intended to honour, even as it affirmed the legitimacy of the newcomers who had created an English-speaking city on the site of Aboriginal settlements. Such examples demonstrate that Pauline

Pauline Johnson, c. 1892.

Pauline Johnson, 1903.

Pauline Johnson, 1907.

G.S. Forsyth, first trade publisher of *Legends of Vancouver*, displaying the book in his bookstore, 349 Hastings Street West, Vancouver, probably December 1913.

Pauline Johnson commemorative stamp, issued March 1961.

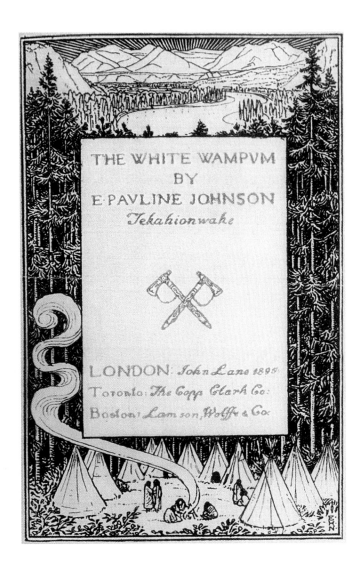

Title page of *The White Wampum*, designed by E.H. New for John Lane, London, 1895.

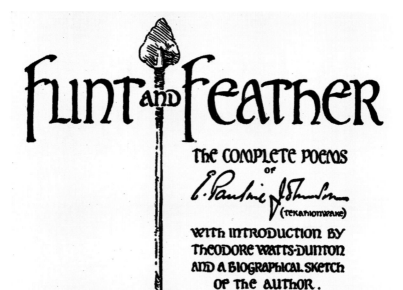

Flint and Feather

The Complete Poems

of

E. Pauline Johnson

(Tekahionwake)

With Introduction by Theodore Watts-Dunton and a Biographical Sketch of the Author.

Illustrated by ♠ J. R. Seavey ♠

Toronto
The Musson Book Company
Limited.

Title page of *Flint and Feather,* misleadingly identifying the book as the complete poems of E. Pauline Johnson. This edition was first published by Musson (Toronto) in 1920, and remained in print into the 1940s.

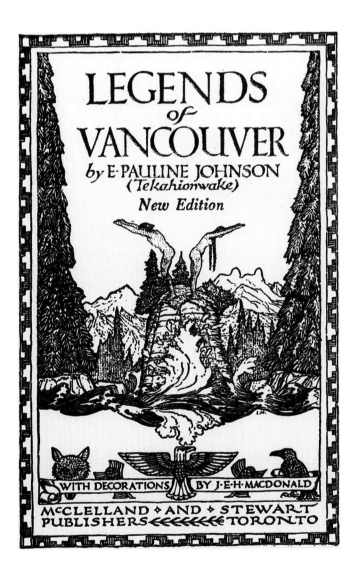

Title page of *Legends of Vancouver*, designed by J.E.H. MacDonald in 1922 for McClelland and Stewart (Toronto). After at least nine printings, this edition was replaced by a new edition in 1961, illustrated by Ben Lim.

Johnson was a conscious wordsmith, and her creations 'the firm handiwork of will' ('Our Brotherhood'). Her language and her narrative forms shore up the sensibilities about the First Nations, women, and Canada that we identified as pivotal in *Paddling Her Own Canoe*. Fresh discoveries about Johnson's style and meaning reward each rereading of her work, whether prose or poetry.

Johnson and her admirers fostered the notion that she was primarily a poet. Indeed she was regularly cited as a key member of the influential so-called Confederation group of literary stars which included Charles G.D. Roberts, Archibald Lampman, Duncan Campbell Scott, and Bliss Carman. Her first published poems, from 1884–5, show that, like most young versifiers, she initially followed the conventions of her day, based on the examples of the great nineteenth-century British poets on whom she was raised, as well as the periodical poets she read in newspapers and magazines. Within a few years, however, she gained greater control and individuality as she explored themes of romantic love, Natives, and nature. During the later 1880s and early 1890s, she struck an individual, radical note in a series of romantic poems whose sexual explicitness enhances the bohemian identity she claimed. Poems like 'Re-Voyage,' with its lovers 'Wave-rocked, and passion tossed,' and 'The Idlers,' which eroticizes the 'splendid, sunburnt throat' of the objectified male lover, help us recognize Johnson as Canada's own 'Daughter of Decadence.' This term was coined by American critic Elaine Showalter to describe women writers of Johnson's generation who 'rescued female sexuality from the [male] decadents' image of romantically doomed prostitutes or devouring Venus flytraps, and represent female desire as a creative force in artistic imagination as well as in biological reproduction.'[39]

Readers of this collection of Johnson's complete poems may be surprised to discover that only a small proportion of her verse directly concerns First Nations material or issues. After early poems arguing for acceptance and reconciliation, she wrote dramatic narratives of Native-to-Native strife and vengeance, such as 'Ojistoh,' which is also remarkable for its portrayal of a woman inflicting death on a would-be rapist. As the crisis in relations between Natives and newcomers deepened after the Northwest Rebellion of 1885, Johnson's words became more direct. In 'The Cry of an Indian Wife,' a Native woman names the injustice inflicted on the tribes, as does a passionate daughter in 'The Cattle Thief.' By 1893 a White man joins the condemnation of genocide in 'Wolverine.' Poetry, however, increasingly yielded to prose as Johnson's preferred genre for Native advocacy. Her few later Indian poems, like the earliest, seem to reincorporate First Nations into normalizing Euro-Canadian conventions, albeit with subtle reminders of difference. Unlike Duncan Campbell Scott, the powerful bureaucrat in the Department of Indian Affairs who supervised Ottawa's assimilationist policies while writing elegiac poems which took for granted the disappearance of his charges, the daughter of Six Nations always hoped for a shared future.

At the same time, Johnson's poems that describe the Canadian landscape without direct reference to its Aboriginal inhabitants demonstrate that, as a poet of nature, she was well in tune with the canonical authors of her generation. In descriptive verse such as 'At Husking Time' and 'Marshlands,' she captures specific moments in the diurnal and seasonal cycles that serve as metaphors for larger human experience. In contrast to the master male poets, her work more often depicts relations between humans and the natural environment as harmonious. Hence, much of Johnson's distinctive contribution to Canadian nature poetry lies in her identity as female. For example, 'The Song My Paddle Sings' celebrates the physical prowess of a solo woman canoeist fearlessly making her way through a sensual, wild landscape which invites collaboration rather than confrontation.

Given the reading public's ongoing fascination with Johnson, as indicated by the broad and frequent dissemination of her works, we would like to suggest that penetration into cultural areas not normally associated with literature is a strong measure of a writer's appeal. With Pauline Johnson, this expansion began during her lifetime, when her name was given to the *Epauline*, a luxury power yacht launched in Vancouver in 1911.[40] Her public significance was dramatically enhanced by her civic funeral attended by Native and White mourners on 10 March 1913, and the interment of her ashes in Vancouver's Stanley Park several hundred feet inland from Siwash Rock, the subject of one of her best-known legends.[41] Here, despite Johnson's wish for a simple grave, a formal memorial was erected in 1922 by the Women's Canadian Club, in a ceremony captured by Fox Movietonews.[42] Often to the consternation of her Six Nations and Brantford supporters, additional commemorative ventures cemented the writer's identification with the West coast. During the First World War the Vancouver *World* used funds donated by Evelyn Johnson to initiate a public subscription for a machine gun for the city's 29th Battalion of the Canadian Expeditionary Corps. Inscribed 'Tekahionwake,' it contributed to the dominion's victory at Ypres and, as Evelyn noted, generally to the 'defense of the Empire and civilization.'[43]

In the 1920s the adoption of the writer's name by a Vancouver choco-
late company, presumably to rival Ontario's Laura Secord candy busi-
ness, furthered Johnson's popular identification with British Columbia
as well as securing her place among Canada's nationalist heroines. The
appearance of her name on schools and roads has not been limited by
provincial boundaries: Ontario detective author Howard Engel created
a fictional Pauline Johnson House as the women's residence in his
equally fictional Secord University.[44] Real jurisdictions have also remem-
bered her. For example, a new residential development in Georgetown,
Ontario, includes Johnson Crescent, along with Berton Boulevard,
Atwood Avenue, Munro Circle, and Grey Owl Run. Johnson's presence
in Canadian art includes the 1933 film *Shadow River*,[45] which similarly
claims her for Canada as a whole. On the literary front, Johnson makes
cameo appearances in books as divergent as L.M. Montgomery's *Anne of
Windy Poplars* (1936), George Bowering's *Caprice* (1987), and Thomas
King's *Green Grass Running Water* (1993).[46]

Although sustained attention to Johnson subsided long before 1961,
the coincidence of the centenary of her birth with the extension of the
federal franchise to status Indians snapped her back into national view.
In March 1961 the Canadian Post Office issued a five-cent commemora-
tive stamp that embraced Johnson as the essential or generic Indian,
symbol of the progress and, not so incidentally, of the assimilation of the
First Nations in Canada. Promotion of Johnson was incorporated into
an agenda of bettering 'race relations,' in the discourse of the period.[47]
In the words of the official brochure:

> This new stamp has been issued to honour Canadians of the Indian race.
> During recent years particularly, Canadian Indians have made tremendous
> advances. They have achieved the federal franchise, made striking practical
> gains in the fields of education, health and sociology, and contributed at
> a vastly accelerated pace to the economic and industrial growth of the
> nation.[48]

While celebrating Johnson, the stamp also misrepresented her. In his
recent study of the 1908 commemoration of the Quebec tercentenary,
historian H.V. Nelles asks whether it is the past or the present which is
the object of such events.[49] In the case of the Johnson stamp, so little
attention was paid to history that the artist neglected even to study avail-
able portraits of Johnson for his images. The stamp, to return to the
words of the brochure, shows 'the profile of the poetess wearing the

high ruffled collar of the Victorian era, superimposed on a background of snow-capped mountains. In the middle distance, a full length likeness of Miss Johnson in tribal costume is shown, the two portraits depicting her two personalities of Indian and Victorian lady.' In fact, neither image presents a recognizable likeness of Johnson: none of her photographs depicts her in either a high ruffled Victorian collar or in Native dress in the pose on the stamp, with both arms raised to the heavens. Moreover, the background of snow-capped mountains links her only with the West coast, ignoring her original affiliation with the Six Nations of southern Ontario.

In the city of Vancouver, commemoration of the Johnson centennial was more overtly problematic. While the Vancouver newspapers printed laudatory individual memoirs by several residents who had known Johnson,[50] other articles by the day's leading literary modernists disparaged her poetry.[51] The poet's name was suggested for the new small theatre erected beside the city's large Queen Elizabeth Theatre but was ultimately rejected in favour of the neutral Vancouver Playhouse. However, such disappointments did not dissuade participants in other celebratory events, including the pilgrimage of Six Nations chiefs to her Stanley Park monument for a commemorative ceremony on 8 July, and the publication of a special Pauline Johnson issue of the *Native Voice*, which carried greetings from major political and public figures. That August the annual Six Nations pageant, which dramatized Johnson's life and work, was filmed by both the National Film Board and Canadian National Railway.[52] In the fall of 1961 the Institute of Iroquoian Studies, which had organized the pilgrimage, sponsored a three-day conference at McMaster University which included an address by Professor Norman Shrive on 'The Place of Pauline Johnson in Canadiana.'[53]

Four decades later, in a different cultural climate, Pauline Johnson is again being recovered, with vastly different results. Postcolonial and feminist commentators in particular have much to say about a Mixed-race daughter of Empire who attempted to continue the role of translator and intermediary favoured by many of her Mohawk ancestors, while simultaneously presenting the case for the New Woman. In the fall of 1999 the public was promised an opera on Pauline's life by Margaret Atwood (who subsequently withdrew from the project). Despite the endurance of a few naysayers,[54] recent press coverage, including the selection of Johnson by *Maclean's* magazine as one of twenty-six 'Canadians who inspired the world,'[55] demonstrates how Johnson's life and work are now revalued in the context of reinvigorated feminism and cultural nationalism.[56] January 2002 saw the world premiere of Simon Johnston's play *Wildcat*, the title taken from the name of Johnson's canoe. We are less impressed by the unreflective ease with which she is being slotted into the category of 'Native American' by critics in the United States, despite her antipathy to the country she viewed as a disloyal and corrupt state.[57]

In the past, Johnson received many tributes in verse, mostly from obscure authors, none of them Native, so far as we know.[58] In recent years, however, she has had a substantial impact on Aboriginal writers, for, as Mi'kmaw author Rita Joe remembers, Johnson was the only Native writer she ever encountered in school.[59] During the 1920s, Cree recitalist Frances Nickawa performed Johnson's poems. For subsequent indigenous writers and public speakers, such as Bernice Loft Winslow ('Dawendine'), born on the Six Nations Reserve in 1902, Johnson was an important example of public success.[60] Women from geographical regions associated with her seem particularly aware of her achievements. Vancouver writer Lee Maracle commended Johnson's handling of the voice of Su-à-pu-luck in *Legends of Vancouver*, and Beth Brant, a Mohawk writer from the Theyindenaga Reserve on the Bay of Quinte, declares 'It is ... time to recognize Johnson for the revolutionary she was,' whose bequest is to have 'walked the writing path clearing the brush for us to follow.'[61] Most impressive is Joan Crate's excellent volume of poems, *Pale as Real Ladies: Poems for Pauline Johnson* (1989, 1991), which draws on her own identification with Johnson as a sister Mixed-race woman poet.

Pauline Johnson devoted much of her writing to the problem of furthering communication between the First Nations and the European newcomers. Storytelling, as she tells us so often, provides a means of conveying truths that are important, if sometimes painful. For example, the legend of 'The Sea-serpent' (one of the many texts for which there is no space in this volume), forcefully condemns European greed and the threat it poses not only to 'red races' who 'are born Socialists' but to Whites themselves.[62] Non-Natives were intended to hear such messages. Johnson warned as well about simple-minded appropriation, whether it be an eagle feather in 'A Night with "North Eagle"' or a clan symbol in 'Hoolool of the Totem Poles.' Exchanges should be meaningfully equivalent, such as those between a Pacific coast chief and the boy dancer in 'The Potlach.'[63] This volume is offered to Canadians of all origins, as well as to readers in other countries, in the same spirit of exchange and desire to further communication. Reading Pauline

Johnson today not only restores proper recognition to a very important early Canadian writer, but also furthers her goal to honour Native culture and values.

Notes

The title of the introduction is a quotation from Johnson's poem 'Our Brotherhood' (1888).

1 Public Archives of British Columbia (PABC), MS-2367, Isabel Ecclestone MacKay, 'Pauline Johnson: A Memory and an Appreciation,' typescript, 1.

2 L.M. Montgomery to Ephraim Weber, 16 July 1933, Paul Gerard Tiessen and Hildi Froese Tiessen, eds., *L.M. Montgomery's Ephraim Weber: Letters 1916–1941* (Waterloo, ON: mlr editions 1999), 148.

3 W.L. Morton, *The Canadian Identity* (Toronto: University of Toronto Press 1961), 111.

4 For a discussion of the differing reception of Christianity by North American Natives, see the editors' introductions to articles by Nancy Shoemaker and Jo-Anne Fiske, in Veronica Strong-Boag, Adele Gleason, and Adele Perry, eds., *Rethinking Canada. The Promise of Women's History*, 4th ed. (Toronto: Oxford University Press 2002).

5 Pauline Johnson to Archie Kains, 20 April 1890, Archibald Kains fonds, NA.

6 On the actual and imagined connection between North American Natives and Celts (such as Boadicea) or Scots, see Veronica Strong-Boag, '"A People Akin to Mine": Indians and Highlanders within the British Empire,' *Native Studies Review* 14, no. 1 (2001): 27–53.

7 Like the Iroquois, the Blackfoot skilfully employed a history of loyalism to the British crown to claim, albeit unsuccesfully, better terms in the new Canadian nation.

8 See Judith Butler, 'Performative Acts and Gender Constitution: An Essay in Phenomenology and Feminist Theory,' in Sue-Ellen Case, ed., *Performing Feminisms: Feminist Critical Theory and Theatre* (Baltimore: Johns Hopkins University Press 1990), 270–82.

9 See Antoinette Burton, *At the Heart of the Empire: Indians and the Colonial Encounter in Late Victorian Britain* (Berkeley: University of California Press 1998) and Judith R. Walkowitz, 'The Indian Woman, The Flower Girl, and the Jew,' *Victorian Studies* (Autumn 1998–9): 3–46.

10 See Carole Gerson, 'Sarah Binks and Edna Jaques: Gender, Parody, and the Construction of Literary Value,' *Canadian Literature* 134 (Fall 1992): 62–73.

11 Archives of Ontario, Emily Pauline Johnson papers, Johnson to Arthur Henry O'Brien, 4 February 1894.

12 On the efforts of friends and the use of this term, see Mrs W. Garland Foster, *The Mohawk Princess* (Vancouver: Lion's Gate 1931), 133.

13 *The Athenaeum,* 28 September 1889. Watts-Dunton was so enamoured of his initial assessment that he cited it at length twenty-four years later, in his memorial introduction to *Flint and Feather* that appears in all editions published after Johnson's death in 1913.

14 H. Hale, 'The White Wampum,' *The Critic,* 4 January 1896, 4–5.

15 Marcus Van Steen, 'E. Pauline Johnson,' introduction to *Legends of Vancouver* (Toronto: McClelland and Stewart 1961), xv. His source is probably Foster (*The Mohawk Princess,* 136–7), who claims that the Trust Fund ordered ten thousand copies on the strength of responses to their solicitation letters sent to Canadian and American authors, prominent individuals, and acquaintances of Pauline.

16 Paul[ine] to Ev[elyn], 8 December 1911, Johnson fonds, McMaster University.

17 E.M. Fleming, Saturday Sunset Presses, to Walter McRaye, 20 September 1912, ibid.

18 Board of Publication Papers, United Church Archives, box 45, ledger for 1904–34: 274. The royalty was 15 cents on the first five thousand sold, and 20 cents thereafter. Thanks to Janet Friskney for this information. Two letters in the Johnson fonds at McMaster University, to Walter McRaye from William Briggs of the Methodist Book and Publishing House, reveal that discussion of these volumes began in January 1913, with McRaye acting on Johnson's behalf. Briggs offered the same terms as those for Nellie McClung's *The Black Creek Stopping House,* in which the author paid all production costs, and received a commission on sales made by the publisher's representatives.

19 Thanks to Janet Friskney for finding the first advertisement in the *Bookseller and Stationer,* February 1927.

20 E. Pauline Johnson to the Musson Book Company, 26 January 1910, Logan Papers, Acadia University. She is responding to their letter of 11 January 1910, Johnson fonds, McMaster University.

21 Sheila Johnston reprints many of the 'lost' poems in *Buckskin and Broadcloth: A Celebration of E. Pauline Johnson – Tekahionwake 1861–1913* (Toronto: Natural Heritage Books 1997).

22 McMaster University, McClelland and Stewart fonds, series A, box 33: Marcus Van Steen to Jack McClelland, 16 February 1962; Richard Pilant to Jack McClelland, 4 February 1962. Pilant's figures refer to William Arthur Deacon's inter-

view with Charles J. Musson (*Globe and Mail*, 3 February 1962) which claims, 'Last year, being the centenary of Pauline Johnson's birth, this firm sold 2,000 copies of her Flint and Feather, which they had published in 1912; and the normal demand for it over those 50 years has averaged 1,500 copies a year.'

23 Nels Hamilton, 'Pauline Johnson Honored But Not for Her Poetry,' *Vancouver Sun*, 10 March 1961; Mordecai Richler, 'Headdresses Jingled But Highbrows Stayed Away,' *Vancouver Sun*, 10 May 1961. Johnson's elderly friend and advocate, Lionel Makovski, thought that the subsequent fuss created excellent publicity, telling Jack McClelland that 'Miss Johnson would have been vastly amused' (19 April 1961), McMaster University, McClelland and Stewart fonds, series A, box 33.

24 See Peter L. Shillingsburg, *Scholarly Editing in the Computer Age* (Ann Arbor: University of Michigan Press 1996), 131–2. Fredson Bowers uses the term 'scholarly reading edition' to describe a text like this one, 'intended to serve two audiences – the scholarly and the generally informed non-professional public.' See his essay, 'Notes on Theory and Practice in Editing Texts,' in Peter Davison, ed., *The Book Encompassed: Studies in Twentieth-Century Bibliography* (Cambridge: Cambridge University Press 1992), 244–57. Robert Stephen Becker makes a useful distinction between 'The Sacred Text' and 'The Sensible Text' in 'Challenges in Editing Modern Literary Correspondence,' *TEXT (Transactions of the Society for Textual Scholarship)* 1 (1981): 257–70.

25 In the notes to the poems, we refer to this as the Chiefswood scrapbook. From about 1888 until 1895 Johnson used this scrapbook as a working document, into which she pasted several photographs and other mementos as well as clipped poems, and from which she occasionally cut pages.

26 See Mary Louise Pratt, *Imperial Eyes: Travel Writing and Transculturation* (London: Routledge 1992).

27 Walter Benjamin, 'The Storyteller: Reflections on the works of Nikolai Leskov,' trans. Harry Zohn, in Hannah Arendt, ed., *Illuminations* (New York: Schocken Books 1969), 83–110; Julie Cruikshank, *The Social Life of Stories: Narrative and Knowledge in the Yukon Territory* (Vancouver: UBC Press 1998), xiii.

28 Ian MacKay, *The Quest of the Folk: Antimodernism and Cultural Selection in Twentieth-Century Nova Scotia* (Montreal: McGill-Queen's University Press 1994).

29 Cruikshank, *Social Life of Stories*, 2.

30 Johnson, 'The Duke of Connaught as Chief of the Iroquois,' *Daily Province Magazine*, 2 July 1910; retitled 'A Royal Mohawk Chief,' *Legends of Vancouver*.

31 Johnson, 'The Deep Waters: A Rare Squamish Legend,' *Vancouver Province Magazine*, 24 September 1910; retitled 'The Deep Waters,' *Legends of Vancouver*.

32 Johnson, 'A Legend of Point Grey,' *Vancouver Province Magazine*, 10 December 1910; retitled 'Point Grey,' *Legends of Vancouver.*

33 'Mother o' the Men,' *Mother's Magazine*, February 1909, included in *The Moccasin Maker*; 'The Lieutenant-Governor's Prize,' *Boys' World*, 20 June 1908.

34 'The Barnardo Boy,' *Boys' World*, 13 August 1910, included in *The Shagganappi.*

35 'Little Wolf-Willow,' ibid., 7 December 1907, included in *The Shagganappi.*

36 'Mothers of a Great Red Race,' *Mother's Magazine*, January 1908.

37 'Her Dominion – A Story of 1867 and Canada's Confederation,' ibid., July 1907.

38 The survival of printed receipts for 'Indian Legends of the Coast' indicates that the title was not finalized until after the manuscript had gone to the printer. E. Pauline Johnson fonds, McMaster University.

39 Elaine Showalter, introduction to *Daughters of Decadence: Women Writers at the Fin de Siècle* (New Brunswick, NJ: Rutgers University Press 1993), xi.

40 Norman Hacking, ed., *Annals of the Royal Vancouver Yacht Club, 1903–1970*, 3rd ed. (Vancouver 1984), 84, 90, 92; unidentified clipping, 'Epauline Launched,' Johnson fonds, McMaster University.

41 Recent coverage of a memorial tribute to Jack Shadbolt links Johnson's funeral to public recognition of art in Vancouver: 'There is some historic precedent for these high-profile tributes to artists in Vancouver. When poet Pauline Johnson died here on [7] March 1913, the whole city was thrown into mourning. Vancouverites flocked to public memorials for the Ontario-born, half-Mohawk writer, whose romantic verses not only helped define this city's sense of itself when it was only 30 years old, but also helped form a distinctive Vancouver aesthetic that balanced all-powerful nature with the memory of First Nations forms and modernist hopes for the future.' Trevor Body, 'Celebrating Shadbolt's Legacy,' *Georgia Straight* (28 January–4 February 1999: 65–6).

42 Movietonews Archives, Fox No. 095.8-C2754.

43 Evelyn Johnson to John Nelson, Vancouver *World*, 18 July 1920, in Mrs W. Garland Foster, *The Mohawk Princess*, 169. See also the correspondence documenting the donation and the *World's* effort to retrieve the gun at the end of the war, 156–70.

44 Howard Engel, *The Suicide Murders* (Toronto: Penguin 1985), 87.

45 NAC, Associated Screen News collection, no. B-632.

46 L.M. Montgomery, *Anne of Windy Poplars* (Toronto: Bantam-Seal 1992), 181. In 1917 Montgomery gave talks on Johnson to both the Hypatia Club, an Uxbridge women's cultural group to which she belonged, and to the Young

People's Guild of the Leaskdale Presbyterian Church. In Bowering's *Caprice*, Johnson is clearly one of the writers satirized in the composite Emily Peachtree Guano (Markham, ON: Penguin 1987), 70–3; Thomas King, *Green Grass Running Water* (Toronto: HarperCollins 1994), 156–9.

47 For example, Blanche Holt-Murison, an old Vancouver friend of Pauline, described the planned pilgrimage of the Six Nations chiefs to Vancouver in a tone of progressive optimism: 'such a vitalizing visit from the chiefs of the Six Nations and their entourage should serve in stimulating measure to symbolize better race relations – not only in Canada but throughout the Commonwealth. It can only generate kindlier publicity and favorable understanding of the new status – under law – of Canada's native Indians.' Holt-Murison to Lionel Makovski, 6 May 1961, McMaster University, McClelland and Stewart papers, series A, box 33.

48 NAC, RG3, v. 3838, file 13-7-72: brochure from the Canadian Post Office on the Johnson stamp, 1961. The issue of 34 million copies was about average for a commemorative stamp. Lobbying by the Iroquois community probably influenced the decision to thus honour Johnson; see Richard Pilant, Institute of Iroquoian Studies, to Jack McClelland, 14 September 1960, McMaster University, McClelland and Stewart papers, series A, box 33.

49 H.V. Nelles, *The Art of Nation-Building: Pageantry and Spectacle at Quebec's Tercentenary* (Toronto: University of Toronto Press 1999), 11–12. See also D.M.R. Bentley, *Mnemographia Canadensis*, vol. 1 (London, ON: Canadian Poetry Press 1999), especially his commentary on stamps commemorating writers, 326–8.

50 See 'Great Figures,' *Vancouver Sun*, 20 February 1961, 'Former Province editor recalls acquaintance,' *Vancouver Province*, 10 March 1961.

51 Hamilton, 'Pauline Johnson Honored But Not for Her Poetry'; Robertson Davies, 'Writer's Diary: Pauline Johnson's art was partly her personality,' *Vancouver Province*, 8 April 1961; Richler, 'Headdresses Jingled but Highbrows Stayed Away.' See Carole Gerson, '"The Most Canadian of all Canadian Poets": Pauline Johnson and the Construction of a National Literature,' *Canadian Literature* 158 (Autumn 1998): 90–108.

52 Both are described by Richard Pilant, Pilant to Jack McClelland, 21 January 1962, McClelland and Stewart papers, McMaster University. We do not know if either of these films has survived.

53 See Norman Shrive, 'What Happened to Pauline?' *Canadian Literature* 13 (Summer 1962): 25–38.

54 In 1999, on the History Channel, Patrick Watson disparaged Johnson when he introduced the biographical documentary produced by Scott Calbeck. He later described her as a 'truly dreadful poet,' *Globe and Mail*, 19 August

2000. Such judgments also permeate his chapter on Johnson in *The Canadians,* which contains many errors.

55 *Maclean's* magazine, 4 September 2000.

56 At the popular level, see Peter Unwin, 'The Mohawk Princess,' *The Beaver,* October–November 1999; Sandra Martin, 'The Persistence of Pauline,' *Globe and Mail,* 19 August 2000; the many appearances of Paul Gessell's article, 'Rediscovering Pauline,' first written for the *Ottawa Citizen* (29 July 2000) and also printed in the *Brantford Expositor* (29 July 2000), *The Montreal Gazette* (27 August 2000), and *The Vancouver Sun* (29 August 2000). Recent academic studies are cited in this book's bibliography. Some of Johnson's poems were selected as the contents of a limited-edition hand-printed book created by Peter Rimmer's typography students at the University College of the Fraser Valley: *Shadow River* (New Westminster, BC: Pine Tree Press 1997).

57 Johnson is the subject of several recent dissertations at American universities, and now appears in reference books such as the *Oxford Companion to Women Writers of the United States* (1995) and the *Dictionary of Literary Biography* no. 175, *Native American Writers of the United States* (1997).

58 Examples we have found include: 'To Brantford's Elocutionist,' anonymous, unidentified clipping, 'To Tekahionwake,' manuscript poem, and Harold Dalby, untitled poem, unidentified Vancouver newspaper, 7 March 1924, all in the Johnson Papers, Trent University Archives; Prof B., '"Little Vancouver" to Pauline Johnson,' 7 April 1899, unidentified clipping, W.A.D.M., 'Legends of Vancouver,' unidentified clipping; A.M. Stephen, 'At Pauline Johnson's Grave,' undated typescript; and Oscar Osland, 'To E. Pauline Johnson,' *Ladies Pictorial Weekly,* n.d., all in the Johnson fonds, McMaster University Archives; Wm. Murray, 'To "Poetry and (poetic) Prose,"' 18 December 1894, manuscript poem, Chiefswood scrapbook; Charles Edward Dedrick, 'To E. Pauline Johnson,' *Canadian Magazine* 1 (1893): 5; Isabel Ecclestone Mackay, 'Pauline Johnson (Tekahionwake),' clipping from unidentified Toronto newspaper, Logan Papers, Acadia; R.D. Cummins, '"Tekahionwake" (E. Pauline Johnson),' *Vancouver Sun,* 14 March 1915; Jessie L. Beattie, 'Message from Pauline,' undated typescript, Brant County Museum.

59 Jeanette Lynes, ed., *Words Out There: Women Poets in Atlantic Canada* (Lockeport, NS: Roseway Publishing), 129–30.

60 R. Stacy's 'Afterword' to Bernice Loft Winslow's *Iroquois Fires* (Ottawa: Penumbra 1995) emphasizes Winslow's oratorical ability, finding her 'less conventional' and 'less sentimental' than Johnson. See also Armand Garnet Ruffo, 'Out of Silence – The Legacy of E. Pauline Johnson: An Inquiry into the Lost and Found Work of Dawendine – Bernice Loft Winslow,' in Christl Verduyn, ed., *Literary Pluralities* (Peterborough, ON: Broadview 1998),

211–23. Like Winslow, Loretta Jobin cites Johnson as an inspiration (see J. Perrault and S. Vance, eds., *Writing the Circle* [Edmonton: NeWest, 1990], 122), as does Maurice Kenny (*On Second Thought* [Norman, OK: University of Oklahoma Press 1995], 21–2). Thomas King's presentation of Johnson in *Green Grass, Running Water* (1993) is more ironic, as is Chief Lindsay Marshall's poem, 'My Paddle Does not Sing' (*Clay Pots and Bones* [1997], 82).

61 Interview with Lee Maracle (27 October 1990) in H. Lutz, *Contemporary Challenges* (Saskatoon: Fifth House 1991), 171; Beth Brant, *Writing as Witness: Essay and Talk* (Toronto: Women's Press 1994), 6–8.

62 Johnson, *Legends of Vancouver* (Toronto: McClelland and Stewart 1928), 60.

63 See 'Trails of the Old Tillicums,' *Vancouver Province Magazine*, 31 December 1910.

POEMS

I. The Early Years: Beginnings to 1888

THE FOURTH ACT

Pine trees sobbing a weird unrest,
In saddened strains,
Crows flying slowly into the West
As daylight wanes;
Breezes that die in a stifled breath,
O, happy breezes, embraced by death.

Fir trees reaching towards the sky
In giant form –
Lift me up with your arms that I
May brave the storm –
O darling unclasp your fair warm hand
'Tis better I should misunderstand.

Turn in pity those tender eyes
Away from me,
The burning sorrow that in them lies
Is misery,
O, gentlest pleader my life has known
Good-bye – The night and I are alone.

'THINK OF ME ...'

Think of me when the sun of life has set
And when purple shades of death draw nigh
Look on my grave with just one sweet regret
And for your little Gypsy breathe a sigh.

Your loving Pauline

MY JEANIE

My Jeanie:
    When Thou art near
The sweetest joys still sweeter seem
The brightest hopes more bright appear
And life is all one happy dream
    When Thou art near.

Your larger half, Pauline E. Johnson

MY LITTLE JEAN

Mine is the fate to watch the evening star,
In yonder dome,
Descending slowly through the cobweb bar
That girts the twilight mysteries afar –
Above your home.

Mine is the fate to turn toward the west
When falls the dew,
When dips the sun beyond the woodland crest
At vesper hour, I think, my loved and best,
Alone of you.

And mine the happy fate to live for aye
Within the dream
Of knowing that the sun lights not a day
But that some thought of yours to me will stray,
My little Jean.

The diamond blaze of glory lures me through
A gilded whirl,
Fame stretches toward me crowns of sapphire blue;
But I must fain resist – and choose but you,
My bonny girl.

Your friendship has sufficed, and held its own
Unsullied still,
What manly voice upon my heart has grown,
What stronger hand can soothe like yours alone
My headstrong will?

Life offers me no love but love for you,
My woman's thought
Was never given to test a faith untrue –
Nor drink of passion's spirits drugged with rue,
Too dearly bought.

They say sometime my wayward heart must rise,
To love so strong,
That friendship will grow cold when other ties
Enslave my heart, that in my soul there lies
An unknown song.

But yet it is unsung, nor do I care
Its notes to glean;
Give in their place your bonny eyes and hair,
Your tender voice, your heart, a jewel rare –
My little Jean.

ROVER

Nurse! will you close the window tight?
    The air is bleak;
I cannot bear its breath to-night,
    I am too weak.

You think that I am worse, dear one?
    Just now you cried;
Your tears mean that before the dawn
    I will have died.

How long you've lived! your hair of snow
    Tells that you've seen
Some three-score years, but I must go
    At seventeen.

So well you've loved and tended me
    Through life's short way,
From my first early infancy,
    To this sad day!

Ah, how the dark pines sigh! I think
    They almost know,
That I am near the river's brink,
    And soon must go.

I do not like their mournful song,
    Nor do I care,
That they are crowns for all the throng
    Of mountains there.

Grey are their rugged peaks, and high;
    I only see
The monotone of deep blue sky,
    The wild fir tree.

The north is closed with jagged crest,
    The east akin
The same stern guards on south and west
    Have shut me in.

Oh, for my home, fanned by the air
    From off the bay!
I'd give a lifetime to be there
    On my last day;

To see for miles along the shore
    The shimmering sand;
To watch the pretty yachts once more
    Come into land;

To hear the hearty sailors sing
    Their gay good-night;
To watch for leagues the sea-gull's wing
    In homeward flight;

To see the light-house white and tall,
    Still and remote;
To hear the brown sandpiper call
    His weird, low note;

To feel the world was wide and gay,
    And heaven as near,
As when I sailed the crescent bay
    This time last year.

A message home from me, you say?
    Yes, they must know
How I have thought of them to-day,
    And loved them so!

Tell them 'goodbye,' and give them this
    Wee mountain-flower,
And say I sent it with a kiss
    In my last hour.

But there's one friend that I must leave
   With fond regret;
I only know how he would grieve –
   My spaniel pet.

My poor brown dog! how he will miss
   My whistle shrill;
He'll wonder where his mistress is,
   Or why so still.

And when he sees you at the gate,
   At home once more,
He'll bark for me and sweetly wait
   Beside the door.

I will not speak or pat his head;
   And he alone
Can't understand that I am dead
   When I go home.

So when in splendor I am laid
   In stately gloom,
Where stars and flower crosses fade
   In snow-white bloom;

When all the lighted candles blend
   With shadows cast,
Bring Rover in – my best-loved friend –
   To look his last.

Then take him in your arms of snow,
   His future place,
And lift him up – perhaps he'll know
   My poor dead face.

No voice, no step, no greetings kind,
   No laughing eyes,
No clue that his dumb, wondering mind
   Can recognize.

But a year hence, when sorrow's flame
   Has ceased to burn,
My dog will watch and wait in vain
   For my return.

THE RIFT

Nature has wept to-day, her pent-up grief
   In tears still trembles on the lily bell;
Remorseless rain-drops fleck its bending leaf,
   And crystallize its yellow coronal.

And from the pansy 'neath the acacia tree
   The purple velvet bloom is dashed away;
The skies are low'ring down so heavily,
   Nature is sadder than a sigh to-day.

Something has hurt your heart and made you grieve,
   The day has been too dark without the sun;
Something has proved too hard; but, oh! believe
   Others have suffered just as you have done.

Some one has sobbed to-day, as you do now;
   Those dry, unending sobs of tearless pain,
And felt the fever-heated pulsing brow,
   That was not cooled by heaven's falling rain.

Some one has asked to-day and been denied,
   And in response sent up the shiv'ring cry
That marks some human wish ungratified;
   The reeds on which they leaned all broken lie.

And some have craved to-day a higher sphere,
   And known the tortures of a pinioned will;
Have felt their efforts baffled, and the clear,
   Hard voice of Fate, ring out against them still.

Some one has lost to-day the gilded prize
   That years endeared unto Ambition's soul;
To-night he bears the hardest agonies
   Of failure in the race to win the goal.

Some one has harder tasks to bear and do,
   Has wilder trials than yours, which he contends;
Some one is farther off from Heaven than you,
   Knows less of kindness, and has fewer friends.

Some one has wept to-day disconsolate,
   In unison with earth has nursed his pain,
And felt the world as harsh and desolate
   As the dark, mournful skies, and dripping rain.

Some one is sad to-night, – uncomforted,
   The heart with all its little woes depressed;
A word, perhaps, she fain had left unsaid
   Is burning still within that patient breast.

Some one is tired to-night, too tired to speak
   Of all the hardships of the dark hours past;
Poor heart and hand have grown so slow and weak
   In struggling for the well-won rest at last.

And you are tired to-night, too tired to know
   The clouds have clustered in a crimson drift;
Too tired to see aloft God's signet bow,
   And o'er its prison arch – an azure rift.

THE RE-INTERMENT OF RED JACKET

   So still the tranquil air,
One scarcely notes the falling of a leaf;
But deeper quiet wraps the dusky Chief
Whose ashes slumber there.

Sweet Indian Summer sleeps,
Trusting a foreign and a paler race
To give her gifted son an honoured place
Where Death his vigil keeps.

Before that slumber fell,
Those ashes in their eloquence had stirred
The stubborn hearts, whose heirs to-day conferred
A Christian burial.

Through war's o'er-clouded skies
His higher flush of oratory 'woke,
And factious schemes succumbed whene'er he spoke
To bid his people rise.

The keenest flint or stone
That barbed the warrior's arrow in its flight,
Could not outreach the limit of his might
That he attained alone.

Early he learned to speak,
With thought so vast, and liberal, and strong,
He blessed the little good and passed the wrong
Embodied in the weak.

So great his mental sight,
That had his form been growing with his mind,
The fir had been within his hand a wand
With superhuman might.

The world has often seen
A master mind pulse with the waning day
That sends his waning nation to decay
Where none can intervene.

And few to-day remain;
But copper-tinted face and smoldering fire
Of wilder life, were left me by my sire
To be my proudest claim.

And so erc Indian Summer sweetly sleeps,
She beckons me where old Niagara leaps;
Superbly she extends her greeting hand,
And smiling speaks to her adopted land;

Saying, 'O, rising nation of the West,
That occupies my land, so richly blest;
O, free, unfettered people that have come
To make America your rightful home,

Forgive the wrongs my children did to you,
And we, the red skins, will forgive you too;
To-day has seen your noblest action done,
The honoured re-entombment of my son.'

THE SEA QUEEN

She does not dwell in far-off verdant lands,
No sailor's bride nor tar's fond lassie she;
No lover and no husband on the sea;
No golden circlet on her dainty hands;
No waiting heart she holds for one afar;
To none a love, to none an ocean star.
Only a little child, with fair blue eyes
That caught their colour from the restless wave,
A baby face, both winsome, bright, and grave,
A guileless cherub clothed in human guise,
Though but a tiny child with virtues few,
A wee small girl, the darling of the crew –
A majesty in embryo of state,
The pretty daughter of the second mate.
Her little heart unmindful of their wrongs,
She laughs, and jests, and shouts their drinking songs;
And, mixed with hymns her angel mother sang,
She uses all their jolly sea-born slang.
At night they hear her pray in lisping tones,
'Protect us, Dod, from 'torms and Davy Jones,
And guide the pilot watch till b'eak of day;

And teep the rats aboard the s'ip alway.'
Untutored infant, motherless, alone,
A baby vagabond that knows no home;
Beloved by all those storm-tossed, hardened men,
Her little life one long, despotic reign;
There's not a man among that loyal crew
But pays the homage to his idol due,
But checks his oaths when those pure footsteps pass,
And says beneath his breath, 'God bless the lass!'
The second mate has taught his child to be
The sailor's pet, the sov'reign of the sea.

IRIS TO FLORETTA

They both live side by side among
The wooded banks of endless song,
Where wild birds carol all day long.

The iris grows beneath the ledge
Of bank all overgrown with sedge
That creeps along the river's edge.

My little girl, so like that flower,
Strong in her purity of power,
Fidelity her richest dower.

With heart and thought of clearer tone
Than her surroundings – where alone
She shines – a gem among the stone.

Her sister twin – the iris blue,
With blossoms clothed in Heaven's hue,
So like her life – so tried and true.

They both live where they daily meet
Temptations through their lives so sweet –
An undercurrent 'round their feet

The stream of love and truth to blend,
A sweetness Heaven alone can send
The iris and my little friend.

A CRY FROM AN INDIAN WIFE

My Forest Brave, my Red-skin love, farewell;
We may not meet to-morrow; who can tell
What mighty ills befall our little band,
Or what you'll suffer from the white man's hand?
Here is your knife! I thought 'twas sheathed for aye.
No roaming bison calls for it to-day;
No hide of prairie cattle will it maim;
The plains are bare, it seeks a nobler game:
'Twill drink the life-blood of a soldier host.
Go; rise and strike, no matter what the cost.
Yet stay. Revolt not at the Union Jack,
Nor raise thy hand against this stripling pack
Of white-faced warriors, marching West to quell
Our fallen tribe that rises to rebel.
They all are young and beautiful and good;
Curse to the war that drinks their harmless blood.
Curse to the fate that brought them from the East
To be our chiefs – to make our nation least
That breathes the air of this vast continent.
Still their new rule and council is well meant.
They but forget we Indians owned the land
From ocean unto ocean; that they stand
Upon a soil that centuries agone
Was our sole kingdom and our right alone.
They never think how they would feel to-day,
If some great nation came from far away,
Wrestling their country from their hapless braves,
Giving what they gave us – but wars and graves.
Then go and strike for liberty and life,
And bring back honour to your Indian wife.
Your wife? Ah, what of that, who cares for me?
Who pities my poor love and agony?

What white-robed priest prays for your safety here,
As prayer is said for every volunteer
That swells the ranks that Canada sends out?
Who prays for vict'ry for the Indian scout?
Who prays for our poor nation lying low?
None – therefore take your tomahawk and go.
My heart may break and burn into its core,
But I am strong to bid you go to war.
Yet stay, my heart is not the only one
That grieves the loss of husband and of son;
Think of the mothers o'er the inland seas;
Think of the pale-faced maiden on her knees;
One pleads her God to guard some sweet-faced child
That marches on toward the North-West wild.
The other prays to shield her love from harm,
To strengthen his young, proud uplifted arm.
Ah, how her white face quivers thus to think,
Your tomahawk his life's best blood will drink.
She never thinks of my wild aching breast,
Nor prays for your dark face and eagle crest
Endangered by a thousand rifle balls,
My heart the target if my warrior falls.
O! coward self I hesitate no more;
Go forth, and win the glories of the war.
Go forth, nor bend to greed of white men's hands,
By right, by birth we Indians own these lands,
Though starved, crushed, plundered, lies our nation low ...
Perhaps the white man's God has willed it so.

IN THE SHADOWS

I am sailing to the leeward,
Where the current runs to seaward
    Soft and slow,
Where the sleeping river grasses
Brush my paddle as it passes
    To and fro.

On the shore the heat is shaking
All the golden sands awaking
    In the cove;
And the quaint sand-piper, winging
O'er the shallows, ceases singing
    When I move.

On the water's idle pillow
Sleeps the overhanging willow,
    Green and cool;
Where the rushes lift their burnished
Oval heads from out the tarnished
    Emerald pool.

Where the very silence slumbers,
Water lilies grow in numbers,
    Pure and pale;
All the morning they have rested,
Amber crowned, and pearly crested,
    Fair and frail.

Here impossible romances,
Indefinable sweet fancies,
    Cluster round;
But they do not mar the sweetness
Of this still September fleetness
    With a sound.

I can scarce discern the meeting
Of the shore and stream retreating,
    So remote;
For the laggard river, dozing,
Only wakes from its reposing
    Where I float.

Where the river mists are rising,
All the foliage baptizing
    With their spray;
There the sun gleams far and faintly,
With a shadow soft and saintly,
    In its ray.

And the perfume of some burning
Far-off brushwood, ever turning
   To exhale
All its smoky fragrance dying,
In the arms of evening lying,
   Where I sail.

My canoe is growing lazy,
In the atmosphere so hazy,
   While I dream;
Half in slumber I am guiding,
Eastward indistinctly gliding
   Down the stream.

THE FIRS

Pine trees sobbing a weird unrest
   In saddened strains;
Crows flying slowly into the west
   As daylight wanes;
Breezes that die in a stifled breath,
Leaving a calm that is still as death.

Fir trees reaching toward the sky
   In giant might;
All day long at your feet I lie
   Awaiting night,
While sweet pine needles are falling down
In silent showers of golden brown.

How waves the blue Canadian air
   Amid your arms?
'Tis not so calm down here as there,
   Because your charms
Enhance the world to a sapphire blue,
And change its tone with its change of hue.

Changed in a thousand trivial ways –
   That shade a life,
Leaving the dregs of yesterdays
   With shadows rife:
Shadows that lie in the fir tops tall,
And fall with the fir cones over all.

For some one's turned their tender eyes
   Away from me,
And dark the sorrow that in them lies
   With misery;
Oh, gentlest pleader my life has known,
I stay as you found me, here – alone.

Alone with the firs and the dying day,
   That lived too long;
Alone with the pines that sing alway
   Their strange, wild song.
Ah, darling ! unclasp your fair, warm hand,
'Tis better I should misunderstand.

EASTER LILIES

Twilight – the ancient city lies asleep;
Below, the waters blackly sullen creep,
Above, the stars in countless thousands peep.

Silent the lesser light now holds her sway,
Nor vanquished sighs, when at to-morrow's ray
This quiet cloud of rest will float away.

Few are the wanderers on the streets to-night,
Flick'ring and dim reflects the corner light,
Beyond the gloom that lurks on left and right.

There lingers still along the alleys quaint,
The echoes of the bells so far and faint,
That crown the night like halo round a saint.

And saint-like, standing there in vestal power,
Peace as her birthright, and God's grace her dower,
Church of St Agnes lifts her grey stone tower.

The portals stand ajar, as one by one
The pilgrims, who the toils of day have done,
Kneel, say a prayer – then seek repose at home.

And enters there with faltering feet and slow,
A girl, whose heart is steeped in secret woe,
Whose hand bears calla lilies, pure as snow.

Up through arched aisles of faintly incensed air,
The Everlasting Lamp is burning, where
She bends her knee below the altar stair.

Only a girl, unknown to you and me,
Only a leaf on Heaven's favoured tree,
Only a drop within the world's great sea.

Only a girl who seeks this one retreat,
To leave her sorrows, with life's bitter-sweet,
Entwined with lilies at her Saviour's feet.

With Easter lilies that she leaves alone
Within that consecrated pile of stone
That stands by moss and lichen overgrown.

That stands, unsullied by surrounding crime,
The gate to Heaven, and the bridge sublime,
The pilgrim treads, that spans the seas of Time.

Ah! weary child of prayers and lily bloom
Would that thy buds could bear on their perfume
The prayers of other hearts enwrapped in gloom.

For as she threads the streets so cold and grey
And in the night St Agnes fades away,
She feels the faith God's Own can hold alway.

It may be, in afflictions hard to bear,
– Her prayers too human for her God to hear –
He sends her Peace, that queen without a peer.

St Agnes with her glories all replete
Will some day take the bitter from the sweet,
And leave her life no longer incomplete.

Twilight – young day is slumbering in the West,
His tissue wings athwart his waxen breast,
Beneath his feet, the city wrapped in rest.

AT THE FERRY

We are waiting in the nightfall by the river's placid rim,
Summer silence all about us, save where swallows' pinions skim
The still grey waters sharply, and the widening circles reach,
With faintest, stillest music, the white gravel on the beach.
The sun has set long, long ago. Against the pearly sky
Elm branches lift their etching up in arches slight and high.
Behind us stands the forest, with its black and lonely pines;
Before us, like a silver thread, the old Grand River winds.
Far down its banks the village lights are creeping one by one;
Far up above, with holy torch, the evening star looks down.

Amid the listening stillness, you and I have silent grown,
Waiting for the river ferry, – waiting in the dusk alone.
At last we hear an eager step, sweet silence reigns no more;
'Tis a barefoot, sun-burnt little boy upon the other shore.
Far through the waning twilight we can see him quickly kneel
To lift the heavy chain, then turn the rusty old cog-wheel;
And the water-logged old ferry-boat moves slowly from the
    brink,
Breaking all the star's reflections with the waves that rise and
    sink;
While the water dripping gently from the rising, falling chains,
Is the only interruption to the quiet that remains
To lull us into golden dreams, to charm our cares away

With its Lethean waters flowing 'neath the bridge of yesterday.
Oh ! the day was calm and tender, but the night is calmer still,
As we go aboard the ferry, where we stand and dream, until
We cross the sleeping river, with its restful whisperings,
And peace falls, like a feather from some passing angel's wings.

'BRANT,' A MEMORIAL ODE

Young Canada with mighty force sweeps on
To gain in power and strength, before the dawn
That brings another era; when the sun
Shall rise again, but only shine upon
Her Indian graves, and Indian memories.
For as the carmine in the twilight skies
Will fade as night comes on, so fades the race
That unto Might and therefore Right gives place,
And as white clouds float hurriedly and high
Across the crimson of a sunset sky,
Although their depths are foamy as the snow,
Their beauty lies in their vermillion glow,
So Canada, thy plumes were hardly won
Without allegiance from thy Indian son,
Thy glories, like the cloud enhance their charm
With red reflections from the Mohawk's arm.
Then meet we as one common Brotherhood,
In peace and love, with purpose understood –
To lift a lasting tribute to the name
Of Brant – who linked his own, with Britain's fame,
Who bade his people leave their valley home,
Where nature in her fairest aspect shone,
Where rolls the Mohawk river, and the land
Is blessed with every good from Heaven's hand,
To sweep the tide of home affections back
And love the land where waves the Union Jack.
What though that home no longer ours! To-day
The Six Red Nations have their Canada,
And rest we here, no cause for us to rise
To seek protection under other skies,

Encircling us an arm both true and brave
Extends from far across the great Salt wave,
Though but a woman's hand 'tis firm and strong
Enough to guard us from all fear of wrong,
A hand on which all British subjects lean –
The loving hand of England's Noble Queen.

['ALAS! HOW DAMNING PRAISE CAN BE!']

alas! how damning praise can be!
This man so scared of spoiling me
Shook all the honey from his pen
Dipped it in acid, and scribbled then –
'No compliments on her I'll laden
She's but a <u>pleasant looking</u> maiden.'

A REQUEST

[To the noble society known as 'The Woman's Auxiliary of
Missions of the Church of England in Canada,' – who are
doing their utmost in the good work of sending Missionaries
to the Crees and Blackfeet – the following lines are respect-
fully and gratefully inscribed.]

Beyond the boundaries of all our mighty inland lakes,
Beyond the old Red River shore, where Manitoba breaks
Into the far and fair North-west its limitless extent,
Last year with cannon, shot, and shell the British soldier went.
Full many a city flocked to bid her gallant boys good-bye,
Cheer after cheer went ringing out, and flags were flaunted
    high;
And well indeed those warriors fought, and surely well they
    bled,
And surely well some sleep to-day within their silent bed.
Perhaps a soldier's medals are of greater honour when
He wins them at the cost of his own fellow-countrymen –

'Tis not my place to question if their laurel wreath still thrives,
If its fragrance is of Indian blood, its glory Indian lives.
I only know some heart still waits with pulse that beats and
    burns
For footsteps of the boy who left but nevermore returns,
Another heart still dwells beyond thy banks, Saskatchewan –
O Indian mother, list'ning for the coming of your son
Who left his home a year ago to fight the Volunteers,
To meet his death from British guns, his death-song British
    cheers.
For you I speak to-day, and ask some noble, faithful hands,
To send another band of men to meet you in your lands.
Not as last year these gallant hearts as dogs of war will go,
No swords within their hands, no cause to bring the after-glow
Of blush to Canada's fair cheek, for none can say as then:
'She treats her Indian wards as foes.' No! These are different
    men,
Their strength is not in rank and file, no martial host they lead,
Their mission is the cross of Christ, their arms the Christian
    creed.
Instead of helmet round their head, a halo shines afar,
'Twill light your prairie pathway up more than the flash of war.
Seek not to find upon this band a coat of crimson glow –
God grant their hands will spotless be as their own robes of
    snow,
O men who go on missions to the North-west Indian lands,
The thorns may pierce your foreheads and the cross may bruise
    your hands,
For though the goal seems far away, reward seems vague and
    dim –
If ye Christianise the least of them, 'Ye do it unto Him,'
And, perhaps, beyond the river brink the waves of death have
    laved,
The jewels in your crown will be the Indian souls you've saved.

FASTING

'Tis morning now, yet silently I stand,
Uplift the curtain with a heavy hand,
Look out while darkness overspreads the way,
   And long for day.

Calm peace is frighted with my mood to-night,
Nor visits my dull chamber with her light,
To guide my senses into her sweet rest
   And leave me blest.

Long hours since the city rocked and sung
Itself to slumber: only the stars swung
Aloft their torches in the midnight skies
   With watchful eyes.

No sound awakes; I, even, breathe no sigh,
Nor hear a single footstep passing by;
Yet I am not alone, for now I feel
   A presence steal

Within my chamber walls; I turn to see
The sweetest guest that courts humanity;
With subtle, slow enchantment draws she near,
   And Sleep is here.

What care I for the olive branch of Peace?
Kind Sleep will bring a thrice-distilled release,
Nepenthe's, that alone her mystic hand
   Can understand.

And so she bends, this welcome sorceress,
To crown my fasting with her light caress.
Ah, sure my pain will vanish at the bliss
   Of her warm kiss.

But still my duty lies in self-denial;
I must refuse sweet Sleep, although the trial

Will reawaken all my depth of pain.
  So once again

I lift the curtain with a weary hand,
With more than sorrow, silently I stand,
Look out while darkness overspreads the way,
  And long for day.

'Go, Sleep,' I say, 'before the darkness die,
To one who needs you even more than I,
For I can bear my part alone, but he
  Has need of thee.

'His poor tired eyes in vain have sought relief,
His heart more tired still, with all its grief;
His pain is deep, while mine is vague and dim,
  Go thou to him.

'When thou hast fanned him with thy drowsy wings,
And laid thy lips upon the pulsing strings
That in his soul with fret and fever burn,
  To me return.'

She goes. The air within the quiet street
Reverberates to the passing of her feet;
I watch her take her passage through the gloom
  To your dear home.

Belovèd, would you knew how sweet to me
Is this denial, and how fervently
I pray that Sleep may lift you to her breast,
  And give you rest –

A privilege that she alone can claim.
Would that my heart could comfort you the same,
But in the censer Sleep is swinging high,
  All sorrows die.

She comes not back, yet all my miseries
Wane at the thought of your calm sleeping eyes –

Wane, as I hear the early matin bell
   The dawn foretell.

And so, dear heart, still silently I stand,
Uplift the curtain with a weary hand,
The long, long night has bitter been and lone,
   But now 'tis gone.

Dawn lights her candles in the East once more,
And darkness flees her chariot before;
The Lenten morning breaks with holy ray,
   And it is day!

LIFE

But yesternight we laughed to view
The stars that sailed in seas of blue –
To-day we wake 'neath greyer skies,
To look on life with diff'rent eyes,
To look on life with diff'rent eyes, with diff'rent eyes –

Alas! how many stars are set,
For which we're longing, watching yet,
O useless hope! O eyes that burn!
The stars you love will not return,
The stars you love will not return.

MY ENGLISH LETTER

When each white moon, her lantern idly swinging,
   Comes out to join the star night-watching band,
Across the grey-green sea, a ship is bringing
   For me a letter, from the Motherland.

Naught would I care to live in quaint old Britain,
    These wilder shores are dearer far to me,
Yet when I read the words that hand has written,
    The parent sod more precious seems to be.

Within that folded note I catch the savour
    Of climes that make the Motherland so fair,
Although I never knew the blessed favour
    That surely lies in breathing English air.

Imagination's brush before me fleeting,
    Paints English pictures, though my longing eyes
Have never known the blessedness of seeing
    The blue that lines the arch of English skies.

And yet my letter brings the scenes I covet,
    Framed in the salt sea winds, aye more in dreams
I almost see the face that bent above it,
    I almost touch that hand, so near it seems.

Near, for the very grey-green sea that dashes
    'Round these Canadian coasts, rolls out once more
To Eastward, and the same Atlantic splashes
    Her wild white spray on England's distant shore.

Near, for the same young moon so idly swinging
    Her threadlike crescent bends the selfsame smile
On that old land from whence a ship is bringing
    My message from the transatlantic Isle.

Thus loves my heart that far old country better,
    Because of those dear words that always come,
With love enfolded in each English letter
    That drifts into my sun-kissed Western home.

EASTER

April 1, 1888

Lent gathers up her cloak of sombre shading
　　In her reluctant hands.
Her beauty heightens, fairest in its fading,
　　As pensively she stands
Awaiting Easter's benediction falling,
　　Like silver stars at night,
Before she can obey the summons calling
　　Her to her upward flight,
Awaiting Easter's wings that she must borrow
　　Ere she can hope to fly –
Those glorious wings that we shall see to-morrow
　　Against the far, blue sky.
Has not the purple of her vesture's lining
　　Brought calm and rest to all?
Has her dark robe had naught of golden shining
　　Been naught but pleasure's pall?
Who knows? Perhaps when to the world returning
　　In youth's light joyousness,
We'll wear some rarer jewels we found burning
　　In Lent's black-bordered dress.
So hand in hand with fitful March she lingers
　　To beg the crowning grace
Of lifting with her pure and holy fingers
　　The veil from April's face.
Sweet, rosy April – laughing, sighing, waiting
　　Until the gateway swings,
And she and Lent can kiss between the grating
　　Of Easter's tissue wings.
Too brief the bliss – the parting comes with sorrow.
　　Good-bye dear Lent, good-bye!
We'll watch your fading wings outlined to-morrow
　　Against the far blue sky.

JOE

An Etching

A meadow brown; across the yonder edge
A zigzag fence is ambling; here a wedge
Of underbush has cleft its course in twain,
Till where beyond it staggers up again;
The long, grey rails stretch in a broken line
Their ragged length of rough, split forest pine,
And in their zigzag tottering have reeled
In drunken efforts to enclose the field,
Which carries on its breast, September born,
A patch of rustling, yellow, Indian corn.
Beyond its shrivelled tassels, perched upon
The topmost rail, sits Joe, the settler's son,
A little semi-savage boy of nine.
Now dozing in the warmth of Nature's wine,
His face the sun has tampered with, and wrought,
By heated kisses, mischief, and has brought
Some vagrant freckles, while from here and there
A few wild locks of vagabond brown hair
Escape the old straw hat the sun looks through,
And blinks to meet his Irish eyes of blue.
Barefooted, innocent of coat or vest,
His grey checked shirt unbuttoned at his chest,
Both hardy hands within their usual nest –
His breeches pockets – so, he waits to rest
His little fingers, somewhat tired and worn,
That all day long were husking Indian corn.
His drowsy lids snap at some trivial sound,
With lazy yawns he slips towards the ground,
Then with an idle whistle lifts his load
And shambles home along the country road
That stretches on, fringed out with stumps and weeds,
And finally unto the backwoods leads,
Where forests wait with giant trunk and bough
The axe of pioneer, the settler's plough.

UNGUESSED

The day is warm and fair;
The early summer air
Is resting in the overhanging trees,
And at our feet there lave
The undulating waves
That wash the shores and fret the sands of many azure seas.

Beneath this tangled bower
We've idled many an hour
And tossed away too many tender days –
I quite content in love
To watch your face above
The netted couch, in which you lie, that softly floats and sways.

Did young Apollo wear
A face than yours more fair,
More purely blonde, in beauty more complete?
Belovèd, will not you
Unclose those eyes of blue
That hold my world and bless and curse the life they render
sweet?

I wonder how you rest
So calmly, when my breast
Is tortured by the efforts that I make
To strangle love and keep
His ensign from my cheek,
To still the passion in my heart just for our friendship's sake.

But perfect calm still lies
Within your sleeping eyes,
O'erveiled by lids that soft betoken rest.
Your lips serenely close
In undisturbed repose,
Nor tremble with the gentle, peaceful heaving of your breast.

Ah! well it is for me
That you, sweet, cannot see

Within my heart so tyrannized by love.
  Ah! well it is for you
  My friendship you deem true,
Nor know how false the friend that bends your sleeping form
  above.

  Some stranger far and lone,
  By you unseen, unknown,
Could give you calmer fondness in my stead,
  For I have drunk the wine
  Distilled from Love's wild vine,
And reeling with its subtle fumes I strike our friendship dead.

OUR BROTHERHOOD

We all maintain some daily trivial service unto man.
We all have possibilities. We all have tried to plan
Some delicate creation. The firm handiwork of will
May assist in its formation, though perchance the artist's skill
Has proved too insufficient to achieve Desire's height.
Our confidence has been too vast, we overreached our might,
We all have dreams unrealized, we all have known the cost
Of prizes won and heights o'ercome, of honours well attained
In places where *we* should have stood – fate failed us, others
  gained.
O! Failure, may we not escape thy black, remorseless wing
That clouds the sunlight of success, our work o'ershadowing?
Why doom to wreck Ambition's barque before it fairly sailed
From ideal shores to ideal lands? Who has not tried – and
  failed?
We all have wakened once, to know the cold and biting truth
That empty is the darling hope we nurtured in our youth.
We all would live in every line with close-shut eyes, and yet
We all can see the fair design is shadowed by – Regret.

THE DEATH-CRY

Moonless the skies, unlit the forest way,
Black hangs the night o'er northern Canada.
Parting the silence comes the hoot of owls,
A stray fox barks – afar some strange dog howls,
In such forebodings crouches death –
                                    A knife
Uplifted in the crisis of hot strife
Has drunk vermillion draughts, its hostile blow
Has stilled the hostile blood of some dark foe,
Noiseless the victor through the midnight creeps
Toward the forest stream which silent sleeps –
Leans he low down above the snake-like flood,
To tell his world that law is blood for blood,
Bold from his parted lips the death-cry leaps
Adown the waters, icily it sweeps,
Weird, strange and chilling, awfulest of cries
That on distant darkness floats – then dies,
The Mohawk listens! all is still as death,
Aye, death itself seems dead – once more that breath
Curdles the air with savage eloquence,
Vibrating through the forest black and dense,
One moment more of gloom, ghostlike and drear,
Then the red warrior's catlike, listening ear
Catches a seeming echo – a reply
From miles adown the stream – his wild death-cry
Has floated with the waters, and 'tis passed
From mouth to mouth, the deed is known at last.
Unmoved he hears the far off eerie wail,
Then turns to take again the midnight trail,
He parts the boughs – bends low his eagle plume
And merges in the depths of forest gloom.

KEEPSAKES

'Keepsakes?' she asked, then grew her sweet eyes grave,
   'Why yes, old-fashioned as it is, my dear,
   I hoard some treasures Cousin Malcolm gave
   To me before he went away last year.

'Three gems he left me, then came a good-bye:
   Then crossed he to that "far-off land" alone,
   But those three treasures are a precious tie
   That binds us through the distance where he's gone.

'One is a plain and heavy hoop of gold:
   To others 'tis an ordinary thing,
   But unto me it means a wealth untold –
   His faith and mine are in that wedding ring.

'I count so royal his untarnished name
   And strive to wear it worthily alway –
   To keep it clothed in honour, just the same
   As Malcom gave it ere he went away.

'Blue blessed eyes and hair of golden light
   My crowning jewel has – so like to his,
   God help me lead our little child aright
   Till I may follow where my darling is.'

THE FLIGHT OF THE CROWS

The autumn afternoon is dying o'er
   The quiet western valley where I lie
Beneath the maples on the river shore,
   Where tinted leaves, blue waters and fair sky
   Environ all; and far above some birds are flying by

To seek their evening haven in the breast
   And calm embrace of silence, while they sing

Te Deums to the night, invoking rest
  For busy chirping voice and tired wing –
And in the hush of sleeping trees their sleeping cradles swing.

In forest arms the night will soonest creep,
  Where sombre pines a lullaby intone,
Where Nature's children curl themselves to sleep,
  And all is still at last, save where alone
  A band of black, belated crows arrive from lands unknown.

Strange sojourn has been theirs since waking day,
  Strange sights and cities in their wanderings blend
With fields of yellow maize, and leagues away
  With rivers where their sweeping waters wend
  Past velvet banks to rocky shores, in cañons bold to end.

O'er what vast lakes that stretch superbly dead,
  Till lashed to life by storm-clouds, have they flown?
In what wild lands, in laggard flight have led
  Their aerial career unseen, unknown,
  Till now with twilight come their cries in lonely monotone?

The flapping of their pinions in the air
  Dies in the hush of distance, while they light
Within the fir tops, weirdly black and bare,
  That stand with giant strength and peerless height,
To shelter fairy, bird and beast throughout the closing night.

Strange black and princely pirates of the skies,
  Would that your wind-tossed travels I could know!
Would that my soul could see, and, seeing, rise
  To unrestricted life where ebb and flow
  Of Nature's pulse would constitute a wider life below!

Could I but live just here in Freedom's arms,
  A kingly life without a sovereign's care!
Vain dreams! Day hides with closing wings her charms,
  And all is cradled in repose, save where
  Yon band of black, belated crows still frets the evening air.

UNDER CANVAS

In Muskoka

Lichens of green and grey on every side;
And green and grey the rocks beneath our feet;
Above our heads the canvas stretching wide;
And over all, enchantment rare and sweet.

Fair Rosseau slumbers in an atmosphere
That kisses her to passionless soft dreams.
O! joy of living we have found thee here,
And life lacks nothing, so complete it seems.

The velvet air, stirred by some elfin wings,
Comes swinging up the waters and then stills
Its voice so low that floating by it sings
Like distant harps among the distant hills.

Across the lake the rugged islands lie,
Fir-crowned and grim; and further in the view
Some shadows seeming swung 'twixt cloud and sky,
Are countless shores, a symphony of blue.

Some northern sorceress, when day is done,
Hovers where cliffs uplift their gaunt grey steeps,
Bewitching to vermilion Rosseau's sun,
That in a liquid mass of rubies sleeps.

The scent of burning leaves, the camp-fire's blaze,
The great logs cracking in the brilliant flame,
The groups grotesque, on which the firelight plays,
Are pictures which Muskoka twilights frame.

And Night, star-crested, wanders up the mere
With opiates for idleness to quaff,
And while she ministers, far off I hear
The owl's uncanny cry, the wild loon's laugh.

WORKWORN

Across the street, an humble woman lives;
To her 'tis little fortune ever gives;
Denied the wines of life, it puzzles me
To know how she can laugh so cheerily.
This morn I listened to her softly sing,
And, marvelling what this effect could bring
I looked: 'twas but the presence of a child
Who passed her gate, and looking in, had smiled.
But self-encrusted, I had failed to see
The child had also looked and laughed to me.
My lowly neighbour thought the smile God-sent,
And singing, through the toilsome hours she went.
O! weary singer, I have learned the wrong
Of taking gifts, and giving naught of song;
I thought my blessings scant, my mercies few,
Till I contrasted them with yours, and you;
To-day I counted much, yet wished it more –
While but a child's bright smile was all your store.

If I had thought of all the stormy days,
That fill some lives that tread less favoured ways,
How little sunshine through their shadows gleamed,
My own dull life had much the brighter seemed;
If I had thought of all the eyes that weep
Through desolation, and still smiling keep,
That see so little pleasure, so much woe,
My own had laughed more often long ago;
If I had thought how leaden was the weight
Adversity lays at my kinsman's gate,
Of that great cross my next door neighbour bears,
My thanks had been more frequent in my prayers;
If I had watched the woman o'er the way,
Workworn and old, who labours day by day,
Who has no rest, no joy to call her own,
My tasks, my heart, had much the lighter grown.

THE LUMBERMAN'S CHRISTMAS

'Well, Carlo, so this here is Chris'mus,
By jingo, I almost forgot,
T'aint what you an' me has been used to,
'Afore we come out here to squat.
Seems jist like the rest of the winter,
The same freezin' air, the same snow,
I guess that we can't be mistaken!
This almanac book says it's so.
Well, Carlo, you lazy old beggar,
Right here in the shanty we'll stay
An' celebrate Chris'mus together,
The loggin' will keep for a day.
We'll hang up this bit o' green cedar
Atop our old keresene light,
It'll make things look somethin' like Chris'mus,
An' brighten us up a great sight.
You're waggin' yer tail, are you, Carlo?
An' puttin' yer head on my knee.
That's one way to say Merry Chris'mus,
An' make believe you're fond o' me:
You scamp, I most think you're not foolin',
I see it right thar in yer eyes.
Don't fail me, old dog, it would kill me,
You're all the possession I prize.

Last Chris'mus – you bet I remember –
We weren't in a shanty that day,
In lumberin' tracts with the railroad
Some sixty an' odd miles away.
No, sir, we were home in the village,
With mother, an' Billy, an' Jack,
An', somehow, I feel like this minute
I kinder jist want to go back.
An' *she* was thar too, an' I loved her;
Yes, Carlo, I'll say so to you,
Because you believe that I'm honest.
An' them that thinks likewise is few.
You see she had promised to marry

Old Jack an' my heart kinder broke,
For tryin' to stand by him squar-like
Meant, love-words must never be spoke.
Somehow it got out, an' the neighbours
Said Jack was suspicious of me;
I carried my heart out too open,
The world as it run by could see.
I stood it until that thar' mornin'
On the Bay, when the storm caught us squar',
I hoped that we both would be drownded,
An' told her my love then and thar'.
Her voice answered strange like an' broken,
Her lips they was white and compressed,
"Oh, Jamie, I'm glad you have spoken,
For, dear one, I loved you the best."
An' then, with the storm devils ragin'
Far out of my arms she was thrown.
O, God, when I come to my senses,
I was safe on the shore – but *alone.*
Alone, with her words still a soundin',
Those wild, lovin' words she jist said,
Alone with the terrible sorrow
Of known' my darlin' was dead.
Alone, with my brave brother Billy,
Who saved my dishonourable life,
For all says I drowned her a purpose
To keep her from bein' Jack's wife.
I think I'd have borne it quite manly,
But when I looked Jack in the face,
He asked me to give the straight ticket,
I told him my love and disgrace;
But never a word did I mention
About them last words that she spoke,
I'd lose him enough, Heaven knows it,
His heart with my own had been broke.
It's hard on me havin' this achin',
This homelessness here in my breast,
But the hardest to bear is the knowin'
That Jack – well – *he thinks like the rest.*
No, Carlo, we won't be returnin'

To them parts for some time to come,
Though knowin' the white-haired old mother
Is waitin' to see us come home;
I guess she looks older this Chris'mus,
An' sadder, mayhap, than I be;
For she an' brave Billy, an' you sir,
Are all that believes now in me.

II. The Prolific Years: 1889–1898

THE HAPPY HUNTING GROUNDS

Into the rose gold westland, its yellow prairies roll,
World of the bison's freedom, home of the Indian's soul.
Roll out, O seas! in sunlight bathed,
Your plains wind-tossed, and grass enswathed.

Farther than vision ranges, farther than eagles fly,
Stretches the land of beauty, arches the perfect sky,
Hemm'd through the purple mists afar
By peaks that gleam like star on star.

Fringing the prairie billows, fretting horizon's line,
Darkly green are slumb'ring wildernesses of pine,
Sleeping until the zephyrs throng
To kiss their silence into song.

Whispers freighted with odour swinging into the air,
Russet needles as censers swing to an altar, where
The angels' songs are less divine
Than duo sung twixt breeze and pine.

Laughing into the forest, dimples a mountain stream,
Pure as the airs above it, soft as a summer dream,
O! Lethean spring thou'rt only found
Within this ideal hunting ground.

Surely the great Hereafter cannot be more than this,
Surely we'll see that country after Time's farewell kiss.
Who would his lovely faith condole?
Who envies not the Red-skin's soul,

Sailing into the cloud land, sailing into the sun,
Into the crimson portals ajar when life is done?
O! dear dead race, my spirit too
Would fain sail westward unto you.

CLOSE BY

So near at hand (our eyes o'erlooked its nearness
In search of distant things)
A dear dream lay – perchance to grow in dearness
Had we but felt its wings
Astir. The air our very breathing fanned
It was so near at hand.

Once, many days ago, we almost held it,
The love we so desired;
But our shut eyes saw not, and fate dispelled it
Before our pulses fired
To flame, and errant fortune bade us stand
Hand almost touching hand.

I sometimes think had we two been discerning,
The by-path hid away
From others' eyes had then revealed its turning
To us, nor led astray
Our footsteps, guiding us into love's land
That lay so near at hand.

So near at hand, dear heart, could we have known it!
Throughout those dreamy hours,
Had either loved, or loving had we shown it,
Response had sure been ours;
We did not know that heart could heart command,
And love so near at hand!

What then availed the red wine's subtle glisten?
We passed it blindly by,
And now what profit that we wait and listen
Each for the other's heart beat? Ah! the cry
Of love o'erlooked still lingers, you and I
Sought heaven afar, we did not understand
'Twas – once so near at hand.

OVERLOOKED

Sleep, with her tender balm, her touch so kind,
                    Has passed me by;
Afar I see her vesture, velvet-lined,
                    Float silently;
O! Sleep, my tired eyes had need of thee!
Is thy sweet kiss not meant to-night for me?

Peace, with the blessings that I longed for so,
                    Has passed me by;
Where'er she folds her holy wings I know
                    All tempests die;
O! Peace, my tired soul had need of thee!
Is thy sweet kiss denied alone to me?

Love, with her heated touches, passion-stirred,
                    Has passed me by.
I called, 'O stay thy flight,' but all unheard
                    My lonely cry;
O! Love, my tired heart had need of thee!
Is thy sweet kiss withheld alone from me?

Sleep, sister-twin of Peace, my waking eyes
                    So weary grow!
O! Love, thou wanderer from Paradise,
                    Dost thou not know
How oft my lonely heart has cried to thee?
But Thou, and Sleep, and Peace, come not to me.

ERIE WATERS

A dash of yellow sand,
Wind-scattered and sun-tanned;
Some waves that curl and cream along the margin of the strand;
And, creeping close to these
Long shores that lounge at ease,
Old Erie rocks and ripples to a fresh sou'-western breeze.

A sky of blue and grey;
Some stormy clouds that play
At scurrying up with ragged edge, then laughing blow away,
Just leaving in their trail
Some snatches of a gale;
To whistling summer winds we lift a single daring sail.

O! wind so sweet and swift,
O! danger-freighted gift
Bestowed on Erie with her waves that foam and fall and lift,
We laugh in your wild face,
And break into a race
With flying clouds and tossing gulls that weave and interlace.

SHADOW RIVER

Muskoka

A stream of tender gladness,
Of filmy sun, and opal-tinted skies;
Of warm midsummer air that lightly lies
In mystic rings,
Where softly swings
The music of a thousand wings
That almost tones to sadness.

Midway 'twixt earth and heaven,
A bubble in the pearly air, I seem

To float upon the sapphire floor, a dream
Of clouds of snow,
Above, below,
Drift with my drifting dim and slow,
As twilight drifts to even.

The little fern-leaf, bending
Upon the brink, its green reflection greets,
And kisses soft the shadow that it meets
With touch so fine,
The border line
The keenest vision can't define;
So perfect is the blending.

The far, fir trees that cover
The brownish hills with needles green and gold,
The arching elms o'erhead, vinegrown and old,
Repictured are
Beneath me far,
Where not a ripple moves to mar
Shades underneath, or over.

Mine is the undertone;
The beauty, strength, and power of the land
Will never stir or bend at my command;
But all the shade
Is marred or made,
If I but dip my paddle blade;
And it is mine alone.

O! pathless world of seeming!
O! pathless life of mine whose deep ideal
Is more my own than ever was the real.
For others Fame
And Love's red flame,
And yellow gold: I only claim
The shadows and the dreaming.

NOCTURNE

Night of Mid-June, in heavy vapours dying,
Like priestly hands thy holy touch is lying
Upon the world's wide brow;
God-like and grand all nature is commanding
The 'peace that passes human understanding';
I, also, feel it now.

What matters it to-night, if one life treasure
I covet, is not mine! Am I to measure
The gifts of Heaven's decree
By my desires? O! life for ever longing
For some far gift, where many gifts are thronging,
God wills, it may not be.

Am I to learn that longing, lifted higher,
Perhaps will catch the gleam of sacred fire
That shows my cross is gold?
That underneath this cross – however lowly,
A jewel rests, white, beautiful and holy,
Whose worth can not be told.

Like to a scene I watched one day in wonder: –
A city, great and powerful, lay under
A sky of grey and gold;
The sun outbreaking in his farewell hour,
Was scattering afar a yellow shower
Of light, that aureoled

With brief hot touch, so marvellous and shining,
A hundred steeples on the sky out-lining,
Like network threads of fire;
Above them all, with halo far outspreading,
I saw a golden cross in glory heading
A consecrated spire:

I only saw its gleaming form uplifting,
Against the clouds of grey to seaward drifting,
And yet I surely know

Beneath the seen, a great unseen is resting,
For while the cross that pinnacle is cresting,
An Altar lies below.

.   .   .   .   .

Night of Mid-June, so slumberous and tender,
Night of Mid-June, transcendent in thy splendour
Thy silent wings enfold
And hush my longing, as at thy desire
All colour fades from round that far-off spire,
Except its cross of gold.

BASS LAKE (MUSKOKA)

Locked by its steeps fir-crowned
    Within the country of the north, there lies
A heron-haunted lake, where seldom sound
    Disturbs the virgin air, save when the sighs
Of gentle pine trees breathe their wind-taught song
Throughout the hours, in cadence lone and long.

Their chanting floats and falls
    Soft as the murmurs purling in a shell
That sings of far-off seas – whose cup enthralls
    The voice of many deeps where waters swell
To everlasting song, and evermore
An echo pearl enclosed repeats it o'er.

Among these wilds treads not
    The foot of fashion, all the littleness
Of social living dies away forgot,
    And scorned by him who seeks this wilderness
For majesty that lies so far beyond
The pale of culture, and its trivial bond.

Upon this rugged shore
    The camper's red log-fire is aglow,
He, who so treasures wood and water lore,

While fortunes could not purchase nor bestow
The purity with which the night endows
His sleep upon his bed of cedar boughs.

No rose-leaf couch is his,
   He spurns the so-called culture that refines
Field blossoms to exotics – sweeter is
   The fragrance of those mighty forest pines,
The littleness of language seems the flower,
The firs are silence, grandeur, soul and power.

Their pulses never die
   Through wide-eyed day or drowsy-lidded night,
When lonely herons flying lakeward cry,
   And some far loon laughs answer in her flight,
O! Northern waters where the muses sing
Of poesy – the poet here is king.

TEMPTATION

How frail is the craft he is steering, how rapid the river
   speeds on,
How many the rocks he is nearing, how luring the water
   god's song.

How gay rings his happy young laughter, as tossed in the play of
   the stream,
Courageous and brave he sails after the fair golden fleece of his
   dream.

Once only, the tears rise to blind him, 'tis when he looks
   backward and sees,
The mother and home far behind him – then trims he again to
   the breeze.

Ah me! the reef under the foam crest was first to grate hard on
   the keel,
He passed it when leaving the home-nest, but sharp was the
   shock he could feel.

Down farther some bold rocks are catching what driftwood the
    waters supply,
With careful and diligent watching he pilots his boat safely by.

And here is a snag where the river runs dizzily onward and fast,
His shallop flies by with a shiver, thank heaven that danger
    is past.

O! horror, he sees in the distance sand bars, is he running
    aground?
But no, with a giant resistance, to clear them he swings the boat
    'round.

Here's a whirlpool, calm seem its terrors, insensibly he is
    drawn in,
His eyes can distinguish no errors, his conscience belittles
    the sin.

Its grasp is the grasp of a demon, and whispering faintly a
    prayer,
With efforts almost superhuman, he pulls from that deadliest
    snare.

The struggle has made him so weary he rests for a space on
    his oar,
And looks from the river now dreary to the sweetness of sky
    and shore.

Red and saffron the clouds glow above him, the sun in a
    splendour descends,
The world looks as though it could love him, and he laughs as
    we laugh on friends.

How brilliant the scene, so much stronger than shadows which
    'round him remain,
He'll watch it but one moment longer, then look to his helm
    again.

And so he lies idle, and drifting, forgetting his lifeboat to steer.
Nor seeing some dark rocks uplifting, sure there can be
    nothing to fear!

O, fool! had he only but striven to turn from that sky colour-
flecked –
Too late, his frail shallop is riven, O, God! on the rocks he is
wrecked.

MISGUIDED

How frail is the craft I am steering, how rapid the river
sweeps on,
How many the rocks I am nearing, how luring the water-god's
song.

The day is but young, yet I travel where currents with dangers
are rife
Though waters are clear and the gravel but borders the river
of Life

With such tiny stones that never hurt the tender soles of my
feet,
I enter my barque and endeavor to master all dangers I meet.

Ah me, the reef under the foam-crest was first to grate hard on
the keel,
I passed it when leaving the home-nest, but sometimes its shock
yet I feel.

Down further some sharp rocks are catching what driftwood the
waters supply
With careful and diligent watching I pilot my boat safely by.

And here is a snag where the river runs dizzily onward and fast,
My shallop flies by with a shiver – Thank Heaven that danger
is past.

O, horror, I see in the distance sand-bars, am I running
aground?
But no, with a giant resistance, to clear them I swing the boat
round.

Here's a whirlpool, calm seem its terrors, insensibly I am
   drawn in.
My eyes can distinguish no errors – my conscience belittles
   the sin.

Its grasp is the grasp of a demon, and whispering faintly a
   prayer,
With errors almost superhuman, I pull from that deadliest
   snare.

The struggle has made me so weary, I rest for a space on my oar,
And look from the river so dreary to the sweetness of sky and
   shore.

How bright are the trees up above me, their colour so
   gorgeously blends,
The sky looks as though it could love me, and I laugh as we
   laugh on friends.

How brilliant its tints, so much stronger than shadows where I
   float and dream,
I'll watch them but one moment longer, then pilot my barque
   down the stream.

And so I lie lazily drifting forgetting my life boat to steer,
Nor seeing some dark rocks uplifting – sure, there can be
   nothing to fear!

O, fool! had I only but striven to turn from that sky colour
   flecked,
Too late, my frail shallop is riven, O, God, on the rocks I am
   wrecked.

FORTUNE'S FAVOURS

Some siren drew
Our charmed canoe
To shores of green 'neath skies of blue

In velvet atmosphere –
The heat extreme,
The sun's fierce gleam,
Forbids us paddling up the stream
So rest we idly here.

Hot waning June
Melts to a swoon
The stillness of this still lagoon
Wherein becalmed we lie,
Our tiny sail
Lifts up her pale
Arms longing that some idle gale
Perchance may wander by.

We lie where dim
Still shadows skim
The rushes on the river's rim
That harbour iris rare,
We whistle low,
Subdued and slow
To call the truant winds to blow
And break the silent air.

Some goddess brings
Upon her wings
The breeze desired as near she swings
Her pinions floating past,
With creaking sound
The boom sways round,
Fresh wind our canvas now has found
It fills – we move at last.

RONDEAU

Some bittersweet that lately grew
When flowers failed and leaves were few,
Tossed through the dull November day

Their saucy coral colours gay
Where wind and rain in dashes blew.

A kindly hand upstretching through
The vines their clusters downward drew
And broke their stems and took away
Some bittersweet.

And brought their berries bright unto
My weary life that lived anew,
Because they made the days less grey.
O! hand that gave, return and stay,
O friend of mine – is all my due
Some bittersweet?

CHRISTMASTIDE

I may not go to-night to Bethlehem,
Nor follow star-directed ways, nor tread
The paths wherein the shepherds walked, that led
To Christ, and peace, and God's good will to men.

I may not hear the Herald Angel's song
Peal through the Oriental skies, nor see
The wonder of that Heavenly company
Announce the King the world had waited long.

The manger throne I may not kneel before,
Or see how man to God is reconciled,
Through pure St Mary's purer, holier child;
The human Christ these eyes may not adore.

I may not carry frankincense and myrrh
With adoration to the Holy One;
Nor gold have I to give the Perfect Son,
To be with those wise kings a worshipper.

Not mine the joy that Heaven sent to them,
For ages since Time swung and locked his gates,
But I may kneel without – the star still waits
To guide me on to holy Bethlehem.

EVERGREENS

A jovial lot are they
Who fill the lumber sleigh,
And by their merriment the woodman gleans
That through the storm and cold,
With boyish hearts and bold,
The little choristers have come to haul the Christmas greens.

And quickly, too, they heap
The boughs where, soft asleep,
A subtle perfume loves to long abide;
So wild and sweet and free,
It always seems to be
Twin sister of the music that we hear at Christmas-tide.

Adown the long white road
The axeman drives his load
Of fragrant greens through puffs and drifts of snow,
Until his happy eyes
See in the twilight skies
The village spire, and well he knows who waits for him below.

Anon he halts before
The church's open door,
And pretty faces greet him with a smile.
Is it the light and heat
That make his pulses beat,
Or but a pair of laughing eyes he meets across the aisle?

WHAT THE SOLDIER SAID

The crisis of the battle neared, the cream of England's sons
Were in the open, fighting, right beneath the Russian guns
That were dealing devastation, with shot that riddled through
The 'Thin red line' of valiant men that less and lesser grew,
But one there was who wavered, as the scarlet column wheeled,
Whose eyes had caught some colours lying in the open field,
He waited not for orders, but he left the ranks to go
To save his comrade, and his flag, to face the Russian foe,
The deadly bayonets glistened, and the cannons thundered
    near,
But his comrade, and his colours he carried to the rear.

Long afterwards, when June was filtering her sunshine through
The little watery clouds afloat in skies of English blue,
It seemed to glow the brighter on a lithe young soldier's face,
As he stood before his sovereign, who leaned with tender grace,
To pin upon his breast a little bit of bronze that bore
These words 'For Valour,' Ah how well he won it in the war.
'See that you wear it nobly,' said his Captain, 'Life won't give
Another such reward as that, so guard it while you live.'
The soldier touched his faded cap, 'Your pardon sir,' said he,
'I'm proud of this wee bit of bronze as any man can be,
It means my honour, sir, and nought on earth I honour more,
But Captain, did you never know I wore a cross before?
It won the glory for me, and I'm none the prouder now
Of the cross upon my bosom, than the cross upon my brow.'

'COMRADES, WE ARE SERVING ...'

Air: 'Onward Christian Soldiers.'

I

Comrades, we are serving,
'Round instruction's throne,

In our youth we're laying
Wisdom's corner stone.
Flood or fire can never
Sweep away the towers,
We are building daily,
In our student hours.

Comrades, we are serving
'Round instruction's throne,
In our youth we're laying,
Wisdom's corner stone.

II

On the very ashes
Sloth has left behind,
Study lays the ground-work,
Of a scholar's mind.
Every lesson mastered,
Like a little stone,
Helps to raise the structure
Knowledge builds alone.

Comrades we are serving, etc.

III

On the firm foundation
That our learning lays,
We construct the stronghold
Of our future days.
Sometimes we will carry
Wisdom's flag unfurled,
Underneath that standard
We can face the world.

Comrades, we are serving, etc.

BEYOND THE BLUE

Speak of you, sir? You bet he did. Ben Fields was far too sound
To go back on a fellow just because he weren't around.
Why, sir, he thought a lot of you, and only three months back
Says he, 'The Squire will some time come a-snuffing out our track
And give us the surprise.' And so I got to thinking then
That any day you might drop down on Rove, and me, and Ben.
And now you've come for nothing, for the lad has left us two,
And six long weeks ago, sir, he went up beyond the blue.

Who's Rove? Oh, he's the collie, and the only thing on earth
That I will ever love again. Why, Squire, that dog is worth
More than you ever handled, and that's quite a piece, I know.
Ah, there the beggar is! – come here, you scalawag! and show
Your broken leg all bandaged up. Yes, sir, it's pretty sore;
I did it, – curse me, – and I think I feel the pain far more
Than him, for somehow I just feel as if I'd been untrue
To what my brother said before he went beyond the blue.

You see, the day before he died he says to me, 'Say, Ned,
Be sure you take good care of poor old Rover when I'm dead,
And maybe he will cheer your lonesome hours up a bit,
And when he takes to you just see that you're deserving it.'
Well, Squire, it wasn't any use. I tried, but couldn't get
The friendship of that collie, for I needed it, you bet.
I might as well have tried to get the moon to help me through,
For Rover's heart had gone with Ben, 'way up beyond the blue.

He never seemed to take to me nor follow me about,
For all I coaxed and petted, for my heart was starving out
For want of some companionship, – I thought, if only he
Would lick my hand or come and put his head aside my knee,
Perhaps his touch would scatter something of the gloom away.
But all alone I had to live until there came a day
When, tired of the battle, as you'd have tired too,
I wished to heaven I'd gone with Ben, 'way up beyond the blue.

.   .   .   .   .

One morning I took out Ben's gun, and thought I'd hunt
    all day,
And started through the clearing for the bush that forward lay,
When something made me look around – I scarce believed
    my mind –
But, sure enough, the dog was following right close behind.
A feeling first of joy, and than a sharper, greater one
Of anger came, at knowing 'twas not me, but Ben's old gun,
That Rove was after, – well, sir, I just don't mind telling you,
But I forgot that moment Ben was up beyond the blue.

Perhaps it was but jealousy – perhaps it was despair,
But I just struck him with the gun and broke the bone right
    there;
And then – my very throat seemed choked, for he began to
    whine
With pain – God knows how tenderly I took that dog of mine
Up in my arms, and tore my old red necktie into bands
To bind the broken leg, while there he lay and licked my hands;
And though I cursed my soul, it was the brightest day I knew,
Or even cared to live, since Ben went up beyond the blue.

I tell you, Squire, I nursed him just as gently as could be,
And now I'm all the world to him, and he's the world to me.
Look sir, at that big, noble soul, right in his faithful eyes,
The square, forgiving honesty that deep down in them lies.
Eh, Squire? What's that you say? *He's got no soul?* I tell you, then,
He's grander and he's better than the mass of what's called
    men;
And I guess he stands a better chance than many of us do
Of seeing Ben some day again, 'way up beyond the blue.

IN APRIL

            I

Outlined in red and saffron
    Against a ground of grey,

Where last year's sedge o'erhangs the edge
    That marks the river's way,
On shores so grey, and dull, and bare,
    On shores so seeming dead –
The lips of life are breathing where
    The willows turn to red,
Enriching all the sombre air
    With glints of gold and red.

II

Without a dash of colour,
    Untouched by red or gold,
The empty days are garbed in greys,
    All passionless and cold,
O ! heart of mine so dull and bare,
    O ! heart so seeming dead,
Thou hast no gems to number where
    Love flashes gold and red,
He never limns the sombre air
    For thee with gold and red.

FOR QUEEN AND COUNTRY
MAY 24th

From east to west the Union Jack has been
Awave all day for country and for Queen.

In aureole of honour stands she high
Upon the pinnacle of history.
No brow that wore the jewel and the gem
In Britain's crown has born that diadem
With such white purity of life and mien
As hers.

To-day her reign seems to have been
A benediction of vast liberties,
That now like many brilliant stars arise

In unity of strength, and with the years
That rolled them over undiscovered spheres –
Have well been forged within a daily flame,
And form a halo round her royal name,
And every shaft in that reflection owes
Its birth to Honour, and with Honour grows,
Until the offspring with the parent stands
Triumphantly within Victoria's hands.

Sweet English mother on old England's throne!
What nobler kingdom can a woman own
Than empires in the heart – and foremost there
Environed by a million tongues of prayer!
How loyalty leaps up in every soul
That calls her Queen – we glory in control
So unabused to serve her subjects best,
That in her blessing she herself is blest.
O! Sorrow, with thy black and sombre wing –
Could we have checked thy mournful whispering –
Could we have chained thy presence and thy voice
Outside her palace walls, had we the choice,
God knows how gladly many of us would
Have died to save our Queen her widowhood.

Through dark, uncertain futures England's shore
May washed with tempests be, yet evermore
Throughout the ages nations will maintain
Her zenith was in good Victoria's reign.
Perchance a thousand years will sweep away
The barriers of time, when some shall say:
'Would we had lived within the age and lands
When sceptres drew their soul from woman's hands.'
O! queenly hands so gentle in your sway,
All Canada cheers on your natal day,
From east to west wave scarlet, white and blue,
In honour of our country and of you.

Time sculptures for us all,
Nor dwells he in king's palaces alone,
But chisels every life into a form

In marbles, streaked or pure – perchance the stone
Is our own making, who can tell, when torn
From Nature's quarries in our early days,
If fate or circumstance our pathway lays?
Or is the power our own to rise and fall?
To-day we mark a statue that has grown
With time's light touch, where nations turn their eyes
To thrones where many royal feet have stood,
And see beneath the arch of English skies
A monument of perfect womanhood.

THE IDLERS

The sun's red pulses beat,
Full prodigal of heat,
Full lavish of its lustre unrepressed;
But we have drifted far
From where his kisses are,
And in this landward-lying shade we let our paddles rest.

The river, deep and still,
The maple-mantled hill,
The little yellow beach whereon we lie,
The puffs of heated breeze,
All sweetly whisper – These
Are days that only come in a Canadian July.

So, silently we two
Lounge in our still canoe,
Nor fate, nor fortune matters to us now:
So long as we alone
May call this dream our own,
The breeze may die, the sail may droop, we care not when
    or how.

Against the thwart, near by,
Inactively you lie,
And all too near my arm your temple bends.

Your indolently crude,
Abandoned attitude,
Is one of ease and art, in which a perfect languor blends.

Your costume, loose and light,
Leaves unconcealed your might
Of muscle, half suspected, half defined;
And falling well aside,
Your vesture opens wide,
Above your splendid sunburnt throat that pulses unconfined.

With easy unreserve,
Across the gunwale's curve,
Your arm superb is lying, brown and bare;
Your hand just touches mine
With import firm and fine,
(I kiss the very wind that blows about your tumbled hair).

Ah! Dear, I am unwise
In echoing your eyes
Whene'er they leave their far-off gaze, and turn
To melt and blur my sight,
For every other light
Is servile to your cloud-grey eyes, wherein cloud shadows burn.

But once, the silence breaks,
But once, your ardour wakes
To words that humanize this lotus-land;
So perfect and complete
Those burning words and sweet,
So perfect is the single kiss your lips lay on my hand.

The paddles lie disused,
The fitful breeze abused,
Has dropped to slumber, with no after-blow;
And hearts will pay the cost,
For you and I have lost
More than the homeward blowing wind that died an hour ago.

DEPTHS

Serene dark pool with all your colours dulled,
Your dreamless waves by twilight slumber-lulled:

Your warmth that flamed because the hot sun hushed
Your lip vermillion, that his kisses crushed,

Wan are the tints he left of gold and gem
For dusk's soft, cloudy greys have smothered them.

Where yonder shore's tree-terraced outlines melt,
The shadows circle like a velvet belt.

And down, far down within the sable deep
A white star-soul awakens from its sleep.

O ! little lake with nightfall interlink't,
Your darkling shores, your margins indistinct –

More in your depth's uncertainty there lies
Than when you image all the sunset dyes.

Like to the poet's soul, you seem to be
A depth no hand can touch, no eye can see.

And melancholy's dusky clouds drift through
The singer's songs, as twilight drifts o'er you.

O! life that saddens for the colours fled,
Within your depths a diamond 'wakes instead.

Perchance in spheres remote, and fair, and far,
There breathes a twin soul to my soul's white star,

Or have we touched already, and passed by
Unconscious that affinity was nigh?

O ! soul, perchance so near me yet unknown,
Some day we'll 'wake within fate's velvet zone.

DAY DAWN

All yesterday the thought of you was resting in my soul,
And when sleep wandered o'er the world that very thought
    she stole
To fill my dreams with splendour such as stars could not eclipse,
And in the morn I wakened with your name upon my lips.

Awakened, my belovèd, to the morning of your eyes,
Your splendid eyes, so full of clouds, wherein a shadow tries
To overcome the flame that melts into the world of grey,
As coming suns dissolve the dark that veils the edge of day.

Cool drifts the air at dawn of day, cool lies the sleeping dew,
But all my heart is burning, for it woke from dreams of you;
And O! these longing eyes of mine look out and only see
A dying night, a waking day, and calm on all but me.

So gently creeps the morning through the heavy air,
The dawn grey-garbed and velvet-shod is wandering everywhere
To wake the slumber-laden hours that leave their dreamless
    rest,
With outspread, laggard wings to court the pillows of the west.

Up from the earth a moisture steals with odours fresh and soft,
A smell of moss and grasses warm with dew, and far aloft
The stars are growing colourless, while drooping in the west,
A late, wan moon is paling in a sky of amethyst.

The passing of the shadows, as they waft their pinions near,
Has stirred a tender wind within the night-hushed atmosphere,
That in its homeless wanderings sobs in an undertone
An echo to my heart that sobbing calls for you alone.

The night is gone, belovèd, and another day set free,
Another day of hunger for the one I may not see.
What care I for the perfect dawn? the blue and empty skies?
The night is always mine without the morning of your eyes.

'HELD BY THE ENEMY'

Oh! dainty little cousin May,
I hear your girlish laughter gay
Each time I near the wide stairway,
Each time I leave the dance.
You little witch, how well I know
The deadly dagger you can throw,
You meet your unprotected foe
With laughter as your lance.

The music murmurs through the rooms
And throbs atween the rich perfumes
That drift from lips of summer blooms,
But sweeter than the flute,
And clearer than the clarionet,
I hear your merry voice, my pet.
Oh! roguish May, where did you get
The laughter of the lute?

I know quite well you're sitting where
The light is shaded from the stair,
For seven dances you've been there
With some poor college boy,
I know so well your feathered fan
Is resting near your mouth, a plan
You always have to tease a man,
The thing you most enjoy.

I know your eyes of melting grey
Are not too often turned his way,
Nor have you very much to say,
But oh, you scamp, you're playing
The very deuce with that poor chap
For whom you never cared a rap,
Unless it was to test the trap
Of coquetry you're laying.

Ah! coz – demoniac divine,
The boy must go – this dance is mine,
I see your eyes with radiance shine
    The while I rescue him
From out the toils he's sure to rue,
For now that I'm alone with you
I know you're loyal, staunch and true
    In heart to Cousin Jim.

TO PEGGY

Dear little girl from far
    Beyond the seas,
From lands where roses are
    You come to these –

These where the birch tree flings
    His ragged coat,
These where the wild pine sings
    With dreamful note –

Ah! Little guest of ours,
    The suns and snows
Greet, mid their wilder flowers,
    An English rose.

TWO WOMEN

She stands where a thousand candles
Broadcast their yellow rays,
Where laugh and song ring all night long
And music sweeps and sways,
A woman pure and peerless as
The diamonds in her hair,
Her regal footsteps never pass
But heroes worship there,

For queen of all 'mid song and light,
She's conquered every heart to-night.

Alone with the night, a woman
Watches a setting star,
Her heaving breast, her lips compressed
Bespeak a soul at war,
In pure and peerless womanhood
She threw her world away,
And suffered for another's good
Self sacrifice to-day,
The victor in a noble fight,
She's queen of but herself to-night.

OCTOBER IN CANADA

Afternoon of autumn lies a'tween me and the hill
    Rising like a giant amethyst a mile away,
Dimmed by opal-tinted airs that intervene until
    All looks like a cobweb mist of purple and of grey.

Lying where the pebbles sprinkle all the river sands,
    I can dip my fingers in the water warm and clear,
Watch the sunlight shimmer in the waves above my hands,
    Watch a snowy little sail that lazily floats near.

Far beyond the flats where some are husking Indian corn,
    I can see the oval, yellow stacks of straw uplift,
Hear the hum of threshing; for since early hours of morn,
    'Round the barns a cloud of amber chaff has been adrift.

Flocks of crows at random fly within the upward air,
    Ebon tufts that dot the clouds athwart a pinkish sky;
Far away the stubble fields are stretching dun and bare,
    Edged with goldenrod and flecked with leaves a-blowing by.

Night comes stealthily and thieves the colours from the hill,
    Nought she leaves upon its brow of amethyst or blue;
Day will soon be over, and the twilight grey and still,
    Whispers very gently that my dreamland darkens too.

'THROUGH TIME AND BITTER DISTANCE'*

Unknown to you, I walk the cheerless shore.
    The cutting blast, the hurl of biting brine
May freeze, and still, and bind the waves at war,
    Ere you will ever know, O! Heart of mine,
That I have sought, reflected in the blue
    Of these sea depths, some shadow of your eyes;
Have hoped the laughing waves would sing of you,
    But this is all my starving sight decries –

I

Far out at sea a sail
    Bends to the freshening breeze,
Yields to the rising gale
    That sweeps the seas;

II

Yields, as a bird wind-tossed,
    To saltish waves that fling
Their spray, whose rime and frost
    Like crystals cling

III

To canvas, mast and spar,
    Till, gleaming like a gem,
She sinks beyond the far
    Horizon's hem.

*For this title the author is indebted to Mr. Charles G.D. Roberts. It occurs in his sonnet 'Rain' [Johnson's note].

IV

Lost to my longing sight,
    And nothing left to me
Save an oncoming night, –
    An empty sea.

AS RED MEN DIE

Captive! Is there a hell to him like this?
A taunt more galling than the Huron's hiss?
He – proud and scornful, he – who laughed at law,
He – scion of the deadly Iroquois,
He – the bloodthirsty, he – the Mohawk chief,
He – who despises pain and sneers at grief,
Here in the hated Huron's vicious clutch,
That even captive he disdains to touch!

Captive! But *never* conquered; Mohawk brave
Stoops not to be to *any* man a slave;
Least, to the puny tribe his soul abhors,
The tribe whose wigwams sprinkle Simcoe's shores.
With scowling brow he stands and courage high,
Watching with haughty and defiant eye
His captors, as they council o'er his fate,
Or strive his boldness to intimidate.
Then fling they unto him the choice;

                          'Wilt thou
Walk o'er the bed of fire that waits thee now –
Walk with uncovered feet upon the coals,
Until thou reach the ghostly Land of Souls,
And, with thy Mohawk death-song please our ear?
Or wilt thou with the women rest thee here?'

His eyes flash like an eagle's, and his hands
Clench at the insult. Like a god he stands.
'Prepare the fire!' he scornfully demands.

He knoweth not that this same jeering band
Will bite the dust – will lick the Mohawk's hand;
Will kneel and cower at the Mohawk's feet;
Will shrink when Mohawk war drums wildly beat.

His death will be avenged with hideous hate
By Iroquois, swift to annihilate
His vile detested captors, that now flaunt
Their war clubs in his face with sneer and taunt,
Not thinking, soon that reeking, red, and raw,
Their scalps will deck the belts of Iroquois.

The path of coals outstretches, white with heat,
A forest fir's length – ready for his feet.
Unflinching as a rock he steps along
The burning mass, and sings his wild war song;
Sings, as he sang when once he used to roam
Throughout the forests of his southern home,
Where, down the Genesee, the water roars,
Where gentle Mohawk purls between its shores,
Songs, that of exploit and of prowess tell;
Songs of the Iroquois invincible.

Up the long trail of fire he boasting goes,
Dancing a war dance to defy his foes.
His flesh is scorched, his muscles burn and shrink,
But still he dances to death's awful brink.
The eagle plume that crests his haughty head
Will *never* droop until his heart be dead.
Slower and slower yet his footstep swings,
Wilder and wilder still his death-song rings,
Fiercer and fiercer through the forest bounds
His voice that leaps to Happier Hunting Grounds.
One savage yell –

        Then loyal to his race,
He bends to death – but *never* to disgrace.

THE LAST PAGE

The story ends, and the book I close –
The well-worn book of The Passing Year –
I've finished reading its weals and woes,
Its bits of briar, its leaves of rose,
The story is done to-day, my dear.

In my hand I hold a book unread,
Uncut the pages of Ninety-one;
Sweet will it be as the year just fled?
As bitter a thing when lying dead,
As the tale just told, the year just done?

I look no more in its covers twain,
The prose is much, and the poems are few,
Yet e're I toss it aside I fain
Would part its pages and turn again
To find where I first read, dear, of you.

The chapter's headed with but your name,
'Twas writ in warmth of the summer shine,
'Till then the story was dull and tame,
But, O! the soul of it since you came
Bewitches me like a wild, rare wine.

Has life another such book for me,
Entrancing, subtle, and sweet as this?
Do chapters sealed in the year to be
Reflect the moments of misery,
Of empty words, or a careless kiss?

In my hand I hold a story new,
Is it grey and grim, or gold and fair?
Will every line speak, dear, of you,
Right unto the end, as now they do,
Or O! will your name be missing there?

THE SNOWSHOER

There's an open plain to southward
Heaped up with a crusty snow,
Drift on drift where the gales uplift
And toss o'er the flats below,
Where the sun flings down his jeweled crown
And the ice fields thieve its glow.

There's a figure lithe and stalwart
That comes o'er the slopes alone,
He tramps along with a step made strong
By muscle, and brain, and bone,
Robust his form, and his heart as warm
As lights from a ruby thrown.

There's a pathway onward stretching
From him to the sun a'set
It lies and gleams like a thing in dreams,
Unmarred by his snowshoe yet,
Turn where he may, there lies the way
Of gold for his feet to fret.

There's a long, long track behind him,
Fields lie to the fore unpressed,
He marks his way by the sun's clear ray
And follows it with a zest,
The phantom glows o'er the roadless snow,
'Twixt him and the yellow west.

OUTLOOKING

A silvery sky, a big, round, laughing moon,
Some bits of cloud that hint at snowing soon,
A pulseless wintry world begirt by night,
Cold, passionlessly white.

Nought else my window frames, no redder hue
Of life. Ah! dear and distant one, can you
Not feel the frozen world throb, melt, and beat,
Warmed by my heart's great heat?

The unrelenting leagues 'twixt you and me,
Transmit they nought of love's intensity?
Can hungry heart flames burn no pathway through
The frozen airs to you?

Where fairy-footed thought its way may steal,
Where love, defying distance still may feel
Soul bend to soul, as in the hours when we
First knew affinity.

THE SEVENTH DAY

Morning lies on all the hills, and all the plains are calm,
Sunday morn that seems to breathe the very soul of balm,
The labour-freighted hours are gone, and now I bow my head
For benedictions on the toil that filled the week just dead.

Sunday morn – and with it comes the wish that now I could
Just listen to the old church bell I heard in childhood
Ring from the little chapel where I knelt in early years,
Ere my life had learned of trials, ere my eyes had learned
    of tears.

Perhaps I'm over tired to-day, perhaps I've not confessed
Some little sin whose weight is lead, but this return of rest
Has touched me with a home-sickness, a fruitless longing for
Just one brief day wherein to be a little child once more;

To run along the narrow path, to climb the little gate
That broke the line of zig-zag fence that bound the old estate,
To wander ankle-deep among the long cut grass that lay
Just where the scythe had toss't it, while it dried to fragrant hay;

To westward see the brown ploughed field in summer fallow lie,
To see my quaintly-fashioned home against the eastward sky,
To feel the placid warmth that fell upon those early hours,
To listen to the mission bell ring from its far off towers.

I wonder if the pathway lies across the meadow still,
And do some other childish feet climb up the dusty hill,
Where stands the holy edifice, where sings a voice divine
Within the bell that calls to-day to other ears than mine.

STAR LAKE (MUSKOKA)

Far from the beaten path, the polished ways,
Where slippered foot of dainty Fashion strays,
Far from the work-encumbered world, whose tie
Binds wealth to one, to others poverty,
Beyond a wilderness unsought, unknown,
Star Lake lies fettered with a belt of stone,
Set like a dew-drop on the rugged skirt
Of forests rock-environed, fir-begirt,
Her regal shores untarnished by the craft
Of cunning man. The north wind never laugh't
Through pines more royal than her edges frame,
That sneer at even Vulcan's hungry flame.
No tempest that adown the nor'land roars
Can ever blast the foothold of these shores;
The cloud-born hurricane bows low to these
Immovable, storm-scorning cedar trees,
Whose aromatic branches sing whene'er
A strolling zephyr threads the virgin air, –
Sing of the lonely years, when all along
These shores, they heard the Indian's hunting song,
And watched his elfish whispering canoe
Flit like a spirit, as they listened to
The fleeing footsteps of the startled deer,
That paused to slake its thirst in waters clear, –
Sing of the lonely years, when wildly rose
The war-cry of the Hurons, when their foes,

The 'Bloody Iroquois,' had reached the North,
And Huron Brave to meet his doom went forth,
Bathed with his blood the sands of Simcoe's shore,
His war-song silenced now for evermore.
Only the heron's call,
The hoot of owl, or loneliest of all,
The plaintive laugh of loons, that wandering
Among the marshes, rest a homeless wing –
These are the voices that, succeeding, reign
Usurpers of the Hurons' old domain;
And soon the wild fowl, too, will hush their cries,
Frighted by pioneers of enterprise,
Scared by the woodman's axe that thirsts to drink
The sap of trees that guard the water's brink,
By voice of sportman's rifle that resounds
Throughout the Redman's erstwhile hunting grounds.
Few are the moons ere these grey cliffs remote
Will echo culture's artificial note;
But Nature only wears this jewel yet:
Within her northern fastnesses deep-set,
Star Lake lies as a matchless cameo,
Cut by God's chisel centuries ago.

THE VAGABONDS

What saw you in your flight to-day,
Crows, awinging your homeward way?

Went you far in carrion quest,
Crows, that worry the sunless west?

Thieves and villains, you shameless things!
Black your record as black your wings.

Tell me, birds of the inky hue,
Plunderous rogues – to-day have you

Seen with mischievous, prying eyes
Lands where earlier suns arise?

Saw you a lazy beck between
Trees that shadow its breast in green,

Teased by obstinate stones that lie
Crossing the current tauntingly?

Fields abloom on the farther side
With purpling clover lying wide –

Saw you there as you circled by,
Vale-environed a cottage lie,

Girt about with emerald bands,
Nestling down in its meadow lands?

Saw you this on your thieving raids?
Speak – you rascally renegades!

Thieved you also away from me
Olden scenes that I long to see?

If, O! crows, you have flown since morn
Over the place where I was born,

Forget will I, how black you were
Since dawn, in feather and character;

Absolve will I, your vagrant band
Ere you enter your slumberland.

RE-VOYAGE

What of the days when we two dreamed together?
   Days marvellously fair,
As lightsome as a skyward floating feather
   Sailing on summer air –
Summer, summer, that came drifting through
Fate's hand to me, to you.

What of the days, my dear? I sometimes wonder
   If you too wish this sky
Could be the blue we sailed so softly under,
   In that sun-kissed July;
Sailed in the warm and yellow afternoon,
With hearts in touch and tune.

Have you no longing to re-live the dreaming,
   Adrift in my canoe?
To watch my paddle blade all wet and gleaming
   Cleaving the waters through?
To lie wind-blown and wave-caressed, until
Your restless pulse grows still?

Do you not long to listen to the purling
   Of foam athwart the keel?
To hear the nearing rapids softly swirling
   Among their stones, to feel
The boat's unsteady tremor as it braves
The wild and snarling waves?

What need of question, what of your replying?
   Oh! well I know that you
Would toss the world away to be but lying
   Again in my canoe,
In listless indolence entranced and lost,
Wave-rocked, and passion-tossed.

Ah me! my paddle failed me in the steering
   Across love's shoreless seas;
All reckless, I had ne'er a thought of fearing
   Such dreary days as these,
When through the self-same rapids we dash by,
My lone canoe and I.

IN DAYS TO COME

If I could know to-day
   That in some far to-morrow you would long
   To hear again the rapids' purling song
About their boulders grey,
   That in some homesick moment you would fain
   Be drifting through this sunlit June again –

If I were sure that you
   Would sometime wish with all your heart to be
   Adrift, and dreaming, while you shared with me
My wandering canoe,
   I would not dread the shore of future days
   That we must touch – then take our sundered ways.

If I could but believe
   That sometime when you see a sunset sky
   You will recall the night that you and I
Watched all the colours weave
   Their wine-like glories 'round the western gate,
   I would not ask a dearer thing of Fate.

I think, could I but know,
   When Indian summer smiles with dusky lip,
   You still will crave to hear my paddle dip
In rapids laughing low –
   Then I would be assured beyond a doubt
   Your heart had not – exactly, barred me out.

THE CAMPER

Night 'neath the northern skies, lone, black, and grim:
Naught but the starlight lies 'twixt heaven, and him.

Of man no need has he, of God, no prayer;
He and his Deity are brothers there.

Above his bivouac the firs fling down
Through branches gaunt and black, their needles brown.

Afar some mountain streams, rockbound and fleet,
Sing themselves through his dreams in cadence sweet,

The pine trees whispering, the heron's cry,
The plover's passing wing, his lullaby.

And blinking overhead the white stars keep
Watch o'er his hemlock bed – his sinless sleep.

AT HUSKING TIME

At husking time the tassel fades
To brown above the yellow blades,
    Whose rustling sheath enswathes the corn
    That bursts its chrysalis in scorn
Longer to lie in prison shades.

Among the merry lads and maids
The creaking ox-cart slowly wades
Twixt stalks and stubble, sacked and torn
At husking time.

The prying pilot crow persuades
The flock to join in thieving raids;
The sly raccoon with craft inborn
His portion steals; from plenty's horn
His pouch the saucy chipmunk lades
At husking time.

THE PILOT OF THE PLAINS

'False,' they said, 'thy Pale-face lover, from the land of waking
   morn;
Rise and wed thy Redskin wooer, nobler warrior ne'er was born;
Cease thy watching, cease thy dreaming,
     Show the white thine Indian scorn.'

Thus they taunted her, declaring, 'He remembers naught of
   thee:
Likely some white maid he wooeth, far beyond the inland sea.'
But she answered ever kindly,
     'He will come again to me,'

Till the dusk of Indian summer crept athwart the western skies;
But a deeper dusk was burning in her dark and dreaming eyes,
As she scanned the rolling prairie,
     Where the foothills fall, and rise.

Till the autumn came and vanished, till the season of the rains,
Till the western world lay fettered in midwinter's crystal chains,
Still she listened for his coming,
     Still she watched the distant plains.

Then a night with nor'land tempest, nor'land snows a-swirling
   fast,
Out upon the pathless prairie came the Pale-face through the
   blast,
Calling, calling, 'Yakonwita,
     I am coming, love, at last.'

Hovered night above, about him, dark its wings and cold and
   dread;
Never unto trail or tepee were his straying footsteps led;
Till benumbed, he sank, and pillowed
     On the drifting snows his head,

Saying, 'O! my Yakonwita call me, call me, be my guide
To the lodge beyond the prairie – for I vowed ere winter died

I would come again, belovèd;
   I would claim my Indian bride.'

'Yakonwita, Yakonwita!' Oh, the dreariness that strains
Through the voice that calling, quivers, till a whisper but
   remains,
'Yakonwita, Yakonwita,
   I am lost upon the plains.'

But the Silent Spirit hushed him, lulled him as he cried anew,
'Save me, save me! O! belovèd, I am Pale but I am true.
Yakonwita, Yakonwita,
   I am dying, love, for you.'

Leagues afar, across the prairie, she had risen from her bed,
Roused her kinsmen from their slumber: 'He has come
   tonight,' she said.
   'I can hear him calling, calling;
   But his voice is as the dead.

'Listen!' and they sate all silent, while the tempest louder grew,
And a spirit-voice called faintly, 'I am dying, love, for you.'
Then they wailed, 'O! Yakonwita.
   He was Pale, but he was true.'

Wrapped she then her ermine round her, stepped without the
   tepee door,
Saying, 'I must follow, follow, though he call for evermore,
Yakonwita, Yakonwita';
   And they never saw her more.

Late at night, say Indian hunters, when the starlight clouds or
   wanes,
Far away they see a maiden, misty as the autumn rains,
Guiding with her lamp of moonlight
   Hunters lost upon the plains.

RONDEAU: THE SKATER

On wings of steel the bold athlete
Brooks rival none, for none so fleet
As speeding under wintry skies,
Before the nor'land gale he flies,
And flying, frets the ice to sleet.

Like Mercury's, his wing'd feet
Skim o'er the river's crystal street,
And dread and danger he defies
On wings of steel.

What though the blast about him beat?
His dauntless heart athrob with heat
Of warm, young blood – his eager eyes
Essay no effort to disguise
That life to him is rare and sweet
On wings of steel.

THE SONG MY PADDLE SINGS

West wind, blow from your prairie nest,
Blow from the mountains, blow from the west.
The sail is idle, the sailor too;
O! wind of the west, we wait for you.
Blow, blow!
I have wooed you so,
But never a favour you bestow.
You rock your cradle the hills between,
But scorn to notice my white lateen.

I stow the sail, unship the mast:
I wooed you long but my wooing's past;
My paddle will lull you into rest.
O! drowsy wind of the drowsy west,
Sleep, sleep,

By your mountain steep,
Or down where the prairie grasses sweep!
Now fold in slumber your laggard wings,
For soft is the song my paddle sings.

August is laughing across the sky,
Laughing while paddle, canoe and I,
Drift, drift,
Where the hills uplift
On either side of the current swift.

The river rolls in its rocky bed;
My paddle is plying its way ahead;
Dip, dip,
While the waters flip
In foam as over their breast we slip.

And oh, the river runs swifter now;
The eddies circle about my bow.
Swirl, swirl!
How the ripples curl
In many a dangerous pool awhirl!

And forward far the rapids roar,
Fretting their margin for evermore.
Dash, dash,
With a mighty crash,
They seethe, and boil, and bound, and splash.

Be strong, O paddle! be brave, canoe!
The reckless waves you must plunge into.
Reel, reel,
On your trembling keel,
But never a fear my craft will feel.

We've raced the rapid, we're far ahead!
The river slips through its silent bed.
Sway, sway,
As the bubbles spray
And fall in tinkling tunes away.

And up on the hills against the sky,
A fir tree rocking its lullaby,
Swings, swings,
Its emerald wings,
Swelling the song that my paddle sings.

AT SUNSET

To-night the west o'er-brims with warmest dyes;
Its chalice overflows
With pools of purple colouring the skies,
Aflood with gold and rose;
And some hot soul seems throbbing close to mine,
As sinks the sun within that world of wine.

I seem to hear a bar of music float
And swoon into the west;
My ear can scarcely catch the whispered note,
But something in my breast
Blends with that strain, till both accord in one,
As cloud and colour blend at set of sun.

And twilight comes with grey and restful eyes,
As ashes follow flame.
But O! I heard a voice from those rich skies
Call tenderly my name;
It was as if some priestly fingers stole
In benedictions o'er my lonely soul.

I know not why, but all my being longed
And leapt at that sweet call;
My heart outreached its arms, all passion thronged
And beat against Fate's wall,
Crying in utter homesickness to be
Near to a heart that loves and leans to me.

RAINFALL

From out the west, where darkling storm-clouds float,
The 'waking wind pipes soft its rising note.

From out the west, o'erhung with fringes grey,
The wind preludes with sighs its roundelay,

Then blowing, singing, piping, laughing loud,
It scurries on before the grey storm-cloud;

Across the hollow and along the hill
It whips and whirls among the maples, till

With boughs upbent, and green of leaves blown wide,
The silver shines upon their underside.

A gusty freshening of humid air,
With showers laden, and with fragrance rare;

And now a little sprinkle, with a dash
Of great cool drops that fall with sudden splash;

Then over field and hollow, grass and grain,
The loud, crisp whiteness of the nearing rain.

PENSEROSO

Soulless is all humanity to me
To-night. My keenest longing is to be
Alone, alone with God's grey earth that seems
Pulse of my pulse and consort of my dreams.

To-night my soul desires no fellowship,
Or fellow-being; crave I but to slip
Through space on space, till flesh no more can bind,
And I may quit for aye my fellow kind.

Let me but feel athwart my cheek the lash
Of whipping wind, but hear the torrent dash
Adown the mountain steep, 'twere more my choice
Than touch of human hand, than human voice.

Let me but wander on the shore night-stilled,
Drinking its darkness till my soul is filled;
The breathing of the salt sea on my hair,
My outstretched hands but grasping empty air.

Let me but feel the pulse of Nature's soul
Athrob on mine, let seas and thunders roll
O'er night and me; sands whirl; winds, waters beat;
For God's grey earth has no cheap counterfeit.

WAVE-WON

To-night, I hunger so
Belovèd one, to know
If you recall and crave again the dream
That haunted our canoe,
And wove its witchcraft through
Our hearts as 'neath the northern night we sailed the northern
    stream.

Ah! dear, if only we
As yesternight could be
Afloat within that light and lonely shell,
To drift in silence till
Heart-hushed, and lulled and still
The moonlight through the melting air flung forth its fatal spell.

The dusky summer night,
The path of gold and white
The moon had cast across the river's breast,
The shores in shadows clad,
The far-away, half-sad
Sweet singing of the whip-poor-will, all soothed our souls to rest.

You trusted, I could feel,
My arm as strong as steel,
So still your upturned face, so calm your breath,
While circling eddies curled,
While laughing rapids whirled
From boulder unto boulder, till they dashed themselves to
    death.

Your splendid eye aflame
Put heaven's stars to shame,
Your god-like head so near my lap was laid –
My hand is burning where
It touched your wind-blown hair,
As sweeping to the rapids' verge, I changed my paddle blade.

The boat obeyed my hand,
Till wearied with its grand
Wild anger, all the river lay aswoon,
And as my paddle dipped
Through pools of pearl it slipped
And swept beneath a shore of shade, beneath a velvet moon.

To-night, again dream you
Our spirit-winged canoe
Is listening to the rapids purling past?
Where in delirium reeled
Our maddened hearts that kneeled
To idolize the perfect world, to taste of love at last.

THE AVENGER

A starless night:
           Thickened with deeds of doom
The black stream serpent-like slips through the gloom
Choked with a Mohawk's blood that trickles slow
From out a well nigh pulseless heart, laid low
By tribal hate and discord – giving rise

To hostile feuds and violent jealousies.
'Twas but a moment's work.

          The Cherokee
Meets with his Mohawk foe; the enmity
Inherited through ages fires the palm
Of each red hand, they face –

          A meaning calm
With venom gorged – then on the night is flung
The deadliest yell that e'er left Indian tongue –
Like wild-cats raged, concurrently they spring,
With tomahawks athirst and glittering;
They close – they struggle – then they leap apart,
Hate as a hell burns madness in each heart.
Some strategy – a crafty, rival strife,
Then parts the darkness to a gleaming knife;
A treacherous manoeuvre –

          On the shore
The Mohawk lifeless lies. The feud is o'er.

Exultingly, the Cherokee now stands,
Appeased his hate, avenged his reeking hands;
With foot upon his writhing victim's throat
He backward flings his head – one long, strange note
Leaves his thin lips – then up to Heaven's height
His war-whoop pierces through the fateful night.

Leagues off, the death-cry 'roused from sleep a son
Of the same sire as is the murdered one,
Nearest of kindred, Indian law demands
The dead must be avenged but by his hands.
The hours drift by – another midnight gloom
Curdles and cringes 'neath impending doom;
With trick of stealth a Mohawk lad slips o'er
The trail – till near a fire-illumed lodge door
He sees a man, a sinewy, ruthless scion
Of Western blood (inhuman as a lion).

The boy's step breaks

The brittle twigs – the red giant starts, awakes,
Then springs erect to meet th' unflinching eye
Of one so youthful, by whose hand to die
Is ignominy – shame – affront – disgrace.
He winces at the insult he, his race
Must take from tribes who tauntingly employ
T'avenge their wrong this fearless stripling boy.
To fate, he offers no resistance; he
Well knows that naught can shatter the decree,
That naught averts the iron Indian law
Of blood for blood, among the Iroquois,
Knows their retaliation firm and fell
Would hound him to the very depths of hell.
Boldly the youth confronts his monstrous foe,
Before whom nations quail – his eyes aglow
With hate and triumph as he hisses through
Locked teeth, 'Last night thou lendest a knife unto
My brother; come I now O! Cherokee,
To give thy bloody weapon back to thee.'
An evil curse – a flash of steel –

A leap –

A thrust above the heart, well aimed and deep,
Plunged to its very hilt in blood, the blade,
While vengeance gloating yells!

The debt is paid.

THE BIRDS' LULLABY

I

Sing to us, cedars; the twilight is creeping
  With shadowy garments, the wilderness through;
All day we have carolled, and now would be sleeping,
  So echo the anthems we warbled to you;

While we swing, swing,
  And your branches sing,
And we drowse to your dreamy whispering.

II

Sing to us, cedars; the night-wind is sighing,
  Is wooing, is pleading, to hear you reply;
And here in your arms we are restfully lying,
  And longing to dream to your soft lullaby;
    While we swing, swing,
    And your branches sing.
  And we drowse to your dreamy whispering.

III

Sing to us, cedars; your voice is so lowly,
  Your breathing so fragrant, your branches so strong;
Our little nest-cradles are swaying so slowly,
  While zephyrs are breathing their slumberous song.
    And we swing, swing,
    While your branches sing,
  And we drowse to your dreamy whispering.

THE PORTAGE

Now for a careful beach atween the towering
  Grey rocks a'yawn like tombs,
Aft lies the lake, blurred by our paddle's scouring,
  Forward the Portage looms,
    Beyond its fastness, a river creeping,
    Then – rapids leaping.

Now for a bracing up of stalwart shoulders
  And now a load to lift;
An uphill tramp through tangled briars and boulders,
  The irksome weight to shift,

And through it all, the far incessant calling
　Of waters falling.

What of the heat? the toil? the sun's red glaring?
　The blistered fingers, too?
What of the muscles teased and strained in bearing
　The fearless fleet canoe?
　　Brief is the labour, then the wild sweet laughter
　　Of rapids after.

THE MARINER

'*Wreck and stray and castaway*' – Swinburne

Once more adrift.
O'er dappling sea and broad lagoon,
O'er frowning cliff and yellow dune,
The long, warm lights of afternoon
　Like jewel dustings sift.

Once more awake.
I dreamed an hour of port and quay,
Of anchorage not meant for me;
The sea, the sea, the hungry sea
　Came rolling up the break.

Once more afloat.
The billows on my moorings press't,
They drove me from my moment's rest,
And now a portless sea I breast,
　And shelterless my boat.

Once more away.
The harbour lights are growing dim,
The shore is but a purple rim,
The sea outstretches grey and grim.
　Away, away, away!

Once more at sea,
The old, old sea I used to sail,
The battling tide, the blowing gale,
The waves with ceaseless under-wail
    The life that used to be.

BRIER

Good Friday

Because, dear Christ, your tender, wounded arm
    Bends back the brier that edges life's long way,
That no hurt comes to heart, to soul no harm,
    I do not feel the thorns so much to-day.

Because I never knew your care to tire,
    Your hand to weary guiding me aright,
Because you walk before and crush the brier,
    It does not pierce my feet so much to-night.

Because so often you have hearkened to
    My selfish prayers, I ask but one thing now,
That these harsh hands of mine add not unto
    The crown of thorns upon your bleeding brow.

WOLVERINE

'Yes, sir, it's quite a story, though you won't believe it's true,
But such things happened often when I lived beyond the Soo.'
And the trapper tilted back his chair and filled his pipe anew.

'I ain't thought of it neither fer this many 'n many a day,
Although it used to haunt me in the years that's slid away;
The years I spent a-trappin' for the good old Hudson's Bay.

'Wild? You bet, 'twas wild then, an' few an' far between
The squatters' shacks, for whites was scarce as furs when things
     is green,
An' only reds an' 'Hudson's' men was all the folk I seen.

'No. Them old Indyans ain't so bad, not if you treat 'em square.
Why, I lived in amongst 'em all the winters I was there,
An' I never lost a copper, an' I never lost a hair.

'But I'd have lost my life the time that you've heard tell about;
I don't think I'd be settin' here, but dead beyond a doubt,
If that there Indyan 'Wolverine' jest hadn't helped me out.

''Twas freshet time, 'way back, as long as sixty-six or eight,
An' I was comin' to the Post that year a kind of late,
For beaver had been plentiful, and trappin' had been great.

'One day I had been settin' traps along a bit of wood,
An' night was catchin' up to me jest faster 'an it should,
When all at once I heard a sound that curdled up my blood.

'It was the howl of famished wolves – I didn't stop to think
But jest lit out across for home as quick as you could wink,
But when I reached the river's edge I brought up at the brink.

'That mornin' I had crossed the stream straight on a sheet of ice
An' now, God help me! There it was, churned up an' cracked
     to dice,
The flood went boiling past – I stood like one shut in a vice.

'No way ahead, no path aback, trapped like a rat ashore,
With naught but death to follow, and with naught but death
     afore;
The howl of hungry wolves aback – ahead, the torrent's roar.

'An' then – a voice, an Indyan voice, that called out clear and
     clean,
"Take Indyan's horse, I run like deer, wolf can't catch Wolverine."
I says, "Thank Heaven." There stood the chief I'd nicknamed
     Wolverine.

'I leapt on that there horse, an' then jest like a coward fled,
An' left that Indyan standin' there alone, as good as dead,
With the wolves a-howlin' at his back, the swollen stream ahead.

'I don't know how them Indyans dodge from death the way
    they do,
You won't believe it, sir, but what I'm tellin' you is true,
But that there chap was 'round next day as sound as me or you.

'He came to get his horse, but not a cent he'd take from me.
Yes, sir, you're right, the Indyans now ain't like they used to be;
We've got 'em sharpened up a bit an' *now* they'll take a fee.

'No, sir, you're wrong, they ain't no "dogs." I'm not through
    tellin' yet;
You'll take that name right back again, or else jest out you get!
You'll take that name right back when you hear all this yarn,
    I bet.

'It happened that same autumn, when some Whites was
    comin' in,
I heard the old Red River carts a-kickin' up a din,
So I went over to their camp to see an English skin.

'They said, "They'd had an awful scare from Injuns," an' they
    swore
That savages had come around the very night before
A-brandishing their tomahawks an' painted up for war.

'But when their plucky Englishmen had put a bit of lead
Right through the heart of one of them, an' rolled him over,
    dead,
The other cowards said that they had come on peace instead.

'"That they (the Whites) had lost some stores, from off their
    little pack,
An' that the Red they peppered dead had followed up their
    track,
Because he'd found the packages an' came *to give them back*.'

'"Oh!" they said, "they were quite sorry, but it wasn't like as if
They had killed a decent Whiteman by mistake or in a tiff,
It was only some old Injun dog that lay there stark an' stiff."

'I said, "You are the meanest dogs that ever yet I seen,"
Then I rolled the body over as it lay out on the green;
I peered into the face – My God! 'twas poor old Wolverine.'

IN GREY DAYS

Measures of oil for others,
   Oil and red wine,
Lips laugh and drink, but never
   Are the lips mine.

Worlds at the feet of others,
   Power gods have known,
Hearts for the favoured round me
   Mine beats, alone.

Fame offering to others
   Chaplets of bays,
I with no crown of laurels,
   Only grey days.

Sweet human love for others,
   Deep as the sea,
God-sent unto my neighbour –
   But not to me.

Sometime I'll wrest from others
   More than all this,
I shall demand from Heaven
   Far sweeter bliss.

What profit then to others,
   Laughter and wine?
I'll have what most they covet –
   Death, will be mine.

IN FRESHET TIME

Rondeau

In freshet time the waters tread
With crafty foot a foreign bed,
On shores whose outlines come and go
As falls or swells the overflow,
The teasel lifts its ragged head
    In freshet time.

The turbid river, mountain-fed,
Laughs while the sun warms overhead,
The thawing flats all spongy grow,
    In freshet time.

Drenched sedges trail with stems outspread
O'er driftwood waterlogged and dead,
The field-mouse burrows deep below,
The wary muskrat plunges low,
And willows turn from grey to red
    In freshet time.

THISTLE-DOWN

Beyond a ridge of pine with russet tips
The west lifts to the sun her longing lips,

Her bushes stain with gold and garnet dye
The shore, the river, and the wide far sky;

Like floods of wine the waters filter through
The reeds that brush our indolent canoe.

I beach the bow where sands in shadows lie;
You hold my hand a space, then speak good-bye.

Upwinds your pathway through the yellow plumes
Of goldenrod, profuse in August blooms

And o'er its tossing sprays you toss a kiss;
A moment more, and I see only this –

The idle paddle you so lately held,
The empty bow your pliant wrist propelled,

Some thistles purpling into violet,
Their blossoms with a thousand thorns afret,

And like a cobweb, shadowy and grey,
Far floats their down – far drifts my dream away.

MOONSET

Idles the night wind through the dreaming firs,
That waking murmur low,
As some lost melody returning stirs
The love of long ago;
And through the far, cool distance, zephyr-fanned,
The moon is sinking into shadow-land.

The troubled night-bird, calling plaintively,
Wanders on restless wing;
The cedars, chanting vespers to the sea,
Await its answering,
That comes in wash of waves along the strand,
The while the moon slips into shadow-land.

O! soft responsive voices of the night
I join your minstrelsy,
And call across the fading silver light
As something calls to me;
I may not all your meaning understand,
But I have touched your soul in shadow-land.

THE CATTLE THIEF

They were coming across the prairie, they were galloping hard
    and fast;
For the eyes of those desperate riders had sighted their man
    at last –
Sighted him off to Eastward, where the Cree encampment lay,
Where the cotton woods fringed the river, miles and miles away.
Mistake him? Never! Mistake him? the famous Eagle Chief!
That terror to all the settlers, that desperate Cattle Thief –
That monstrous, fearless Indian, who lorded it over the plain,
Who thieved and raided, and scouted, who rode like a
    hurricane!
But they've tracked him across the prairie; they've followed him
    hard and fast;
For those desperate English settlers have sighted their man
    at last.

Up they wheeled to the tepees, all their British blood aflame,
Bent on bullets and bloodshed, bent on bringing down
    their game;
But they searched in vain for the Cattle Thief: that lion had left
    his lair,
And they cursed like a troop of demons – for the women alone
    were there.
'The sneaking Indian coward,' they hissed; 'he hides while yet
    he can;
He'll come in the night for cattle, but he's scared to face a *man.*'
'Never!' and up from the cotton woods rang the voice of
    Eagle Chief;
And right out into the open stepped, unarmed, the Cattle
    Thief.
Was that the game they had coveted? Scarce fifty years had
    rolled
Over that fleshless, hungry frame, starved to the bone and old;
Over that wrinkled, tawny skin, unfed by the warmth of blood.
Over those hungry, hollow eyes that glared for the sight of food.

He turned, like a hunted lion: 'I know not fear,' said he;

And the words outleapt from his shrunken lips in the language
    of the Cree.
'I'll fight you, white-skins, one by one, till I kill you *all*,' he said;
But the threat was scarcely uttered, ere a dozen balls of lead
Whizzed through the air about him like a shower of metal rain,
And the gaunt old Indian Cattle Thief dropped dead on the
    open plain.
And that band of cursing settlers gave one triumphant yell,
And rushed like a pack of demons on the body that writhed
    and fell.
'Cut the fiend up into inches, throw his carcass on the plain;
Let the wolves eat the cursed Indian, he'd have treated us
    the same.'
A dozen hands responded, a dozen knives gleamed high,
But the first stroke was arrested by a woman's strange, wild cry.
And out into the open, with a courage past belief,
She dashed, and spread her blanket o'er the corpse of the
    Cattle Thief;
And the words outleapt from her shrunken lips in the language
    of the Cree,
'If you mean to touch that body, you must cut your way through
    me.'
And that band of cursing settlers dropped backward one by one,
For they knew that an Indian woman roused, was a woman to let
    alone.
And then she raved in a frenzy that they scarcely understood,
Raved of the wrongs she had suffered since her earliest
    babyhood:
'Stand back, stand back, you white-skins, touch that dead man
    to your shame;
You have stolen my father's spirit, but his body I only claim.
You have killed him, but you shall not dare to touch him now
    he's dead.
You have cursed, and called him a Cattle Thief, though you
    robbed him first of bread –
Robbed him and robbed my people – look there, at that
    shrunken face,
Starved with a hollow hunger, we owe to you and your race.
What have you left to us of land, what have you left of game,
What have you brought but evil, and curses since you came?

How have you paid us for our game? how paid us for our land?
By a *book*, to save our souls from the sins *you* brought in your
    other hand.
Go back with your new religion, we never have understood
Your robbing an Indian's *body*, and mocking his *soul* with food.
Go back with your new religion, and find – if find you can –
The *honest* man you have ever made from out a *starving* man.
You say your cattle are not ours, your meat is not our meat;
When *you* pay for the land you live in, *we'll* pay for the meat
    we eat.
Give back our land and our country, give back our herds of
    game;
Give back the furs and the forests that were ours before you
    came;
Give back the peace and the plenty. Then come with your new
    belief,
And blame, if you dare, the hunger that *drove* him to be a thief.'

AT CROW'S NEST PASS

At Crow's Nest Pass the mountains rend
Themselves apart, the rivers wend
    A lawless course about their feet,
    And breaking into torrents beat
In useless fury where they blend
    At Crow's Nest Pass.

The nesting eagle, wise, discreet,
Wings up the gorge's lone retreat
And makes some barren crag her friend
    At Crow's Nest Pass.

Uncertain clouds, half-high, suspend
Their shifting vapours, and contend
    With rocks that suffer not defeat;
    And snows, and suns, and mad winds meet
To battle where the cliffs defend
    At Crow's Nest Pass.

BENEDICTUS

Something so tender fills the air to-day.
What it may be, or mean, no voice can say,
But all the harsh, hard things seem far away.

Something so restful lies on lake and shore,
The world seems anchored, and life's petty war
Of haste and labour gone for evermore.

Something so holy lies upon the land,
Like to a blessing from a saintly hand,
A peace we feel, though cannot understand.

FIRE FLOWERS

And only where the forest fires have sped,
   Scorching relentlessly the cool north lands,
A sweet wild flower lifts its purple head,
And, like some gentle spirit sorrow-fed,
   It hides the scars with almost human hands.

And only to the heart that knows of grief,
   Of desolating fire, of human pain,
There comes some purifying sweet belief,
Some fellow-feeling beautiful, if brief.
   And life revives, and blossoms once again.

THE GOPHER

A merry little rascal, with a saucy little way,
Who dresses like a hypocrite, in soft, religious grey.

He pilfers in the harvest fields, he steals the very best,
And monkeys with his conscience, as they're apt to do out west.

HARVEST TIME

Pillowed and hushed on the silent plain,
Wrapped in her mantle of golden grain,

Wearied of pleasuring weeks away,
Summer is lying asleep to-day, –

Where winds come sweet from the wild-rose briers
And the smoke of the far-off prairie fires;

Yellow her hair as the goldenrod,
And brown her cheeks as the prairie sod;

Purple her eyes as the mists that dream
At the edge of some laggard sun-drowned stream;

But over their depths the lashes sweep,
For Summer is lying to-day asleep.

The north wind kisses her rosy mouth,
His rival frowns in the far-off south,

And comes caressing her sunburnt cheek,
And Summer awakes for one short week, –

Awakes and gathers her wealth of grain,
Then sleeps and dreams for a year again.

HIS MAJESTY, THE WEST WIND

Once in a fit of mental aberration
I wrote some stanzas to the western wind,
A very stupid, maudlin invocation
That into ears of audiences I've dinned.

A song about a sail, canoe and paddle,
Recited I, in sailor flannels dressed,

And when they heard it people would skiddadle,
Particularly those who had been west.

For they, alas, had knowledge. I was striving
To write of something I had never known,
That I had ne'er experienced – the driving
Of western winds across a prairie blown.

I never thought when grinding out those stanzas,
I'd live to swallow pecks of prairie dust,
That I'd deny my old extravaganzas,
And wish his Majesty distinctly – cussed.

KICKING-HORSE RIVER

It does not care for grandeur,
    And it does not care for state,
It flips its little fingers
    In the very face of fate;
And when its course is thwarted
    Its current set at bay,
It just kicks up its saucy heels
    And takes another way.

It laughs among the monarchs,
    It giggles at the kings.
It dances in the gorges,
    While a comic song it sings;
It ripples into waterfalls,
    It tipples into spray,
And when they raise their eyebrows up
    It – takes another way.

It does not care a button
    For the granite or the rocks.
It never gets discouraged,
    For it's never in a box.

When mountains contradict it,
   And canyons have their say,
It kicks a little higher,
   And – takes another way.

LITTLE VANCOUVER

Little Vancouver was born in the west,
The healthiest baby on Canada's breast.
What matter if once in its cradle it lay
Its life all but doomed on its christening day,
Its poor little body fire-fevered lay tost,
And Canada mourned her sweet infant as lost.
But little Vancouver just shook its small head,
And said 'I'm laid up but you bet I'm not dead.'

And motherly Canada nursed the wee youth,
And bought it a railroad to cut its first tooth.
And soon it grew out of its swaddling bands,
To slip from the lap and the old nurse's hands,
To toddle away in its two little shoes,
While all its grown relatives soon heard the news,
That the sturdy young westerner nothing depresses,
For little Vancouver is in its short dresses.

Little Vancouver is royal of birth,
And a coronet carries of national worth
That some day she may wear, and surprise the whole nation,
By causing the Queen's City full abdication
Of sceptre and kingdom, for some time or other.
This pretty young Princess will rival her mother;
Though aged but eight summers, this fact you can't down,
That little Vancouver is heir to the crown.

Little Vancouver is growing apace,
And a miniature is of the Queen City's face;
She's tall, and she's strong, and surpassingly fair,
And about her a certain imperial air

That suggests old Toronto must look to her merits,
For this little child the title inherits,
And not many years may have overhead flown,
E'er little Vancouver may sit on the throne.

THE PRAIRIE

I may not catch the largeness of its meaning,
So infinite and perfected the whole,
But this child-wisdom I am slowly gleaning,
That through its silence I can reach its soul.

I stand and watch its limitless outreaching,
Its velvet brownness to the sky unroll,
And though I may not understand its teaching,
Its silence has revealed to me its soul.

SILHOUETTE

The sky-line melts from russet into blue,
Unbroken the horizon, saving where
A wreath of smoke curls up the far, thin air,
And points the distant lodges of the Sioux.

Etched where the lands and cloudlands touch and die
A solitary Indian tepee stands,
The only habitation of these lands,
That roll their magnitude from sky to sky.

The tent poles lift and loom in thin relief,
The upward floating smoke ascends between,
And near the open doorway, gaunt and lean,
And shadow-like, there stands an Indian Chief.

With eyes that lost their lustre long ago,
With visage fixed and stern as fate's decree,

He looks towards the empty west, to see
The never-coming herd of buffalo.

Only the bones that bleach upon the plains,
Only the fleshless skeletons that lie
In ghastly nakedness and silence, cry
Out mutely that naught else to him remains.

WHERE LEAPS THE STE MARIE

I

What dream you in the night-time
   When you whisper to the moon?
What say you in the morning?
   What do you sing at noon?
When I hear your voice uplifting,
Like a breeze through branches sifting,
And your ripples softly drifting
   To the August airs a-tune.

II

Lend me your happy laughter,
   Ste Marie, as you leap;
Your peace that follows after
   Where through the isles you creep.
Give to me your splendid dashing,
Give your sparkles and your splashing,
Your uphurling waves down crashing,
   Then, your aftermath of sleep.

THE WOLF

Like a grey shadow lurking in the light,
He ventures forth along the edge of night;
With silent foot he scouts the coulee's rim
And scents the carrion awaiting him.
His savage eyeballs lurid with a flare
Seen but in unfed beasts which leave their lair
To wrangle with their fellows for a meal
Of bones ill-covered. Sets he forth to steal,
To search and snail and forage hungrily;
A worthless prairie vagabond is he.
Luckless the settler's heifer which astray
Falls to his fangs and violence a prey;
Useless her blatant calling when his teeth
Are fast upon her quivering flank – beneath
His fell voracity she falls and dies
With inarticulate and piteous cries,
Unheard, unheeded in the barren waste,
To be devoured with savage greed and haste.
Up the horizon once again he prowls
And far across its desolation howls;
Sneaking and satisfied his lair he gains
And leaves her bones to bleach upon the plains.

CURTAIN

Scene, final;
    Setting, modern;
        House, interior.
Left centre, window open to the west;
Right centre, swing door (showing some exterior
And eastern garden seats where one may rest).

Dramatis Personae,
    Two wand'ring spirits
Who speak their lines, then flit across the stage,

Trusting the audience to applaud their merits,
Hoping their failures earn not failure's wage.

Enter
The 'Gentle Reader' with this paper –
Then, warning tinkle of the curtain-bell;
The footlights lower; something like a vapour
Comes to the eyes that westward look farewell;
The rising audience dons its coat and filing
(The 'Gentle Reader' stays until the close);
Then with the customary bowing, smiling,
Exit Miss Poetry and Mr Prose.

MARSHLANDS

A thin wet sky, that yellows at the rim,
And meets with sun-lost lip the marsh's brim.

The pools low lying, dank with moss and mould,
Glint through their mildews like large cups of gold.

Among the wild rice in the still lagoon,
In monotone the lizard shrills his tune.

The wild goose, homing, seeks a sheltering,
Where rushes grow, and oozing lichens cling.

Late cranes with heavy wing, and lazy flight,
Sail up the silence with the nearing night.

And like a spirit, swathed in some soft veil,
Steals twilight and its shadows o'er the swale.

Hushed lie the sedges, and the vapours creep,
Thick, grey and humid, while the marshes sleep.

SOU'WESTER

Taut sheet and filling sail,
And sweet wild wind that frolics fast,
As strains the canvas, strains the mast,
To piping breeze a-blowing past,
   A-growing to a gale.

For'ard the breakers churn,
The whitecaps whip to lines of cream,
They beat and break along our beam,
And like the shadow of a dream
   The shore drops down astern.

BOOTS AND SADDLES

'Boots and saddles' – the well-known call,
A stir in paddock, and box, and stall,
A flutter of something felt by all,
   A madness none can name.

'Boots and saddles' – you can see the brisk
Exchange of bills and the silver disk;
For what is a race without a risk,
   To lord, or lad, or dame?

'Boots and saddles' – the rustle spreads,
The fever reels to a thousand heads,
The man that hopes and the man that dreads
   The chance of the coming game.

'Boots and saddles' – the horses line,
Blood and beauty and speed combine
For the coming contest, wild as wine,
   And hot as fiercest flame.

'Boots and saddles' – ah, that's the sound;
The long, clear notes on the air resound;
The blood upleaps and the pulses bound
  With a madness none can tame.

THE FAVOURITE

I think she knows she is trim and neat,
From her slender head to her slender feet.
I think she knows of her silken coat,
Of her arching neck, of her dainty throat.
For she holds her head with a regal pride
Of contrariness that she cannot hide.

I almost think that she strains to reach
The God-like gift of our human speech.
I think she knows she is nobler far
Than half the mammon about her are.
Yet this splendid, royal-blooded thing
Is slave to the track and betting ring.

'Tis little she needs of whirling lash,
Of stinging spur in the headlong dash;
Her gleaming eye, her sensitive ear,
Her flanks athrob with every cheer,
Are far too fine for the urging heel,
For this beautiful, speechless beast can feel.

I think that she sees beyond our ken,
Beyond the minds of women and men.
I think she sneers at our hollow show,
At our littleness; but this I know,
That she understands the breathless pause,
The ringing cheers and the wild applause,
The sweet renown of a glory won,
Of a triumph gained, of a race well run.

IN THE BOXES

It isn't so much in the cost of her gown;
   It isn't the colour or shade,
That causes her rival to stare up and down,
From the tip of her shoe to her smart bonnet crown;
   But it's all in the way it is made.

It may be of chiffon, of silk, or of lace,
   The rarest that weaver can weave;
It may be of cloth, or of cotton; but trace
The jealousy rife in each feminine face
   If she has one yard more in each sleeve.

She may be imposing, or proper, or pert;
   Her eyes may be brown, blue or black.
Be she pretty or plain, be she flippant or flirt,
It matters but little, so long as her skirt
   Has five organ plaits in the back.

She may bet with the boys, or plunge into the pools,
   Or else be religious and staid;
But her sweet little Ladyship stands there and rules,
For her gown is the envy of sages and fools;
   But it's all in the way it is made.

THE LAST HURDLE

Another sixty seconds, and the contest will be ended,
Neck and neck, nose and nose, with nostrils wide distended.

Swinging up the quarter-mile, with equal chance of winning,
They take the rise in splendid style, and cross the flat a-spinning.

But one has dropped an inch behind – your blood begins to
   curdle,
'Till you realize your horse is first to take the final hurdle.

PERSPECTIVE

I

Mantle of yellow and gown of green
  The late May days have donned,
With far fresh reaches of grass between,
  And the blue of the lake beyond.

II

The wide sun-eyes of the dandelion
  To the humid airs respond,
And the ships go slipping along the line
  Of blue on the lake beyond.

THE WHITE AND THE GREEN

I

It is winter in the Lakeland, and the sleeping islands lie,
Wrapped in pearl-embroidered ermine, crowned with milk-
    white ivory.
For many days have come and gone, and many hours are old,
Since the plover passed to southward at the coming of the cold.

II

It is summer in the Lakeland, and the islands lie serene,
All garmented in emerald, within a world of green.
For many days have come and gone, and many hours are old,
Since the plover passed to northward, and the April suns
    were gold.

DAWENDINE

There's a spirit on the river, there's a ghost upon the shore,
They are chanting, they are singing through the starlight
    evermore,
As they steal amid the silence.
        And the shadows of the shore.

You can hear them when the Northern candles light the
    Northern sky,
Those pale, uncertain candle flames, that shiver, dart and die,
Those dead men's icy finger tips,
        Athwart the Northern sky.

You can hear the ringing war-cry of a long-forgotten brave
Echo through the midnight forest, echo o'er the midnight
    wave,
And the Northern lanterns tremble
        At the war-cry of that brave.

And you hear a voice responding, but in soft and tender song;
It is Dawendine's spirit singing, singing all night long;
And the whisper of the night wind
        Bears afar her Spirit song.

And the wailing pine trees murmur with their voice attuned
    to hers,
Murmur when they 'rouse from slumber as the night wind
    through them stirs;
And you listen to their legend,
        And their voices blend with her's.

There was feud and there was bloodshed near the river by the hill;
And Dawendine listened, while her very heart stood still:
Would her kinsman or her lover
        Be the victim by the hill?

Who would be the great unconquered? who come boasting how
    he dealt

Death? and show his rival's scalplock fresh and bleeding at
 his belt.
Who would say, 'O Dawendine!
  Look upon the death I dealt?'

And she listens, listens, listens – till a war-cry rends the night,
Cry of her victorious lover, monarch he of all the height;
And his triumph wakes the horrors,
  Kills the silence of the night.

Heart of her! it throbs so madly, then lies freezing in her breast,
For the icy hand of death has chilled the brother she loved best;
And her lover dealt the death-blow;
  And her heart dies in her breast.

And she hears her mother saying, 'Take thy belt of wampum
 white;
Go unto yon evil savage while he glories on the height;
Sing and sue for peace between us:
  At his feet lay wampum white.

'Lest thy kinsmen all may perish, all thy brothers and thy sire
Fall before his mighty hatred as the forest falls to fire;
Take thy wampum pale and peaceful,
  Save thy brothers, save thy sire.'

And the girl arises softly, softly slips toward the shore;
Loves she well the murdered brother, loves his hated foeman
 more,
Loves, and longs to give the wampum;
  And she meets him on the shore.

'Peace,' she sings, 'O mighty victor, Peace! I bring thee
 wampum white.
Sheathe thy knife whose blade has tasted my young kinsman's
 blood to-night
Ere it drink to slake its thirsting,
  I have brought thee wampum white.'

Answers he, 'O Dawendine! I will let thy kinsmen be,
I accept thy belt of wampum; but my hate demands for me
That they give their fairest treasure,
    Ere I let thy kinsmen be.

'Dawendine, for thy singing, for thy suing war shall cease;
For thy name, which speaks of dawning, *Thou* shalt be the dawn
    of peace;
For thine eyes whose purple shadows tell of dawn,
    My hate shall cease.

Dawendine, Child of Dawning, hateful are thy kin to me;
Red my fingers with their heart blood, but my heart is red
    for thee:
Dawendine, Child of Dawning,
    Wilt thou fail or follow me?'

And her kinsmen still are waiting for her returning from the
    night,
Waiting, waiting for her coming with her belt of wampum white;
But forgetting all, she follows,
    Where he leads through day or night.

There's a spirit on the river, there's a ghost upon the shore,
And they sing of love and loving through the starlight
    evermore,
As they steal amid the silence,
    And the shadows of the shore.

OJISTOH

I am Ojistoh, I am she, the wife
Of him whose name breathes bravery and life
And courage to the tribe that calls him chief.
I am Ojistoh, his white star, and he
Is land, and lake, and sky – and soul to me.

Ah! But they hated him, those Huron braves,
Him who had flung their warriors into graves,
Him who had crushed them underneath his heel,
Whose arm was iron, and whose heart was steel
To all – save me, Ojistoh, chosen wife
Of my great Mohawk, white star of his life.

Ah! but they hated him, and councilled long
With subtle witchcraft how to work him wrong;
How to avenge their dead, and strike him where
His pride was highest, and his fame most fair.
Their hearts grew weak as women at his name:
They dared no war-path since my Mohawk came
With ashen bow, and flinten arrow-head
To pierce their craven bodies; but their dead
Must be avenged. Avenged? They dared not walk
In day and meet his deadly tomahawk;
They dared not face his fearless scalping knife;
So – Niyoh!* – then they thought of me, his wife.

O! evil, evil face of them they sent
With evil Huron speech: 'Would I consent
To take of wealth? be queen of all their tribe?
Have wampum, ermine?' Back I flung the bribe
Into their teeth, and said, 'While I have life
Know this – Ojistoh is the Mohawk's wife.'

Wah! how we struggled! But their arms were strong.
They flung me on their pony's back, with thong
Round ankle, wrist, and shoulder. Then upleapt
The one I hated most: his eye he swept
Over my misery, and sneering said,
'Thus, fair Ojistoh, we avenge our dead.'

And we rode, rode as a sea wind-chased,
I, bound with buckskin to his hated waist,
He, sneering, laughing, jeering, while he lashed
The horse to foam, as on and on we dashed.

* God, in the Mohawk language [Johnson's note].

Plunging through creek and river, bush and trail,
On, on we galloped like a northern gale.
At last, his distant Huron fires aflame
We saw, and nearer, nearer still we came.

I, bound behind him in the captive's place,
Scarcely could see the outline of his face.
I smiled, and laid my cheek against his back:
'Loose thou my hands,' I said. 'This pace let slack.
Forget we now that thou and I are foes.
I like thee well, and wish to clasp thee close;
I like the courage of thine eye and brow;
I like thee better than my Mohawk now.'

He cut the cords; we ceased our maddened haste
I wound my arms about his tawny waist;
My hand crept up the buckskin of his belt;
His knife hilt in my burning palm I felt;
One hand caressed his cheek, the other drew
The weapon softly – 'I love you, love you,'
I whispered, 'I love you as my life.'
And – buried in his back his scalping knife.

Ha! how I rode, rode as a sea wind-chased,
Mad with sudden freedom, mad with haste,
Back to my Mohawk and my home. I lashed
That horse to foam, as on and on I dashed.
Plunging through creek and river, bush and trail,
On, on I galloped like a northern gale.
And then my distant Mohawk's fires aflame
I saw, as nearer, nearer still I came,
My hands all wet, stained with a life's red dye,
But pure my soul, pure as those stars on high –
'My Mohawk's pure white star, Ojistoh, still am I.'

BECALMED

I

Idle summer along the river,
Idle airs on the wide lagoon,
Sails that sleep where winds should sweep,
The long-dead winds with their long-dead tune.

II

Idle crickets that shrill their singing
Beneath the brow of the cooling hill,
The sun-bathed strand, the far in-land,
A'dream in the noontide, warm and still.

III

Idle cranes in the distant marshes,
With folded wing in the restful glooms,
And up in the glade, in under-shade –
Wild bees a'whirr 'round the clover-blooms.

IV

Idle sails that aloft are flapping
Athwart the mast in their restlessness,
The far off clouds above the shrouds
Drift on – we only are motionless.

THE LIFTING OF THE MIST

All the long day the vapours played
    At blindfold in the city streets,
Their elfin fingers caught and stayed
    The sunbeams, as they wound their sheets
Into a filmy barricade
    'Twixt earth and where the sunlight beats.

A vagrant band of mischiefs these,
   With wings of grey and cobweb gown;
They live along the edge of seas,
   And creeping out on foot of down,
They chase and frolic, frisk and tease
   At blind-man's buff with all the town.

And when at eventide the sun
   Breaks with a glory through their grey,
The vapour-fairies, one by one,
Outspread their wings and float away
In clouds of colouring, that run
   Wine-like along the rim of day.

Athwart the beauty and the breast
   Of purpling airs they twirl and twist,
Then float away to some far rest,
   Leaving the skies all colour-kiss't –
A glorius and a golden West
   That greets the Lifting of the Mist.

THE SONGSTER

Music, music with throb and swing,
   Of a plaintive note, and long;
'Tis a note no human throat could sing,
No harp with its dulcet golden string, –
Nor lute, nor lyre with liquid ring,
   Is sweet as the robin's song.

He sings for love of the season
   When the days grow warm and long,
For the beautiful God-sent reason
   That his breast was born for song.

Calling, calling so fresh and clear,
   Through the song-sweet days of May;
Warbling there, and whistling here,

He swells his voice on the drinking ear,
On the great, wide, pulsing atmosphere
   Till his music drowns the day.

He sings for love of the season
   When the days grow warm and long,
For the beautiful God-sent reason
   That his breast was born for song.

THE GOOD OLD N. P.

(*Air – The Red, White, and Blue*)

I

Now rise up men of the nation,
   Rise up at your country's command,
Come forward whatever your station,
   And shoulder-to-shoulder we'll stand.
We may differ in creed and in colour,
   French and English and Red men are we,
But we're one for our cause and our country,
   We are one for the good old N. P.

Chorus
Then three cheers for the good old N. P.,
   Give a hearty three times three,
We are one for our cause and our country,
   We are one for the good old N. P.

II

It has nourished the son of the city,
   It has nourished the son of the soil,
Surrounded the workman with plenty,
   Awarding with wages his toil.
It has fed both the lordly and lowly,
   And Master and Man will agree,

And its foes are admitting, though slowly,
　　Success means the good old N. P.

Chorus

　　　III

So rally ye sons of Protection,
　　And shoulder-to-shoulder we'll stand,
We'll gather from every direction,
　　From seaboard and lakeside and land;
For the tariff that fostered and fed us,
　　From the hour of its birth we began
To know, to prosperity it led us
　　And we'll stand by it now to a man.

Chorus

LULLABY OF THE IROQUOIS

Little brown baby-bird, lapped in your nest,
　　Wrapped in your nest,
　　Strapped in your nest,
Your straight little cradle-board rocks you to rest;
　　Its hands are your nest;
　　Its bands are your nest;
It swings from the down-bending branch of the oak;
You watch the camp flame, and the curling grey smoke;
But, oh, for your pretty black eyes sleep is best, –
Little brown baby of mine, go to rest.

Little brown baby-bird swinging to sleep,
　　Winging to sleep,
　　Singing to sleep,
Your wonder-black eyes that so wide open keep,
　　Shielding their sleep,
　　Unyielding to sleep,

The heron is homing, the plover is still,
The night-owl calls from his haunt on the hill,
Afar the fox barks, afar the stars peep, –
Little brown baby of mine, go to sleep.

THE CORN HUSKER

Hard by the Indian lodges, where the bush
   Breaks in a clearing, through ill-fashioned fields,
She comes to labour, when the first still hush
   Of autumn follows large and recent yields.

Age in her fingers, hunger in her face,
   Her shoulders stooped with weight of work and years,
But rich in tawny colouring of her race,
   She comes a-field to strip the purple ears.

And all her thoughts are with the days gone by,
   Ere might's injustice banished from their lands
Her people, that to-day unheeded lie,
   Like the dead husks that rustle through her hands.

LOW TIDE AT ST ANDREWS

(*New Brunswick*)

The long red flats stretch open to the sky,
Breathing their moisture on the August air.
The seaweeds cling with flesh-like fingers where
The rocks give shelter that the sands deny;
And wrapped in all her summer harmonies
St Andrews sleeps beside her sleeping seas.

The far-off shores swim blue and indistinct,
Like half-lost memories of some old dream.
The listless waves that catch each sunny gleam

Are idling up the waterways land-linked,
And, yellowing along the harbour's breast,
The light is leaping shoreward from the west.

And naked-footed children, tripping down,
Light with young laughter, daily come at eve
To gather dulse and sea clams and then heave
Their loads, returning laden to the town,
Leaving a strange grey silence when they go, –
The silence of the sands when tides are low.

THE QUILL WORKER

Plains, plains, and the prairie land which the sunlight floods
    and fills,
To the north the open country, southward the Cypress Hills;
Never a bit of woodland, never a rill that flows,
Only a stretch of cactus beds, and the wild, sweet prairie rose;
Never a habitation, save where in the far south-west
A solitary tepee lifts its solitary crest,
Where Neykia in the doorway, crouched in the red sunshine,
Broiders her buckskin mantle with the quills of the porcupine.

Neykia, the Sioux chief's daughter, she with the foot that flies,
She with the hair of midnight and the wondrous midnight eyes,
She with the deft brown fingers, she with the soft, slow smile,
She with the voice of velvet and the thoughts that dream
    the while –
'Whence come the vague to-morrows? Where do the yesters fly?
What is beyond the border of the prairie and the sky?
Does the maid in the Land of Morning sit in the red sunshine,
Broidering her buckskin mantle with the quills of the
    porcupine?'

So Neykia, in the westland, wonders and works away,
Far from the fret and folly of the 'Land of Waking Day.'
And many the pale-faced trader who stops at the tepee door

For a smile from the sweet, shy worker, and a sigh when the
    hour is o'er.
For they know of a young red hunter who oftentimes has stayed
To rest and smoke with her father, though his eyes were on
    the maid;
And the moons will not be many ere she in the red sunshine
Will broider his buckskin mantle with the quills of the
    porcupine.

HIS SISTER'S SON

.   .   .   .   .

For they killed the best that was in me
When they said I must not return
To my father's lodge, to my mother's arms:
When my heart would burn – and burn!
For when dead is a daughter's womanhood
There is nothing left that is grand and good.

.   .   .   .   .

TRAVERSE BAY

Outside, a sweep of waves and winds that roar
    Beneath storm-threatened skies,
But here, a harbour sheltered by a shore
    That circles crescent wise
Like some young moon that left its aerial lands
To shape and spill its silver on these sands.

I stand and watch the line of liquid blue
    Where skies and waters meet
The long green waves that crowd the nearer view
    And break about my feet.
The waters lift and heave, then drop away
Beaten and breathless, sweeping up the bay.

And all the wonder of this wind-swept sea,
   And its tempestuous sky,
Its hidden past, its unknown history,
   Its centuries gone by –
Rise and proclaim the Infinite, until
The doubt within my heart grows hushed – then still.

THE MOUSE'S MESSAGE

Two little mice and a great big mouse
Went journeying away together,
And they came, at last, to a little grey house
And their hearts were light as a feather,
For they said 'Here a dear little boy-boy lives,
We would like to kiss and to squeeze,
And Pauline said
He would give us a bed
And a great big piece of cheese.'

For she called him her sweetheart – so she did,
Her dear little love of a Brownie,
And she sent us East with Gerald to feast,
Till we all get slick and downy.
And she said we must hug little Gerald, for her,
And nibble his cheeks so cheery,
And kiss him twice
Like good little mice
Because he's his old girl's Dearie.

THE INDIAN CORN PLANTER

He needs must leave the trapping and the chase,
   For mating game his arrows ne'er despoil,
And from the hunter's heaven turn his face,
   To wring some promise from the dormant soil.

He needs must leave the lodge that wintered him,
   The enervating fires, the blanket bed –
The women's dulcet voices, for the grim
   Realities of labouring for bread.

So goes he forth beneath the planter's moon
   With sack of seed that pledges large increase,
His simple pagan faith knows night and noon,
   Heat, cold, seedtime and harvest shall not cease.

And yielding to his needs, this honest sod,
   Brown as the hand that tills it, moist with rain,
Teeming with ripe fulfilment, true as God,
   With fostering richness, mothers every grain.

CANADIAN BORN

We first saw light in Canada, the land beloved of God;
We are the pulse of Canada, its marrow and its blood:
And we, the men of Canada, can face the world and brag
That we were born in Canada beneath the British flag.

Few of us have the blood of kings, few are of courtly birth,
But few are vagabonds or rogues of doubtful name and worth;
And all have one credential that entitles us to brag –
That we were born in Canada beneath the British flag.

We've yet to make our money, we've yet to make our fame,
But we have gold and glory in our clean colonial name;
And every man's a millionaire if only he can brag
That he was born in Canada beneath the British flag.

No title and no coronet is half so proudly worn
As that which we inherited as men Canadian born.
We count no man so noble as the one who makes the brag
That he was born in Canada beneath the British flag.

The Dutch may have their Holland, the Spaniard have his
   Spain,
The Yankee to the south of us must south of us remain;
For not a man dare lift a hand against the men who brag
That they were born in Canada beneath the British flag.

THE LEGEND OF QU'APPELLE VALLEY

I am the one who loved her as my life,
   Had watched her grow to sweet young womanhood;
Won the dear privilege to call her wife,
   And found the world, because of her, was good.
I am the one who heard the spirit voice,
   Of which the paleface settlers love to tell;
From whose strange story they have made their choice
   Of naming this fair valley the 'Qu'Appelle.'

She had said fondly in my eager ear –
   'When Indian summer smiles with dusky lip,
Come to the lakes, I will be first to hear
   The welcome music of thy paddle dip.
I will be first to lay in thine my hand,
   To whisper words of greeting on the shore;
And when thou would'st return to thine own land,
   I'll go with thee, thy wife for evermore.'

Not yet a leaf had fallen, not a tone
   Of frost upon the plain ere I set forth,
Impatient to possess her as my own –
   This queen of all the women of the North.
I rested not at even or at dawn,
   But journeyed all the dark and daylight through –
Until I reached the Lakes, and, hurrying on,
   I launched upon their bosom my canoe.

Of sleep or hunger then I took no heed,
   But hastened o'er their leagues of waterways;

But my hot heart outstripped my paddle's speed
  And waited not for distance or for days,
But flew before me swifter than the blade
  Of magic paddle ever cleaved the Lake,
Eager to lay its love before the maid,
  And watch the lovelight in her eyes awake.

So the long days went slowly drifting past;
  It seemed that half my life must intervene
Before the morrow, when I said at last –
  'One more day's journey and I win my queen!'
I rested then, and, drifting, dreamed the more
  Of all the happiness I was to claim, –
When suddenly from out the shadowed shore,
  I heard a voice speak tenderly my name.

'Who calls?' I answered; no reply; and long
  I stilled my paddle blade and listened. Then
Above the night wind's melancholy song
  I heard distinctly that strange voice again –
A woman's voice, that through the twilight came
  Like to a soul unborn – a song unsung.
I leaned and listened – yes, she spoke my name,
  And then I answered in the quaint French tongue,
'Qu'Appelle? Qu'Appelle?' No answer, and the night
  Seemed stiller for the sound, till round me fell
The far-off echoes from the far-off height –
  'Qu'Appelle?' my voice came back, 'Qu'Appelle?
  Qu'Appelle?'
This – and no more; I called aloud until
  I shuddered as the gloom of night increased,
And, like a pallid spectre wan and chill,
  The moon arose in silence in the east.

I dare not linger on the moment when
  My boat I beached beside her tepee door;
I heard the wail of women and of men, –
  I saw the death-fires lighted on the shore.
No language tells the torture or the pain,
  The bitterness that flooded all my life, –

When I was led to look on her again,
  That queen of women pledged to be my wife.
To look upon the beauty of her face,
  The still closed eyes, the lips that knew no breath;
To look, to learn, – to realize my place
  Had been usurped by my one rival – Death.
A storm of wrecking sorrow beat and broke
  About my heart, and life shut out its light
Till through my anguish some one gently spoke,
  And said, 'Twice did she call for thee last night.'
I started up – and bending o'er my dead,
  Asked when did her sweet lips in silence close.
'She called thy name – then passed away,' they said,
  'Just on the hour whereat the moon arose.'

Among the lonely Lakes I go no more,
  For she who made their beauty is not there;
The paleface rears his tepee on the shore
  And says the vale is fairest of the fair.
Full many years have vanished since, but still
  The voyageurs beside the campfire tell
How, when the moonrise tips the distant hill,
  They hear strange voices through the silence swell.
The paleface loves the haunted lakes they say,
  And journeys far to watch their beauty spread
Before his vision; but to me the day,
  The night, the hour, the seasons are all dead.
I listen heartsick, while the hunters tell
  Why white men named the valley The Qu'Appelle.

III. The Later Years: 1899–1913

'GIVE US BARABBAS'

There was a man – a Jew of kingly blood,
  But of the people – poor and lowly born,
Accused of blasphemy of God, He stood
  Before the Roman Pilate, while in scorn
The multitude demanded it was fit
  That one should suffer for the people, while
Another be released, absolved, acquit,
  To live his life out virtuous or vile.

'Whom will ye have – Barabbas or this Jew?'
  Pilate made answer to the mob, 'The choice
Is yours; I wash my hands of this, and you,
  Do as you will.' With one vast ribald voice
The populace arose and, shrieking, cried,
  'Give us Barabbas, we condone his deeds!'
And He of Nazareth was crucified –
  Misjudged, condemned, dishonoured for their needs.

And down these nineteen centuries anew
  Comes the hoarse-throated, brutalized refrain,
'Give us Barabbas, crucify the Jew!'
  Once more a man must bear a nation's stain, –
And that in France, the chivalrous, whose lore
  Made her the flower of knightly age gone by.

Now she lies hideous with a leprous sore
　　No skill can cure – no pardon purify.

And an indignant world, transfixed with hate
　　Of such disease, cries, as in Herod's time,
Pointing its finger at her festering state,
　　'Room for the leper, and her leprous crime!'
And France, writhing from years of torment, cries
　　Out in her anguish, 'Let this Jew endure,
Damned and disgraced, vicarious sacrifice.
　　The honour of my army is secure.'

And, vampire-like, that army sucks the blood
　　From out a martyr's veins, and strips his crown
Of honour from him, and his herohood
　　Flings in the dust, and cuts his manhood down.
Hide from your God, O! ye that did this act!
　　With lesser crimes the halls of Hell are paved.
Your army's honour may be still intact,
　　Unstained, unsoiled, unspotted, – but unsaved.

WINNIPEG – AT SUNSET

Sink in your pillows, O! Sun-King that reigns
　　From east unto west,
Bury your yellow head out on the plain's
　　Wind-beaten breast.

Sink in your cradle of colour and cloud,
　　King of the day,　·
Leaving us only the shadow and shroud
　　Of on-coming grey.

Twilight is lingering over the rim
　　Of prairie and sky,
Its purple and amethyst, born in the dim
　　Horizon, to die.

The city is blinking her myriad eyes
   Of glimmering lights,
And the wintry moon in the wintry skies
   Sails up the heights.

While her thousand vassals of stars step forth
   The night to greet,
Where the city – queen of the west and north –
   Stands at their feet.

She who in garment of icicles dressed
   Regally reigns,
Queen of the prairie-land, queen of the west,
   Queen of the plains.

'H.M.S.'

Oh! They're only little letters, but they mean a mighty lot
Not explained in dictionary, nor expressed in polyglot;
And I've learned a little lesson that I never knew before,
That we can't turn up our noses at a British Man-o'-War.

Chorus: –

   For there's that about the sailors, and there's that about
     the ship,
   That makes you think a while before you give her any lip;
   And you've only got to see her, and I bet that you'll confess
   That she's mighty full of meaning, is an H.M.S.

I've arrived at the conclusion that it really wouldn't pay
To kick up a rebellion were she anchored in the Bay;
For I think she's built for business, and likes a little gore,
And I'd hardly like to quarrel with a British Man-o'-War.

For I think you'd be unhappy if you weren't the best of friends,
For to have her for an enemy would hardly suit your ends;

In fact, I never saw the thing that I respected more,
Or wished so much to chum with, as a British Man-o'-War.

And if she's not a friend of yours, just leave her quite alone,
Don't come around and tease her if you prize your blood and
    bone;
For I'm under the impression that the day you would deplore
When you started out to meddle with a British Man-o'-War.

And if she's got an eye on you, a-cruising round your coast,
You'd better waken up a bit, and look to every post;
For I'm pretty jolly certain that you can't lie round and snore,
If your harbour's lying open to a British Man-o'-War.

And if you've had a little tiff, why! do the thing that's wise:
Just call around, take off your hat, and then apologize;
Don't foster any foolish pride, although you may feel sore;
Take my advice – don't monkey with a British Man-o'War.

THE RIDERS OF THE PLAINS

Who is it lacks the knowledge? Who are the curs that dare
To whine and sneer that they do not fear the whelps in the
    Lion's lair?
But we of the North will answer, while life in the North remains,
Let the curs beware lest the whelps they dare are the Riders of
    the Plains;
For these are the kind whose muscle makes the power of the
    Lion's jaw,
And they keep the peace of our people and the honour of
    British law.

A woman has painted a picture, – 'tis a neat little bit of art
The critics aver, and it roused up for her the love of the big
    British heart.

'Tis a sketch of an English bulldog that tigers would scarce
　　attack,
And round and about and beneath him is painted the Union
　　Jack,
With its blaze of colour, and courage, its daring in every fold,
And underneath is the title, 'What we have we'll hold.'
'Tis a picture plain as a mirror, but the reflex it contains
Is the counterpart of the life and heart of the Riders of the
　　Plains;
For like to that flag and that motto, and the power of that
　　bulldog's jaw,
They keep the peace of our people and the honour of British law.

These are the fearless fighters, whose life in the open lies,
Who never fail on the prairie trail 'neath the Territorial skies,
Who have laughed in the face of the bullets and the edge of the
　　rebels' steel,
Who have set their ban on the lawless man with his crime
　　beneath their heel;
These are the men who battle the blizzards, the suns, the rains,
These are the famed that the North has named the 'Riders of
　　the Plains,'
And theirs is the might and the meaning and the strength of
　　the bulldog's jaw,
While they keep the peace of the people and the honour of
　　British law.

These are the men of action, who need not the world's renown,
For their valour is known to England's throne as a gem in the
　　British crown;
These are the men who face the front, whose courage the world
　　may scan,
The men who are feared by the felon, but are loved by the
　　honest man;
These are the marrow, the pith, the cream, the best that the
　　blood contains,
Who have cast their days in the valiant ways of the Riders of the
　　Plains;
And theirs is the kind whose muscle makes the power of old
　　England's jaw,

And they keep the peace of her people and the honour of
British law.

Then down with the cur that questions, – let him slink to his
craven den, –
For he daren't deny our hot reply as to 'who are our mounted
men.'
He shall honour them east and westward, he shall honour them
south and north,
He shall bare his head to that coat of red wherever that red
rides forth.
'Tis well that he knows the fibre that the great North-West
contains,
The North-West pride in her men that ride on the Territorial
plains, –
For of such as these are the muscles and the teeth in the
Lion's jaw,
And they keep the peace of our people and the honour of
British law.

RONDEAU: MORROW-LAND

In Morrow-Land there lies a day
In shadows clad, in garments grey
When sunless hours will come, My Dear
And skies will lose their lustre clear
Because I shall be leagues away.

Has Fate no other – kindlier way?
No gentler hands on me to lay,
Than I to go – than you stay here
In Morrow-Land?

And O! These days will be so dear –
Throughout the cold and coming year,
This Passion Week of gold and grey
Will haunt my heart and bless my way
In Morrow-Land.

TO C.H.W.

I

In Heidelberg, where you were born
The sunshine must be fine and rare
To leave such warmth within your heart
Such warmth of yellow in your hair,
To touch your thought and soul with that
Which neither suns nor stars impart,
That strange, exquisite gift of God,
That fine and fairy thing called art.
Did Fate decree your art and mine
Should weave into a future skein
When you were born in Heidelberg
And I was born in Vain?

II

In Heidelberg where you were born
The day dawn must wear strange disguise
Now, it has left its wealth of grey
And melting shadows in your eyes
From whose deep sombre beauty all
Your soul God-given speaks the clear
Unblemished strength of all your art
And writes that soul, a soul sincere.
Did Fate decree your promise hour
Meet mine of storm and stress and rain
When you were born in Heidelberg
And I was born in Vain?

HEIDLEBURGH

In Heidleburgh, where you were born,
The day dawn must wear strange disguise;

Since it has left is wealth of grey and melting shadows
In your eyes.
Did Fate decreee your art and mine
Should weave into a future skein,
When you were born in Heidleburgh
And I was born in vain?

In Heidleburgh, where you were born,
The sunshine must be fine and rare
To leave its wealth of golden sunshine
In your hair.
Did Fate decree your promise hour
Greet mine of storm and stress and rain,
When you were born in Heidleburgh
And I was born in vain?

HIS MAJESTY THE KING

I

There's a man in the Isle of England, he's the Lord of a vast
   Empire –
The son of a woman dear, and dead, the son of a noble sire.
A man who was born a Briton, born in the British hearts to dwell;
And they call him the King of England – but, he reigns in the
   West as well.

II

There's a man in the Isle of England, whose rule we are proud
   to own,
In the purple, and gold, and ermine, and the splendour of
   England's throne.
He has come to the heart of a nation too vast for the tongue
   to tell,
And they call him the King of England, but he's Lord of the
   North as well.

III

There's an Arm in the Isle of England, an Arm that is strong
   and grand,
It circles the world with a wealth of love outstretched from the
   Motherland.
'Tis the sword and shield of the children that over the oceans
   dwell –
'Tis the Arm of the King of England, but, 'tis the Arm of the
   East as well.

IV

There's a man in the Isle of England, who holds in his kingly
   hand
The reigns of a power, great and good, but those reins are a
   silken strand.
And the South, in its silken harness, will learn in his love to
   dwell,
For the man who is King of England is the Lord of the South
   as well.

V

And we of the North, East, South, and Westland, we'll battle,
   we'll dare, we'll do;
We will die for the King of England when the Empire wants
   us to.
Then cheer for the man in the British Isles till the ends of the
   earth shall ring,
For, as we fought for the Queen of England, we will fight for
   England's King.

A PRODIGAL

My heart forgot its God for love of you,
   And you forgot me, other loves to learn;
Now through a wilderness of thorn and rue
   Back to my God I turn.

And just because my God forgets the past,
   And in forgetting does not ask to know
Why I once left His arms for yours, at last
   Back to my God I go.

MADE IN CANADA

What is the creed and the calling that we of the north uphold?
It is never the cry for power, it is never the greed of gold.
Let the east, and south, and west contend, like wolves, for a
   maverick bone,
But Canada for the Canadians is the creed that we call our own.

Good wines are at Kaiser Wilhelm's, good cakes are at Uncle
   Sam's,
And in dear old Britain's larders are the best of plums and jams.
But beef and bread, and a blanket, a pipe, a mug and a fire,
Are the things that we have in Canada; what more can a man
   desire?

We don't need the marts of Europe, nor the trade of the
   eastern isles,
We don't need the Yankee's corn and wine, nor the Asiatic's
   smiles,
For what so good as our home-made cloth, and under the wide
   blue dome,
Will you tell me where you have tasted bread like the bread that
   is baked at home?

And we are the young and strong, and who so fit for the fight
   as we?
With our hands of steel and our iron heel and our hearts like
   the oaken tree.
For we are the home-bred, home-fed men, the pride of a
   princely land,
And the things that are made in Canada are the things that her
   sons demand.

So this is the creed and calling that we of the north uphold;
It is never the cry for power, it is never the greed of gold.
Let the east, and the south, and west contend, like wolves, for a
    maverick's bone,
But Canada for the Canadians is the creed that we call our own.

THE ART OF ALMA-TADEMA

There is no song his colours cannot sing,
    For all his art breathes melody, and tunes
The fine, keen beauty that his brushes bring
    To murmuring marbles and to golden Junes.

The music of those marbles you can hear
    In every crevice, where the deep green stains
Have sunken when the grey days of the year
    Spilled leisurely their warm, incessant rains

That, lingering, forget to leave the ledge,
    But drenched into the seams, amid the hush
Of ages, leaving but the silent pledge
    To waken to the wonder of his brush.

And at the Master's touch the marbles leap
    To life, the creamy onyx and the skins
Of copper-coloured leopards, and the deep,
    Cool basins where the whispering water wins

Reflections from the gold and glowing sun,
    And tints from warm, sweet human flesh, for fair
And subtly lithe and beautiful, leans one –
    A goddess with a wealth of tawny hair.

AT HALF-MAST

You didn't know Billy, did you? Well, Bill was one of the boys,
The greatest fellow you ever seen to racket an' raise a noise, –
An' sing! Say, you never heard singing 'nless you heard Billy sing.
I used to say to him, 'Billy, that voice that you've got there'd
    bring
A mighty sight more bank-notes to tuck away in your vest,
If only you'd go on the concert stage instead of a-ranchin'
    West.'
An' Billy he'd jist go laughin', and say as I didn't know
A robin's whistle in springtime from a barnyard rooster's crow.
But Billy could sing, an' I sometimes think that voice lives
    anyhow, –
That perhaps Bill helps with the music in the place he's gone
    to now.

The last time that I seen him was the day he rode away;
He was goin' acrost the plain to catch the train for the East
    next day.
'Twas the only time I ever seen poor Bill that he didn't laugh
Or sing an' kick up a rumpus an' racket around, and chaff,
For he'd got a letter from his folks that said for to hurry home,
For his mother was dyin' away down East an' she wanted Bill
    to come.
Say, but the feller took it hard, but he saddled up right away,
An' started across the plains to take the train for the East,
    next day.
Sometimes I lie awake a-nights jist a-thinkin' of the rest,
For that was the great big blizzard day, when the wind come
    down from west,
An' the snow piled up like mountains an' we couldn't put foot
    outside,
But jist set into the shack an' talked of Bill on his lonely ride.
We talked of the laugh he threw us as he went at the break
    o' day,
An' we talked of the poor old woman dyin' a thousand
    mile away.

Well, Dan O'Connell an' I went out to search at the end of the
  week,
Fer all of us fellers thought a lot, – a lot that we darsn't speak.
We'd been up the trail about forty mile, an' was talkin' of
  turning back,
But Dan, well, he wouldn't give in, so we kep' right on to the
  railroad track.
As soon as we sighted them telegraph wires says Dan, 'Say, bless
  my soul!
Ain't that there Bill's red handkerchief tied half way up that
  pole?'
Yes, sir, there she was, with her ends a-flippin' an' flyin' in the
  wind,
An' underneath was the envelope of Bill's letter tightly pinned.
'Why, he must a-boarded the train right here,' says Dan, but I
  kinder knew
That underneath them snowdrifts we would find a thing or two;
Fer he'd writ on that there paper, 'Been lost fer hours, – all
  hope is past.
You'll find me, boys, where my handkerchief is flyin' at
  half-mast.'

THE CITY AND THE SEA

I

To none the city bends a servile knee;
  Purse-proud and scornful, on her heights she stands,
And at her feet the great white moaning sea
  Shoulders incessantly the grey-gold sands, –
One the Almighty's child since time began,
  And one the might of Mammon, born of clods;
For all the city is the work of man,
  But all the sea is God's.

II

And she – between the ocean and the town –
  Lies cursed of one and by the other blest:
Her staring eyes, her long drenched hair, her gown,
  Sea-laved and soiled and dank above her breast.
She, image of her God since life began,
  She, but the child of Mammon, born of clods,
Her broken body spoiled and spurned of man,
  But her sweet soul is God's.

GOLDEN – OF THE SELKIRKS

A trail upwinds from Golden;
It leads to a land God only knows,
To the land of eternal frozen snows,
That trail unknown and olden.

And they tell a tale that is strange and wild –
Of a lovely and lonely mountain child
That went up the trail from Golden.

A child in the sweet of her womanhood,
Beautiful, tender, grave and good
As the saints in time long olden.

And the days count not, nor the weeks avail;
For the child that went up the mountain trail
Came never again to Golden.

And the watchers wept in the midnight gloom,
Where the cañons yawn and the Selkirks loom,
For the love that they knew of olden.

And April dawned, with its suns aflame,
And the eagles wheeled and the vultures came
And poised o'er the town of Golden.

God of the white eternal peaks,
Guard the death while the vulture seeks! –
God of the days so olden.

For only God in His greatness knows
Where the mountain holly above her grows,
On the trail that leads from Golden.

GOODBYE

Sounds of the seas grow fainter,
   Sounds of the sands have sped;
The sweep of gales,
The far white sails,
   Are silent, spent and dead.

Sounds of the days of summer
   Murmur and die away,
And distance hides
The long, low tides,
   As night shuts out the day.

GUARD OF THE EASTERN GATE

Halifax sits on her hills by the sea
   In the might of her pride, –
Invincible, terrible, beautiful, she
   With a sword at her side.

To right and to left of her, battlements rear
   And fortresses frown;
While she sits on her throne without favour or fear,
   With her cannon as crown.

Coast guard and sentinel, watch of the weal
   Of a nation she keeps;
But her hand is encased in a gauntlet of steel,
   And her thunder but sleeps.

LADY ICICLE

Little Lady Icicle is dreaming in the north-land
And gleaming in the north-land, her pillow all aglow;
   For the frost has come and found her
   With an ermine robe around her
Where little Lady Icicle lies dreaming in the snow.

Little Lady Icicle is waking in the north-land,
And shaking in the north-land her pillow to and fro;
   And the hurricane a-skirling
   Sends the feathers all a-whirling
Where little Lady Icicle is waking in the snow.

Little Lady Icicle is laughing in the north-land,
And quaffing in the north-land her wines that over-flow;
   All the lakes and rivers crusting
   That her finger-tips are dusting,
Where little Lady Icicle is laughing in the snow.

Little Lady Icicle is singing in the north-land,
And bringing from the north-land a music wild and low;
   And the fairies watch and listen
   Where her silver slippers glisten,
As little Lady Icicle goes singing through the snow.

Little Lady Icicle is coming from the north-land,
Benumbing all the north-land where'er her feet may go;
   With a fringe of frost before her
   And a crystal garment o'er her,
Little Lady Icicle is coming with the snow.

LADY LORGNETTE

I

Lady Lorgnette, of the lifted lash,
   The curling lip and the dainty nose,
The shell-like ear where the jewels flash,
   The arching brow and the languid pose,
The rare old lace and the subtle scents,
   The slender foot and the fingers frail, –
I may act till the world grows wild and tense,
   But never a flush on your features pale.
The footlights glimmer between us two, –
   You in the box and I on the boards, –
I am only an actor, Madame, to you,
   A mimic king 'mid his mimic lords,
For you are the belle of the smartest set,
     Lady Lorgnette.

II

Little Babette, with your eyes of jet,
   Your midnight hair and your piquant chin,
Your lips whose odours of violet
   Drive men to madness and saints to sin, –
I see you over the footlights' glare
   Down in the pit 'mid the common mob, –
Your throat is burning, and brown, and bare,
   You lean, and listen, and pulse, and throb;
The viols are dreaming between us two,
   And my gilded crown is no make-believe,
I am more than an actor, dear, to you,
   For you called me your king but yester eve,
And your heart is my golden coronet,
     Little Babette.

PRAIRIE GREYHOUNDS

C.P.R. 'No. I,' Westbound

I swing to the sunset land –
The world of prairie, the world of plain,
The world of promise and hope and gain,
The world of gold, and the world of grain,
  And the world of the willing hand.

I carry the brave and bold –
The one who works for the nation's bread,
The one whose past is a thing that's dead,
The one who battles and beats ahead,
  And the one who goes for gold.

I swing to the 'Land to Be,'
I am the power that laid its floors,
I am the guide to its western stores,
I am the key to its golden doors,
  That open alone to me.

C.P.R. 'No. 2,' Eastbound

I swing to the land of morn;
The grey old east with its grey old seas,
The land of leisure, the land of ease,
The land of flowers and fruits and trees,
  And the place where we were born.

Freighted with wealth I come;
For he who many a moon has spent
Far out west on adventure bent,
With well-worn pick and a folded tent,
  Is bringing his bullion home.

I never will be renowned,
As my twin that swings to the western marts,
For I am she of the humbler parts,
But I am the joy of the waiting hearts;
  For I am the Homeward-bound.

THE SLEEPING GIANT

(*Thunder Bay, Lake Superior*)

When did you sink to your dreamless sleep
   Out there in your thunder bed?
Where the tempests sweep,
And the waters leap,
   And the storms rage overhead.

Were you lying there on your couch alone
   Ere Egypt and Rome were born?
Ere the Age of Stone,
Or the world had known
   The Man with the Crown of Thorn.

The winds screech down from the open west,
   And the thunders beat and break
On the amethyst
Of your rugged breast, –
   But you never arise or wake.

You have locked your past, and you keep the key
   In your heart 'neath the westing sun,
When the mighty sea
And its shore will be
   Storm-swept till the world is done.

A TOAST

There's wine in the cup, Vancouver,
   And there's warmth in my heart for you,
While I drink to your health, your youth, and your wealth,
   And the things that you yet will do.
In a vintage rare and olden,
   With a flavour fine and keen,
Fill the glass to the edge, while I stand up to pledge
   My faith to my western queen.

Then here's a Ho! Vancouver, in wine of the bonniest hue,
  With a hand on my hip and the cup at my lip,
And a love in my life for you.
  For you are a jolly good fellow, with a great, big heart, I know;
So I drink this toast
To the 'Queen of the Coast.'
  Vancouver, here's a Ho!

And here's to the days that are coming,
  And here's to the days that are gone,
And here's to your gold and your spirit bold,
  And your luck that has held its own;
And here's to your hands so sturdy,
  And here's to your hearts so true,
And here's to the speed of the day decreed
  That brings me again to you.

Then here's a Ho! Vancouver, in wine of the bonniest hue,
  With a hand on my hip and the cup at my lip,
And a love in my life for you.
  For you are a jolly good fellow, with a great, big heart, I know;
So I drink this toast
To the 'Queen of the Coast.'
  Vancouver, here's a Ho!

YOUR MIRROR FRAME

Methinks I see your mirror frame,
  Ornate with photographs of them.
Place mine therein, for, all the same,
  I'll have my little laughs at them.

For girls may come, and girls may go,
  I think I have the best of them;
And yet this photograph I know
  You'll toss among the rest of them.

I cannot even hope that you
   Will put me in your locket, dear;
Nor costly frame will I look through,
   Nor bide in your breast pocket, dear.

For none your heart monopolize,
   You favour such a nest of them.
So I but hope your roving eyes
   Seek mine among the rest of them.

For saucy sprite, and noble dame,
   And many a dainty maid of them
Will greet me in your mirror frame,
   And share your kisses laid on them.

And yet, sometimes I fancy, dear,
   You hold me as the best of them.
So I'm content if I appear
   To-night with all the rest of them.

THE TRAIN DOGS

Out of the night and the north;
   Savage of breed and of bone,
Shaggy and swift comes the yelping band,
Freighters of fur from the voiceless land
   That sleeps in the Arctic zone.

Laden with skins from the north,
   Beaver and bear and raccoon,
Marten and mink from the polar belts,
Otter and ermine and sable pelts –
   The spoils of the hunter's moon.

Out of the night and the north,
   Sinewy, fearless and fleet,
Urging the pack through the pathless snow,
The Indian driver, calling low,
   Follows with moccasined feet.

Ships of the night and the north,
  Freighters on prairies and plains,
Carrying cargoes from field and flood
They scent the trail through their wild red blood,
  The wolfish blood in their veins.

WHEN GEORGE WAS KING

Cards, and swords, and a lady's love,
That is a tale worth reading,
An insult veiled, a downcast glove,
And rapiers leap unheeding.
  And 'tis O! for the brawl,
  The thrust, the fall,
And the foe at your feet a-bleeding.

Tales of revel at wayside inns,
The goblets gaily filling,
Braggarts boasting a thousand sins,
Though none can boast a shilling.
  And 'tis O! for the wine,
  The frothing stein,
And the clamour of cups a-spilling.

Tales of maidens in rich brocade,
Powder and puff and patches,
Gallants lilting a serenade
Of old-time trolls and catches.
  And 'tis O! for the lips
  And the finger tips,
And the kiss that the boldest snatches.

Tales of buckle and big rosette,
The slender shoe adorning,
Of curtseying through the minuet
With laughter, love, or scorning.
  And 'tis O! for the shout
  Of the roustabout,
As he hies him home in the morning.

Cards and swords, and a lady's love,
Give to the tale God-speeding,
War and wassail, and perfumed glove,
And all that's rare in reading.
   And 'tis O! for the ways
   Of the olden days,
And a life that was worth the leading.

THE CATTLE COUNTRY

Up the dusk-enfolded prairie,
   Foot-falls, soft and sly,
Velvet cushioned, wild and wary,
   Then – the coyote's cry.

Rush of hoofs, and roar and rattle,
   Beasts of blood and breed,
Twenty thousand frightened cattle,
   Then – the wild stampede.

Pliant lasso circling wider
   In the frenzied flight –
Loping horse and cursing rider,
   Plunging through the night.

Rim of dawn the darkness losing
   Trail of blackened soil;
Perfume of the sage brush oozing
   On the air like oil.

Foothills to the Rockies lifting
   Brown, and blue, and green,
Warm Alberta sunlight drifting
   Over leagues between.

That's the country of the ranges,
   Plain and prairie land,
And the God who never changes
   Holds it in His hand.

THE TRAIL TO LILLOOET

Sob of fall, and song of forest, come you here on haunting
    quest,
Calling through the seas and silence, from God's country of
    the west?
Where the mountain pass is narrow, and the torrent white and
    strong,
Down its rocky-throated cañon, sings its golden-throated song.

You are singing there together through the God-begotten
    nights,
And the leaning stars are listening above the distant heights
That lift like points of opal in the crescent coronet
About whose golden setting sweeps the trail to Lillooet.

Trail that winds and trail that wanders, like a cobweb hanging
    high,
Just a hazy thread outlining mid-way of the stream and sky,
Where the Fraser River cañon yawns its pathway to the sea,
But half the world has shouldered up between its song and me.

Here, the placid English August, and the sea-encircled miles;
There – God's copper-coloured sunshine beating through the
    lonely aisles
Where the waterfalls and forest voice for ever their duet,
And call across the cañon on the trail to Lillooet.

THE MAN IN CHRYSANTHEMUM LAND

There's a brave little berry-brown man
At the opposite side of the earth;
Of the White, and the Black, and the Tan,
He's the smallest in compass and girth.
O! he's little, and lively, and Tan,
And he's showing the world what he's worth.
For his nation is born, and its birth

Is for hardihood, courage, and sand,
   So you take off your cap
   To the brave little Jap
Who fights for Chrysanthemum Land.

Near the house that the little man keeps,
There's a Bug-a-boo building its lair;
It prowls, and it growls, and it sleeps
At the foot of his tiny back stair.
But the little brown man never sleeps,
For the Brownie will battle the Bear –
He has soldiers and ships to command;
   So take off your cap
   To the brave little Jap
Who fights for Chrysanthemum Land.

Uncle Sam stands a-watching near by,
With his finger aside of his nose –
John Bull with a wink in his eye,
Looks round to see how the wind blows –
O! jolly old John, with his eye
Ever set on the East and its woes.
More than hoeing their own little rows
These wary old wags understand,
   But they take off their caps
   To the brave little Japs
Who fight for Chrysanthemum Land.

Now he's given us Geishas, and themes
For operas, stories, and plays,
His silks and his chinas are dreams,
And we copy his quaint little ways;
O! we look on his land in our dreams,
But his value we failed to appraise,
For he'll gather his laurels and bays –
His Cruisers and Columns are manned,
   And we take off our caps
   To the brave little Japs
Who fight for Chrysanthemum Land.

CANADA

(*Acrostic*)

Crown of her, young Vancouver; crest of her, old Quebec;
Atlantic and far Pacific sweeping her, keel to deck.
North of her, ice and arctics; southward a rival's stealth;
Aloft, her Empire's pennant; below, her nation's wealth.
Daughter of men and markets, bearing within her hold,
Appraised at highest value, cargoes of grain and gold.

AUTUMN'S ORCHESTRA

(*Inscribed to One Beyond Seas*)

Know by the thread of music woven through
This fragile web of cadences I spin,
That I have only caught these songs since you
Voiced them upon your haunting violin.

The Overture

October's orchestra plays softly on
The northern forest with its thousand strings,
And Autumn, the conductor wields anon
The Golden-rod – the baton that he swings.

The Firs

There is a lonely minor chord that sings
Faintly and far along the forest ways,
When the firs finger faintly on the strings
Of that rare violin the night wind plays,
Just as it whispered once to you and me
Beneath the English pines beyond the sea.

Mosses

The lost wind wandering, forever grieves
  Low overhead,
Above grey mosses whispering of leaves
  Fallen and dead.
And through the lonely night sweeps their refrain
Like Chopin's prelude, sobbing 'neath the rain.

The Vine

The wild grape mantling the trail and tree,
festoons in graceful veils its drapery,
Its tendrils cling, as clings the memory stirred
By some evasive haunting tune, twice heard.

The Maple

I

It is the blood-hued maple straight and strong,
Voicing abroad its patriotic song.

II

Its daring colours bravely flinging forth
The ensign of the Nation of the North.

Hare-Bell

Elfin bell in azure dress,
Chiming all day long,
Ringing through the wilderness
Dulcet notes of song.
Daintiest of forest flowers
Weaving like a spell –
Music through the Autumn hours,
Little Elfin bell.

The Giant Oak

And then the sound of marching armies 'woke
Amid the branches of the soldier oak,
And tempests ceased their warring cry, and dumb
The lashing storms that muttered, overcome,
Choked by the heralding of battle smoke,
When these gnarled branches best their martial drum.

Aspens

A sweet high treble threads its silvery song,
Voice of the restless aspen, fine and thin
It trills its pure soprano, light and long –
Like the vibretto of a mandolin.

Finale

The cedars trees have sung their vesper hymn,
And now the music sleeps –
Its benediction falling where the dim
Dusk of the forest creeps.
Mute grows the great concerto – and the light
Of day is darkening, Good-night, Good-night.
But through the night time I shall hear within
The murmur of these trees,
The calling of your distant violin
Sobbing across the seas,
And waking wind, and star-reflected light
Shall voice my answering. Good-night, Good-night.

THE HOMING BEE

You are belted with gold, little brother of mine,
    Yellow gold, like the sun
That spills in the west, as a chalice of wine
    When feasting is done.

You are gossamer-winged, little brother of mine,
　　Tissue winged, like the mist
That broods where the marshes melt into a line
　　Of vapour sun-kissed.

You are laden with sweets, little brother of mine,
　　Flower sweets, like the touch
Of hands we have longed for, of arms that entwine,
　　Of lips that love much.

You are better than I, little brother of mine,
　　Than I, human-souled,
For you bring from the blossoms and red summer shine,
　　For others, your gold.

THE LOST LAGOON

It is dusk on the Lost Lagoon,
And we two dreaming the dusk away,
Beneath the drift of a twilight grey,
Beneath the drowse of an ending day,
And the curve of a golden moon.

It is dark in the Lost Lagoon,
And gone are the depths of haunting blue,
The grouping gulls, and the old canoe,
The singing firs, and the dusk and – you,
And gone is the golden moon.

O! lure of the Lost Lagoon, –
I dream to-night that my paddle blurs
The purple shade where the seaweed stirs,
I hear the call of the singing firs
In the hush of the golden moon.

LA CROSSE

(*Acrostic*)

Crown Prince born of the forest courts –
A child of the stealthy Redskin Race,
Now you are throned as the King of Sports –
Acclaimed as ruler, while yet the trace
Dark and savage, of Indian blood,
Arrows its way with a tiger's grace –
Surging your veins with its headlong flood.

Nature has made you a virile thing –
Agile and lithe, that no time can tame,
Tawny your sire, but your mothering
Indian and Paleface, both may claim,
Owing your birth to the wilds remote –
National game of the robust North,
A panther, wrapped in a racehorse coat –
Live with its blood you are forging forth.

Sinew of deer in your woven net,
Pulse of the ash in your curving frame,
Obeying the master-hand firm set
Renews the birth you cannot forget
That crowns you Canada's kingly game.

THE ARCHERS

I

Stripped to the waist, his copper-coloured skin
Red from the smouldering heat of hate within,
Lean as a wolf in winter, fierce of mood –
As all wild things that hunt for foes, or food –
War paint adorning breast and thigh and face,
Armed with the ancient weapons of his race,

A slender ashen bow, deer sinew strung,
And flint-tipped arrow each with poisoned tongue, –
Thus does the Red man stalk to death his foe,
And sighting him strings silently his bow,
Takes his unerring aim, and straight and true
The arrow cuts in flight the forest through,
A flint which never made for mark and missed,
And finds the heart of his antagonist.
Thus has he warred and won since time began,
Thus does the Indian bring to earth his man.

II

Ungarmented, save for a web that lies
In fleecy folds across his impish eyes,
A tiny archer takes his way intent
On mischief, which is his especial bent.
Across his shoulder lies a quiver, filled
With arrows dipped in honey, thrice distilled
From all the roses brides have ever worn
Since that first wedding out of Eden born.
Beneath a cherub face and dimpled smile
This youthful hunter hides a heart of guile;
His arrows aimed at random fly in quest
Of lodging-place within some blameless breast.
But those he wounds die happily, and so
Blame not young Cupid with his dart and bow:
Thus has he warred and won since time began,
Transporting into Heaven both maid and man.

BRANDON

(*Acrostic*)

Born on the breast of the prairie, she smiles to her sire – the
    sun,
Robed in the wealth of her wheat-lands, gift of her mothering
    soil,

Affluence knocks at her gateways, opulence waits to be won.
Nuggets of gold are her acres, yielding and yellow with spoil,
Dream of the hungry millions, dawn of the food-filled age,
Over the starving tale of want her fingers have turned the page;
Nations will nurse at her storehouse, and God gives her grain
    for wage.

THE KING'S CONSORT

I

Love, was it yesternoon, or years agone,
   You took in yours my hand,
And placed me close beside you on the throne
   Of Oriental lands?

The truant hour came back at dawn to-day,
   Across the hemispheres,
And bade my sleeping soul retrace its way
   These many hundred years.

And all my wild young life returned and ceased
   The years that lie between,
When you were King of Egypt, and The East,
   And I was Egypt's queen.

II

I feel again the lengths of silken gossamer enfold
My body and my limbs in robes of emerald and gold.
I feel the heavy sunshine, and the weight of languid heat
That crowned the day you laid the royal jewels at my feet.

You wound my throat with jacinths, green and glist'ning
   serpent-wise,
My hot, dark throat that pulsed beneath the ardour of your eyes;
And centuries have failed to cool the memory of your hands
That bound about my arms those massive, pliant golden bands.

You wreathed around my wrists long ropes of coral and of jade,
And beaten gold that clung like coils of kisses love-inlaid;
About my naked ankles tawny topaz chains you wound,
With clasps of carven onyx, ruby-rimmed and golden bound.

But not for me the Royal Pearls to bind about my hair,
'Pearls were too passionless,' you said, for one like me to wear,
I must have all the splendour, all the jewels warm as wine,
But pearls so pale and cold were meant for other flesh than
    mine.

But all the blood-warm beauty of the gems you thought my due
Were pallid as a pearl beside the love I gave to you;
O! Love of mine come back across the years that lie between,
When you were King of Egypt – Dear, and I was Egypt's Queen.

CALGARY OF THE PLAINS

Not of the seething cities with their swarming human hives,
Their fetid airs, their reeking streets, their dwarfed and
    poisoned lives,
Not of the buried yesterdays, but of the days to be,
The glory and the gateway of the yellow West is she.

The Northern Lights dance down her plains with soft and
    silvery feet,
The sunrise gilds her prairies when the dawn and daylight
    meet;
Along her level lands the fitful southern breezes sweep,
And beyond her western windows the sublime old mountains
    sleep.

The Redman haunts her portals, and the Paleface treads her
    streets,
The Indian's stealthy footstep with the course of commerce
    meets,
And hunters whisper vaguely of the half forgotten tales
Of phantom herds of bison lurking on her midnight trails.

Not hers the lore of olden lands, their laurels and their bays;
But what are these, compared to one of all her perfect days?
For naught can buy the jewel that upon her forehead lies –
The cloudless sapphire Heaven of her territorial skies.

THE BALLAD OF YAADA

(*A Legend of the Pacific Coast*)

There are fires on Lulu Island, and the sky is opalescent
With the pearl and purple tinting from the smouldering
of peat.
And the Dream Hills lift their summits in a sweeping, hazy
crescent,
With the Capilano cañon at their feet.

There are fires on Lulu Island, and the smoke, uplifting, lingers
In a faded scarf of fragrance as it creeps across the day,
And the Inlet and the Narrows blur beneath its silent fingers,
And the cañon is enfolded in its grey.

But the sun its face is veiling like a cloistered nun at vespers;
As toward the altar candles of the night a censer swings,
And the echo of tradition wakes from slumbering and whispers,
Where the Capilano river sobs and sings.

It was Yaada, lovely Yaada, who first taught the stream its
sighing,
For 'twas silent till her coming, and 'twas voiceless as the shore;
But throughout the great forever it will sing the song undying
That the lips of lovers sing for evermore.

He was chief of all the Squamish, and he ruled the coastal
waters –
And he warred upon her people in the distant Charlotte Isles;
She, a winsome basket weaver, daintiest of Haida daughters,
Made him captive to her singing and her smiles.

Till his hands forgot to havoc and his weapons lost their lusting,
Till his stormy eyes allured her from the land of Totem Poles,
Till she followed where he called her, followed with a woman's
  trusting,
To the cañon where the Capilano rolls.

And the women of the Haidas plied in vain their magic power,
Wailed for many moons her absence, wailed for many moons
  their prayer,
'Bring her back, O Squamish foeman, bring to us our Yaada
  flower!'
But the silence only answered their despair.

But the men were swift to battle, swift to cross the coastal water,
Swift to war and swift of weapon, swift to paddle trackless miles,
Crept with stealth along the cañon, stole her from her love and
  brought her
Once again unto the distant Charlotte Isles.

But she faded, ever faded, and her eyes were ever turning
Southward toward the Capilano, while her voice had hushed
  its song,
And her riven heart repeated words that on her lips were
  burning:
'Not to friend – but unto foeman I belong.

'Give me back my Squamish lover – though you hate, I still must
  love him.
Give me back the rugged cañon where my heart must ever be –
Where his lodge awaits my coming, and the Dream Hills lift
  above him,
And the Capilano learned its song from me.'

But through long-forgotten seasons, moons too many to be
  numbered,
He yet waited by the cañon – she called across the years,
And the soul within the river, though the centuries had
  slumbered,
Woke to sob a song of womanly tears.

For her little lonely spirit sought the Capilano cañon,
When she died among the Haidas in the land of Totem Poles,
And you yet many hear her singing to her lover-like companion,
If you listen to the river as it rolls.

But 'tis only when the pearl and purple smoke is idly swinging
From the fires on Lulu Island to the hazy mountain crest,
That the undertone of sobbing echoes through the river's
    singing,
In the Capilano cañon of the West.

SONG

The night-long shadows faded into grey,
    Then silvered into glad and gold sunlight,
Because you came to me, like a new day
    Born of the beauty of an autumn night.

The silence that enfolded me so long
    Stirred to the sweetest music life has known,
Because you came, and coming woke the song
    That slumbered through the years I was alone.

So have you brought the silver from the shade,
    The music and the laughter and the day,
So have you come to me, and coming made
    This life of mine a blossom-bordered way.

'AND HE SAID, FIGHT ON'

Time and its ally, Dark Disarmament
    Have compassed me about,
Have massed their armies, and on battle bent
    My forces put to rout,
But though I fight alone, and fall, and die,
    Talk terms of Peace? Not I.

They war upon my fortress, and their guns
    Are shattering its walls,
My army plays the coward's part, and runs,
    Pierced by a thousand balls,
They call for my surrender, I reply,
    'Give quarter now? Not I.'

They've shot my flag to ribbons, but in rents
    It floats above the height.
Their ensign shall not crown my battlements
    While I can stand and fight.
I fling defiance at them as I cry,
    'Capitulate? Not I.'

AFTERMATH

The wide, warm acres stretching lazily,
Roll out their russet silence to the sea,
Bared to the winds that whisper ceaselessly
Of homing time and landward-lying things.

Along the uplands, vagrant locusts whirr
Themselves through sunshine, and within the blur
Of purple distances, the faint, far stir
Of some lone haymaker that scythes and sings.

Across the marsh, reclaimed from the seas that creep
Against the sheltering dykes, the droning sweep
Of sickles, where the long salt grasses sleep,
Hushed in the peace that near fulfillment brings.

RECLAIMED LANDS

The long, flat lands out reach, field after field,
    Low-lying at the hem
Of snarling seas that beat against the shield
    Of dykes that shelter them.

No more the landward-lifting waves will drown
    These shores with storms and tide;
The guardian earth they cannot battle down;
    The sea is shut outside.

I hear the voices of the days long gone
    Clamour and call to me,
O love, the shelter of your arms alone
    Shuts out the wolfish sea!

TO WALTER MCRAYE

This to the friend I love, who up life's trail
Rode side by side with me through gallant days
And who yet journeys near, that I may hail
Him as he passes through the old byways.

This to the friend who loves me, who would fain
Halt me from mounting for my lonely ride,
Who would give vast possessions to detain
Me on the range this side the Great Divide.

       .   .   .   .   .   .

But I shall pledge you in this stirrup cup
Before I ride into the far sunset –
I shall not fail you at the Great Round Up
O! friend of mine, who never failed me yet.

THE BALLAD OF LALOO

This is Laloo, chief of the tribe whose feet
Follow the murmuring Illecillewaet,
As through the mighty Selkirk Range it strays
Singing, and sighing down its waterways.

Laloo who was the man, before these grim
Canyons and crags crushed the soul of him,
Tortured his heart and bleached his red blood pale
Before his feet passed up the long, long trail.

Chief was Laloo and well beloved of men
But best beloved of lovely Ollienn
She the sweet mountain flower of her race
Fleetest of foot and loveliest of face.

Daring, but dutiful, winsome and sweet
This daughter of the Illecillewaet.

IV. Anonymous and Pseudonymous Poems

BOTH SIDES

SHE

I'd been having a whacking flirtation
  With a boy not twenty years old:
And although I am five years his senior,
  That ugly fact need not be told.
I know that he literally worshipped
  Me; and just to tell you the truth,
I rather enjoyed the outpouring
  Of this wild first love of his youth.
How I liked my shy, innocent lover!
  But – wretched young villain! – I learned
That when chaffed by the fellows he called me
  His 'auntie' when my back was turned.

HE

I was desperately, madly, devoutly
  In love with a woman so fair
That, as usual, I thought her an angel,
  With halos encircling her hair.
She was older than I – but what of it?
  Her age but enhanced her, for then
Was she not *so* unselfish, preferring

A boy to society men?
But one day I got over my 'spasm,'
    And out of love's arms I soon slid
When I heard that, when chaffed by some women,
    She called me a 'snippy young kid.'

IN THE SHADOWS: MY VERSION

I am sailing down the river
Calm my craft moves, not a quiver
    Do I feel.
Save when the rocky point and jagged
Through the boiling rapids, ragged
    Scrapes the keel.

Night-hawks high above me, screaming
Love's eyes turn upon me, beaming
    Trustfully.
All about us night is falling
On the shore a child is squalling
    Bustfully.

Willowy copse and densest umbrage
Cast long shadows, and the foliage
    Tinged with red
Forms a background for a bumpkin
Sitting on a yellow pumpkin
    Scratching head.

Joyful are the leaping waters
And my boat, light, 'teeter-totters'
    On the foam.
And the blue-bloused granger fellow
Smock shock-ful of apples mellow
    Shambles home.

From the Locks as paddling westward
Soon I feel a weakness vestward
   So we lunch,
Leaving naught of all the luncheon
Only sighing for a puncheon
   Of good punch.

Into light from out the shadow
Home is reached, and I'm so glad, oh!
   But 'twas bliss.
As we leave the boat house, homing
Naughty thought, I, in the gloaming,
   Snatch a kiss.

     By the Pasha.

LENT

Whence this horrible stagnation?
Not one single invitation
   Ever comes,
Though before Ash Wednesday morning
Tired to death was I adorning
   These At Homes.

Balls and 'shines' with steady measure
Every night required 'The pleasure
   Of my Co.'
Now – upon a shelf reposes
Folded up as meek as Moses
   My dress clo'.

All throughout the Lenten season
Tho' I can't define the reason,
   I must rest,
Gradually I'm growing thinner
And a flabby one course dinner
   I digest.

So I somewhat long for Easter
When my appetite may feast her
  Full extent
(When society's more sunny
Tho' I'm saving lots of money
  During Lent).

No new ties, nor gloves, nor flowers,
No swell suppers – no late hours
  I enjoy –
Every night I turn in early
(I'm in fact my mother's curly-
  Headed boy).

        Woeful Jack

A TURNED DOWN PAGE

There's a turned down page, as someone says,
  In every human life –
A hidden story of happier days,
  Of peace amidst the strife;

A folded-down leaf, that the world knows not,
  A love dream rudely crushed;
The sight of a face that is not forgot,
  Although the voice be hush'd;

The far-distant sounds of a harp's soft strings –
  An echo in the air;
The hidden pages may be full of such things –
  Of things that once were fair.

There's a hidden page in each life, and mine
  A story might unfold;
But the end was sad of the dream divine –
  It better rests untold!

PROSE

OUTDOOR PASTIMES FOR WOMEN

The day has departed when it was considered ungentle and masculine for women to participate in outdoor sports. Within the latter half of this practical century America, at least, has decreed that feminine beauty and feminine health are synonymous, and to attain these woman-kind clamoured long and loudly at the iron portals so jealously closed by that most exacting of monsters, Good Form, betwixt her and her brethren, who themselves regarded the luxury of sports afield as their exclusive right. But the moment man championed the beauty of colour, of splendidly-developed figures, of firm flesh and a springy, tireless footstep as the truest attributes of girlish loveliness the difficulty ended. Women, like men, learned to despise the beauty (?) of idleness, of list-less hands, of pallid cheeks, of languid, doughy figures, and they wel-comed the time when men, in conjunction with Mrs Grundy, accorded to the world of women the privilege of healthful exercises, where strong life-giving airs and genial sunshine need not be filtered through the glass and garniture of four square walls before it became refined (?) suf-ficiently for feminine lungs to inhale and feminine faces to be bared to.

Years ago that dainty, essentially lady-like game, la grace, and that queen of elegance in pastimes, archery, comprised the limit of outdoor sports for women. Perhaps these were diversified by a mild bout at shut-tlecock and battledore; but as for a sport that would tone up one's mus-cles, harden one's flesh, develop the chest and send the blood bounding with life and warmth through one's veins, why, our grandmothers would have turned to their tambour work, their spinning wheels and embroi-dery frames in horror at the very mention of such things.

Then appeared that insidious and, alas! insipid thing, croquet, invented more for the purpose of furthering bad tempers and flirtations than physical development. But it was the thin edge of the wedge after all, and as such one should respect it, for close upon its heels followed lawn tennis, as it was called in its infancy, and from this little seedling burst forth the blooming bouquet of health-giving games, and namby-pamby, inane young girlhood awakened to the realization that the present age demanded of her nothing more perfect than the physique of the goddesses of ancient Greece. That Diana who

Dropped her silvery bow
Upon the meadows low

was far more of an ideal beauty than the wasp-waisted, bepowdered, bepatched caricature of robustness that femininity boasted in 'ye olden times.'

And to-day there is little indeed from which we are barred out – riding, sailing, swimming, rowing, paddling, cricketing, fishing, and even shooting, and the latest thing approved – cycling; but in enumerating these all on a wild midwinter night one feels the pulse of a hot national blood athrob in one's veins, that demands with every heart beat a special mention of Canadian national winter sports, in which both lads and lassies participate. And one instinctively yields to the impulse, saying, 'And now abideth these three – skating, tobogganing and snowshoeing,' but the greatest of these is snowshoeing, particularly on a night when a cold northern moon hangs aloft and the world beneath it looks like a big Christmas card with its crystallized pine trees and its fringes of icicles glittering and shimmering in the pale cold light.

Then our youth doffs its feathers and finery, dons its blanket coat, worsted toque, and shod with shoes aboriginal tramps forth through forest and field with a care-free gait, the sturdy step and rollicking laughter known only to rosiest health and – Canada. And what maiden is there in our strong young country who considers her feet too fragile to be encased in three pairs of woollen stockings, then bound about with a pair of gay moccasins and strapped to the network of a big, unwieldy snowshoe! And what is there in the first steps she takes that transforms those huge duck-footed looking shoes into a web of wings that skim over field and fence and drift, with the ease of Hiawatha's magic moccasins and the delicious vigour that Canada's daughters alone possess.

Few girls look prettier in evening dress than in a blanket suit (the most sensible thing ever devised for weathering a northern climate). The short light skirt and loose double-breasted coat, each bordered with the brilliant stripes and 'button-hole' stitched edges, look very little like the homely couch covers for which they were originally manufactured. And, some way or other, the face that laughs out at you from its nest of upturned coat collar and little curls astray from the confines of the brilliant toque has a certain gypsy likeness, a touch of sauciness and merry vitality one seldom sees in a ballroom. And, oh! what an irresistible bit of colour she is, from the tassel on her toque to the gaily-embroidered toe of her moccasin. True, the latter may not be quite as Cinderella-like as the French heeled slipper that her little foot will fill at the Governor's ball to-morrow night, but it is close and pliable and warm, and la Canadienne loves her buckskin shoon, heelless and flat as it may be.

Given a moonlit night, an atmosphere when the mercury drops to zero, or as much below as it can, a 5-mile stretch of drifted snow, an escort stalwart and brave, whose hand is strong, whose arm is muscular, whose foot is fleet and tireless, and little Lady Canada is content. She will snap her fingers at Fate, laugh in the face of Fortune and tramp for hours by the side of the big jovial lad, racing him down hill, having her small mittened fingers smothered in his brawny paw as he assists her up that long, long slope and over that high and marvellously frequent fence. Then comes the little stretch of forest land where the black cedars shut out the moonlight and the way is very uncertain. They halt. He raises his face, lays his hand, cup shaped, across his lips and gives a weird, long call. Through the shadows and cedars floats a reply from their comrades who have tramped far forward. He responds, they double it, and after a little argument, in which she asserts that she 'can see as plainly as if it were day, and that she can get along famously by herself, thank you,' he takes her hand authoritatively and trudges along, winding in and out among the trees and making the way far more difficult than need be.

A STRONG RACE OPINION:
ON THE INDIAN GIRL IN MODERN FICTION

Every race in the world enjoys its own peculiar characteristics, but it scarcely follows that every individual of a nation must possess these prescribed singularities, or otherwise forfeit in the eyes of the world their nationality. Individual personality is one of the most charming things to be met with, either in a flesh and blood existence, or upon the pages of fiction, and it matters little to what race an author's heroine belongs, if he makes her character distinct, unique and natural.

The American book heroine of today is vari-coloured as to personality and action. The author does not consider it necessary to the development of her character, and the plot of the story to insist upon her having American-coloured eyes, an American carriage, an American voice, American motives, and an American mode of dying; he allows her to evolve an individuality ungoverned by nationalisms – but the outcome of impulse and nature and a general womanishness.

Not so the Indian girl in modern fiction, the author permits her character no such spontaneity, she must not be one of womankind at large, neither must she have an originality, a singularity that is not definitely 'Indian.' I quote 'Indian' as there seems to be an impression amongst authors that such a thing as tribal distinction does not exist among the North American aborigines.

The term 'Indian' signifies about as much as the term 'European,' but I cannot recall ever having read a story where the heroine was described as 'a European.' The Indian girl we meet in cold type, however, is rarely distressed by having to belong to any tribe, or to reflect any tribal characteristics. She is merely a wholesome sort of mixture of any band existing between the Mic Macs of Gaspé and the Kwaw-Kewlths of British Columbia, yet strange to say, that notwithstanding the numerous tribes, with their aggregate numbers reaching more than 122,000 souls in Canada alone, our Canadian authors can cull from this huge revenue of character, but one Indian girl, and stranger still that this lonely little heroine never had a prototype in breathing flesh-and-blood existence!

It is a deplorable fact, but there is only one of her. The story-writer who can create a new kind of Indian girl, or better still portray a 'real live' Indian girl who will do something in Canadian literature that has never been done, but once. The general author gives the reader the impression that he has concocted the plot, created his characters, arranged his action, and at the last moment has been seized with the idea that the regulation Indian maiden will make a very harmonious background whereon to paint his pen picture, that, he, never having met this interesting individual, stretches forth his hand to his library shelves, grasps the first Canadian novelist he sees, reads up his subject, and duplicates it in his own work.

After a half dozen writers have done this, the reader might as well leave the tale unread as far as the interest touches upon the Indian character, for an unvarying experience tells him that this convenient personage will repeat herself with monotonous accuracy. He knows what she did and how she died in other romances by other romancers, and she will do and die likewise in his (she always does die, and one feels relieved that it is so, for she is too unhealthy and too unnatural to live).

The rendition of herself and her doings gains no variety in the pens of manifold authors, and the last thing that they will ever think of will be to study 'The Indian Girl' from life, for the being we read of is the offspring of the writer's imagination and never existed outside the book covers that her name decorates. Yes, there is only one of her, and her name is 'Winona.' Once or twice she has borne another appellation, but it always has a 'Winona' sound about it. Even Charles Mair, in that masterpiece of Canadian-Indian romances, 'Tecumseh,' could not resist 'Winona.' We meet her as a Shawnee, as a Sioux, as a Huron, and then, her tribe unnamed, in the vicinity of Brockville.

She is never dignified by being permitted to own a surname, although, extraordinary to note, her father is always a chief, and had he ever existed, would doubtless have been as conservative as his contemporaries about the usual significance that his people attach to family name and lineage.

In addition to this most glaring error this surnameless creation is possessed with a suicidal mania. Her unhappy, self-sacrificing life becomes such a burden to both herself and the author that this is the only means by which they can extricate themselves from a lamentable tangle, though, as a matter of fact suicide is an evil positively unknown among Indians. To-day there may be rare instances where a man crazed by liquor might destroy his own life, but in the periods from whence 'Winona's' character is sketched self-destruction was unheard of. This seems to be a fallacy which the best American writers have fallen a prey to. Even Helen Hunt Jackson, in her powerful and beautiful romance of 'Ramona,' has weakened her work deplorably by having no less than three Indians suicide while maddened by their national wrongs and personal grief.

The hardest fortune that the Indian girl of fiction meets with is the inevitable doom that shadows her love affairs. She is always desperately in love with the young white hero, who in turn is grateful to her for services rendered the garrison in general and himself in particular during red days of war. In short, she is so much wrapped up in him that she is treacherous to her own people, tells falsehoods to her father and the other chiefs of her tribe, and otherwise makes herself detestable and dishonourable. Of course, this white hero never marries her! Will some critic who understands human nature, and particularly the nature of authors, please tell the reading public why marriage with the Indian girl is so despised in books and so general in real life? Will this good farseeing critic also tell us why the book-made Indian makes all the love advances to the white gentleman, though the real wild Indian girl (by the way, we are never given any stories of educated girls, though there are many such throughout Canada) is the most retiring, reticent, noncommittal being in existence!

Captain Richardson, in that inimitable novel, 'Wacousta,' scarcely goes as far in this particular as his followers. To be sure he has his Indian heroine madly in love with young de Haldimar, a passion which it goes without saying he does not reciprocate, but which he plays upon to the extent of making her a traitor to Pontiac inasmuch as she betrays the secret of one of the cleverest intrigues of war known in the history of America, namely, the scheme to capture Fort Detroit through the means of an exhibition game of lacrosse. In addition to this de Haldimar makes a cat's paw of the girl, using her as a means of communication between his fiancée and himself, and so the excellent author permits his Indian girl to get herself despised by her own nation and disliked by the reader. Unnecessary to state, that as usual the gallant white marries his fair lady, whom the poor little red girl has assisted him to recover.

Then comes another era in Canadian-Indian fiction, wherein G. Mercer Adam and A. Ethelwyn Wetherald have given us the semi-historic novel 'An Algonquin Maiden.' The former's masterly touch can be recognized on every page he has written; but the outcome of the combined pens is the same old story. We find 'Wanda' violently in love with Edward MacLeod, she makes all the overtures, conducts herself disgracefully, assists him to a reunion with his fair-skinned love, Helene; then betakes herself to a boat, rows out into the lake in a thunderstorm, chants her own death-song, and is drowned.

But, notwithstanding all this, the authors have given us something exceedingly unique and novel as regards their red heroine. They have sketched us a wild Indian girl who kisses. They, however, forgot to tell us where she learned this pleasant fashion of emotional expression; though two such prominent authors who have given so much time to the study of Indian customs and character, must certainly have noticed the entire ignorance of kissing that is universal among the Aborigines. A wild Indian never kisses; mothers never kiss their children even, nor lovers their sweethearts, husbands their wives. It is something absolutely unknown, unpractised.

But 'Wanda' was one of the few book Indian girls who had an individuality and was not hampered with being obliged to continually be national first and natural afterwards. No, she was not national; she did things and said things about as un-Indian like as Bret Harte's 'M'liss:' in fact, her action generally resembles 'M'liss' more than anything else; for 'Wanda's' character has the peculiarity of being created more by the dramatis personae in the play than by the authors themselves. For example: Helene speaks of her as a 'low, untutored savage,' and Rose is guilty of remarking that she is 'a coarse, ignorant woman, whom you cannot admire, whom it would be impossible for you to respect;' and these comments are both sadly truthful, one cannot love or admire a heroine that grubs in the mud like a turtle, climbs trees like a raccoon, and tears and soils her gowns like a madwoman.

Then the young hero describes her upon two occasions as a 'beautiful little brute.' Poor little Wanda! not only is she non-descript and ill-starred, but as usual the authors take away her love, her life, and last and most terrible of all, her reputation; for they permit a crowd of men-friends of the hero to call her a 'squaw,' and neither hero nor authors deny that she is a 'squaw.' It is almost too sad when so much prejudice exists against the Indians, that any one should write an Indian heroine with such glaring accusations against her virtue, and no contradictory statements either from writer, hero, or circumstance. 'Wanda' had without doubt the saddest, unsunniest, unequal life ever given to Canadian readers.

Jessie M. Freeland has written a pretty tale published in *The Week*; it is called 'Winona's Tryst,' but Oh! grim fatality, here again our Indian girl duplicates her former self. 'Winona' is the unhappy victim of violent love for Hugh Gordon, which he does not appreciate or return. She assists him, serves him, saves him in the usual 'dumb animal' style of book Indians. She manages by self abnegation, danger, and many heart-aches to restore him to the arms of Rose McTavish, who of course he has loved and longed for all through the story. Then 'Winona' secures the time honoured canoe, paddles out into the lake and drowns herself.

But Miss Freeland closes this pathetic little story with one of the simplest, truest, strongest paragraphs that a Canadian pen has ever written, it is the salvation of the otherwise threadbare development of plot, Hugh Gordon speaks, 'I solemnly pledge myself in memory of Winona to do something to help her unfortunate nation. The rightful owners of the soil, dispossessed and driven back inch by inch over their native prairies by their French and English conquerors; and he kept his word.'

Charles Mair has enriched Canadian Indian literature perhaps more than any of our authors, in his magnificent drama, 'Tecumseh.' The character of the grand old chief himself is most powerfully and accurately drawn. Mair has not fallen into that unattractive fashion of making his Indians 'assent with a grunt' – or look with 'eyes of dog-like fidelity' or to appear 'very grave, very dignified, and not very immaculately clean.' Mair avoids the usual commonplaces used in describing Indians by those who have never met or mixed with them. His drama bears upon every page evidence of long study and life with the people whom he has written of so carefully, so truthfully.

As for his heroine, what portrayal of Indian character has ever been more faithful than that of 'Iena.' Oh! happy inspiration vouchsafed to the author of 'Tecumseh' he has invented a novelty in fiction – a white man who deserves, wins and reciprocates the Indian maiden's love – who says, as she dies on his bosom, while the bullet meant for him stills and tears her heart.

> 'Silent for ever! Oh, my girl! my girl!
> Those rich eyes melt; those lips are sunwarm still –
> They look like life, yet have no semblant voice.
> Millions of creatures throngs and multitudes
> Of heartless beings, flaunt upon the earth,
> There's room enough for them, but thou, dull fate –
> Thou cold and partial tender of life's field,
> That pluck'st the flower, and leav'st the weed to thrive –
> Thou had'st not room for her! Oh, I must seek
> A way out of the rack – I need not live,
> * * * * but she is dead –
> And love is left upon the earth to starve,
> My object's gone, and I am but a shell,
> A husk, and empty case, or anything
> What may be kicked about the world.'

After perusing this refreshing white Indian drama the reader has but one regret, that Mair did not let 'Iena' live. She is the one 'book' Indian girl that has Indian life, Indian character, Indian beauty, but the inevitable doom of death could not be stayed even by Mair's sensitive Indian-loving pen. No, the Indian girl must die, and with the exception of 'Iena' her heart's blood must stain every page of fiction whereon she appears. One learns to love Lefroy, the poet painter; he never abuses by coarse language and derisive epithets his little Indian love, 'Iena' accepts delicately and sweetly his overtures, Lefroy prizes nobly and honourably her devotion. Oh! Lefroy, where is your fellowman in fiction? 'Iena,' where is your prototype? Alas, for all the other pale-faced lovers, they are indifferent, almost brutal creations, and as for the red skin girls that love them, they are all fawn eyed, unnatural, unmaidenly idiots and both are merely imaginary make-shifts to help out romances, that would be immeasurably improved by their absence.

Perhaps, sometimes an Indian romance may be written by someone who will be clever enough to portray national character without ever having come in contact with it. Such things have been done, for are we not told that Tom Moore had never set foot in Persia before he wrote Lalla Rookh? and those who best know what they affirm declare that remarkable poem as a faithful and accurate delineation of Oriental scenery, life and character. But such things are rare, half of our authors who write up Indian stuff have never been on an Indian reserve in their lives, have never met a 'real live' Redman, have never even read Parkman, Schoolcraft or Catlin; what wonder that their conception of a people that they are ignorant of, save by heresay, is dwarfed, erroneous and delusive.

And here follows the thought – do authors who write Indian romances love the nation they endeavour successfully or unsuccessfully to describe? Do they, like Tecumseh, say, 'And I, who love your nation, which is just, when deeds deserve it,' or is the Indian introduced into literature but to lend a dash of vivid colouring to an otherwise tame and sombre picture of colonial life: it looks suspiciously like the latter reason, or why should the Indian always get beaten in the battles of romances, or the Indian girl get inevitably the cold shoulder in the wars of love?

Surely the Redman has lost enough, has suffered enough without additional losses and sorrows being heaped upon him in romance. There are many combats he has won in history from the extinction of the Jesuit Fathers at Lake Simcoe to Cut Knife Creek. There are many girls who have placed dainty red feet figuratively upon the white man's neck from the days of Pocahontas to those of little 'Bright Eyes,' who captured all Washington a few seasons ago. Let us not only hear, but read something of the North American Indian 'besting' some one at least once in a decade, and above all things let the Indian girl of fiction develop from the 'doglike,' 'fawnlike,' 'deer-footed,' 'fire-eyed,' 'crouching,' 'submissive' book heroine into something of the quiet, sweet womanly woman she is, if wild, or the everyday, natural, laughing girl she is, if cultivated and educated; let her be natural, even if the author is not competent to give her tribal characteristics.

FORTY-FIVE MILES ON THE GRAND

Ontario boasts many a beautiful inland river, whose waters fret shores
historically famous and naturally picturesque, but the royal little stream
that laughs and slumbers alternately through the south-western coun-
ties, that tosses its current wildly about rocky coast and midstream boul-
der, that hurls itself into spray, whirlpool and rapid, then, tired and
silent, slips into dark, still pools and long, yellow sand reaches – Ah! who
would not know it was The Grand River? with its romantic forests, its
legend-thronged hills, its wide and storied flats, its tradition-fraught val-
leys? This was the great domain of that most powerful of North American
nations, the Iroquois, who, after joining their forces and fortunes with
Britain, subsequent to the American war of independence, received as
indemnity the vast tract of country lying within the limits of six miles bor-
dering on either side of the Grand from its source to its mouth, although,
with all the alleged wealth of this ancient people, they count to-day as
their sole landed possessions only a few thousand acres, but a small por-
tion of which fronts on the waters that are inseparably linked with the red
man and his traditions. In olden days, when the industrious beaver
dammed the creeks, and bears haunted the almost impenetrable forests,
when the shy red deer stole lightly down to slake its thirst in the crystal
stream, and only the Indian's moccasined foot left its imprint along the
shore, the Grand was a narrow, turbulent, forest watercourse, abounding
in fish of all kinds, and navigable only by the birch bark canoe and the
old, native 'dug-out,' which even to-day may be seen in many unbridged,
ferryless localities, especially along the Iroquois reserve tracts. But for
many a by-gone year the Grand has been a broad, semi-sluggish stretch of
water, owing to many mills and their requisite dams backing the water
into the wide, still stretches for miles up stream, above which many rip-
ples and rills of the erstwhile rapids sing and purl to the birch-crowned
banks, like souvenirs of the long ago, and although these rapids cannot
boast the fascination of danger, or the charm of peril, their rollicking
laughter is a delight to the canoeist's ear, and their devious, boulder-
fraught course a test of his paddle's skill. The canoeist who has not 'run'
the Grand, who has never pitched canvas on its lovely shores, who has
never hoisted a sail to its treacherous and coquettish winds, scarcely
deserves the name, and he certainly has a future sporting ground rife
with surprises and delights, which is well worth a long trip to traverse.

Canoeing has sprung into marvellous popularity in Canada within the last five years, and, apart from the great sporting centres, there exist no clubs of more active organization than those of Galt and Brantford, on the Grand. A stretch of some thirty-five miles of water lies between these points, and a lovelier run cannot be found in the Province. It can be covered in a few hours, for the rapids follow each other thick and fast, and the stern paddler must keep pretty wide awake, or his craft will come to grief in the twinkling of an eye, on one of the myriad rock shelves, or tiny, innocent-looking boulders that throng the river bed.

One warm June morning two of us made the run in a little, cruising Peterbo' that we had shipped by rail across country the previous day. Our taut little craft slipped between the rocky shores upon which the slumbering old town of Galt crowds its grey stone houses, and in the fourth of an hour we had left streets and buildings and people behind the rolling hills and pasture lands, and were dancing along on the sunny breast of the Grand that very soon changed its shores from green country sides and meadow lands, to wild, cedar-crested banks, where shy birds hushed their song at the sound of our voices, and where pathless woods and underbrush stretched along the very water's edge.

A few miles of placid water, on the surface of which our paddles dipped audibly, and then the 'waking of waves amid stream, a visibly accelerated movement of shores slipping astern, a soft whisper of bows cutting rapidly through hurrying waters, and then, O, sweetest of all music, the far-off laughter of a rapid, rollicking and scampering among its stones. Nearer, nearer it came; the ripple grew into a roar, the sweet, wild laughter arose into boisterous, tempestuous merriment, and in another moment we swirled round a bend, dashing headlong into a tossing, twirling mass of waters that fretted and fumed themselves into eddies and whirlpools and showers of pearly spray, with a petulance that defied restraint.

Without a word we gripped our paddles with fingers like iron, I heard the hurried plunge of the stern blade, and with the knowledge of the pliant wrist and mighty muscle that was master of rapid, paddle and Peterboro', and which had piloted me through many a more dangerous run than this, I knelt steady and straight, while we bounded through, swerving one moment to the right to escape a boulder, then next, running to the left to avoid a shoal. More than once I thought we were over, but that sturdy little canoe never failed us, bringing up at the foot of the rapid with scarcely a quart of water shipped, but with two breathless, wind-blown, spray-showered people, kneeling fore and aft, and wearing expressions of mingled surprise and triumph. And this was but the beginning of the end; following closely, came rapid after rapid, with a quarter mile breathing space between, until eleven of these noisy, frolicsome fellows had linked themselves into one long chain, covering seven miles, and then, in apparently utter weariness, the waters sank to slumber in great, deep pools, sluggish and curentless as a lagoon.

We paddled on, disturbing great cranes that rose on indolent wings, flapped lazily by, and settled once more in the marshes when we had passed. Only the voices of the land-locked springs, trickling their way to the river, and the quaint cry of the sandpipers scurrying along shore arose on the warm June air, until the stream, jealous of these rivals, laughed out once more into the rapids and natural dams, the shooting of which drenched us to the throats. But with all their quarrelling and tempestuous fury they failed to overthrow our basswood, and the sole complaint we had against them was that they were not dangerous and frequent enough to suit our venturesome spirits.

We slipped very slowly into Brantford, for many waste waters, dams and mill races take the life out of the stream above the town. But if it lacks character above, it certainly regains its natural temper and tone, as it whirls away from the little city, like a steed broken loose from chafing harness, and whatever bondage it suffers to serve the good townsfolk, is but a tonic and stimulant to further vivacity, and rejuvenates all its upstream vitality. The river takes a huge loop here, forming so perfect a horseshoe that at the end of eleven miles, it is only two and a half across country to the point you started from. A short portage brings you to the canal, up which you paddle with perfect ease, having performed the extraordinary feat of running more than thirteen miles, bringing up at the starting point with not a paddle stroke against stream. This is the favourite run of the Brantford Canoe Club, who invade the river three times each summer, with flags waving, club colours flying, and each little craft laden down with fantastic devices in Chinese lanterns and torch effects. The flotilla musters fifty-five strong, and probably no club in Canada claims a more interesting or historic route, for an annual cruise.

The city lies scarcely a mile astern, before the lovely ridge of hills known as Tutela Heights outline their crests against the sky. They were the old-time haunts of the now extinct Indian tribe, whose language even is comparatively a dead one. There remains but one old woman, living on the Six Nations Reserve, twenty miles down stream, who speaks this forgotten tongue, and, were it not for the indefatigable zeal and study manifested by Mr Horatio Hale, the eminent Indianologist, this quaint dialect would have remained forever unrecorded.

In the midst of these hills that have many a time echoed the eerie death cry that told of up-stream murders and bloodshed; when the red man only lived and hunted and died, before the curtain dropped on that wild wood scene, and the action changed amid other stage settings, there stands an old-fashioned white frame cottage, with faded green shutters, a wide verandah, and a drowsy air of yesterday hanging about its eaves and half-neglected gardens. It was for many years the home of Alexander Graham Bell, of telephone fame and from this house to Brantford, two and a half miles distant, the trial wire was stretched. When a little child I often heard my father relate this story of the initial performance over this unperfected wire that was to grow with years into a necessity more important than at that time they even dared to hope. The young scientist, anxious, but confident, had bidden a number of guests to dine at the quaint Bell homestead, and to participate in the pleasure of the experiment.

Young Graham and my father personally tacked much of the wire, with non-conducting staples to the fences and trees between the Heights and the city, spending much of the afternoon at the work. Succeeding the dinner came the experiment, which was very satisfactory, the operator in the city being able to distinguish the voices of each guest, until my father was requested to speak in Mohawk.

'Can't hear,' said the city operator.

The greeting was repeated.

'Something's wrong,' said the city man.

Another Mohawk sentence from my father.

'What's that?' from the city.

More Mohawk.

City man, 'Oh! I say professor, you might have invited me, how many cases did you open?'

A wild roar of laughter from 'The Heights,' and young Graham's voice over my father's shoulder 'You've insulted the chief.' Apologies from the city man, and general amusement at both ends of the line. With what horror the simple-minded old Tutelas would have regarded that bewitched bit of wire that carried the human voice across those silent hills of theirs, that have nurtured the greatness of race, and the power of intellect. A century ago the Tutela roved here in the pride of heritage and health, a century hence, and who shall say what the world will not owe to this gifted young pale face whose feet have wandered through many days among those heights and valleys? The redman's doom has overtaken the Tutela, the white man has overtaken his ambition, and to-day both race and genius are unknown to the beautiful hills that alone remain unchanging and unchanged, lifting forever their purple heads, while the river purls and whispers a ceaseless lullaby about their feet.

A few miles further down stream, and the spire of the 'Old Mohawk' church looks somberly out through the trees. Probably no church in America has been more frequently written up than this century-old building. A long and exhaustive write-up has already appeared in these columns, so it may be here sufficient to mention that it was built especially for the Mohawks in Brant's time. The Bible, law, silver communion service, bell, and British coat-of-arms being presented by Queen Ann, many years prior to its erection.

One more notable spot to pass, and the paddles of the cruisers redip in home waters. To the right, low and level stretch 'the fields and meadows of Bow Park' the model stock farm of the province. Some of the cattle on these lands have a world-wide reputation, and as the gorgeous fleet sails past, the brilliant flags and lanterns are stared at in wonderment by meek-eyed Jerseys and robust Holsteins, a single one of which is worth more bank notes than all the graceful craft put together.

But the gay canoeists care little for past histories of nations, for genius, for stock farms. To them the rapids are dearer than yesterday's romance; they love laughter more than money. And when the portage is made, and they begin their grand triumphal entry into town, when the old lagoon banks are thronged with spectators who watch with eager eyes the torches and fireworks, when the rollicking choruses are started, and the sluggish canal is converted into a bit of Venice dropped down into the new world, the quiet old river is left far behind, left to its hills and its twilights, to its long winding, through flats and marshes and forests, past village and town and the lonely reserve of the Iroquois; on, on, until with irresistible longing, it is lost in the great hungry arms of Lake Erie.

A RED GIRL'S REASONING

'Be pretty good to her, Charlie, my boy, or she'll balk sure as shooting.'

That was what old Jimmy Robinson said to his brand new son-in-law, while they waited for the bride to reappear.

'Oh! you bet, there's no danger of much else. I'll be good to her, help me Heaven,' replied Charlie McDonald, brightly.

'Yes, of course you will,' answered the old man, 'but don't you forget, there's a good big bit of her mother in her, and,' closing his left eye significantly, 'you don't understand these Indians as I do.'

'But I'm just as fond of them, Mr Robinson,' Charlie said assertively, 'and I get on with them too, now, don't I?'

'Yes, pretty well for a town boy; but when you have lived forty years among these people, as I have done; when you have had your wife as long as I have had mine – for there's no getting over it, Christine's disposition is as native as her mother's, every bit – and perhaps when you've owned for eighteen years a daughter as dutiful, as loving, as fearless, and, alas! as obstinate as that little piece you are stealing away from me to-day – I tell you, youngster, you'll know more than you know now. It is kindness for kindness, bullet for bullet, blood for blood. Remember, what you are, she will be,' and the old Hudson Bay trader scrutinized Charlie McDonald's face like a detective.

It was a happy, fair face, good to look at, with a certain ripple of dimples somewhere about the mouth, and eyes that laughed out the very sunniness of their owner's soul. There was not a severe nor yet a weak line anywhere. He was a well-meaning young fellow, happily dispositioned, and a great favourite with the tribe at Robinson's Post, whither he had gone in the service of the Department of Agriculture, to assist the local agent through the tedium of a long census-taking.

As a boy he had had the Indian relic-hunting craze, as a youth he had studied Indian archaeology and folk-lore, as a man he consummated his predilections for Indianology by loving, winning and marrying the quiet little daughter of the English trader, who himself had married a native woman some twenty years ago. The country was all backwoods, and the Post miles and miles from even the semblance of civilization, and the lonely young Englishman's heart had gone out to the girl who, apart from speaking a very few words of English, was utterly uncivilized and uncultured, but had withal that marvellously innate refinement so universally possessed by the higher tribes of North American Indians.

Like all her race, observant, intuitive, having horror of ridicule, consequently quick at acquirement and teachable in mental and social habits, she had developed from absolute pagan indifference into a sweet, elderly Christian woman, whose broken English, quiet manner, and still handsome copper-coloured face, were the joy of old Robinson's declining years.

He had given their daughter Christine all the advantages of his own learning – which, if truthfully told, was not universal; but the girl had a fair common education, and the native adaptability to progress.

She belonged to neither and still to both types of the cultured Indian. The solemn, silent, almost heavy manner of the one so commingled with the gesticulating Frenchiness and vivacity of the other, that one unfamiliar with native Canadian life would find it difficult to determine her nationality.

She looked very pretty to Charles McDonald's loving eyes, as she reappeared in the doorway, holding her mother's hand and saying some happy words of farewell. Personally she looked much the same as her sisters, all Canada through, who are the offspring of red and white parentage – olive-complexioned, grey-eyed, black-haired, with figure slight and delicate, and the wistful, unfathomable expression in her whole face that turns one so heart-sick as they glance at the young Indians of to-day – it is the forerunner too frequently of 'the white man's disease,' consumption – but McDonald was pathetically in love, and thought her the most beautiful woman he had ever seen in his life.

There had not been much of a wedding ceremony. The priest had cantered through the service in Latin, pronounced the benediction in English, and congratulated the 'happy couple' in Indian, as a compliment to the assembled tribe in the little amateur structure that did service at the post as a sanctuary.

But the knot was tied as firmly and indissolubly as if all Charlie McDonald's swell city friends had crushed themselves up against the chancel to congratulate him, and in his heart he was deeply thankful to escape the flower-pelting, white gloves, rice-throwing, and ponderous stupidity of a breakfast, and indeed all the regulation gimcracks of the usual marriage celebrations, and it was with a hand trembling with absolute happiness that he assisted his little Indian wife into the old muddy buckboard that, hitched to an underbred-looking pony, was to convey them over the first stages of their journey. Then came more adieus, some hand-clasping, old Jimmy Robinson looking very serious just at the last, Mrs Jimmy, stout, stolid, betraying nothing of visible emotion, and then the pony, roughshod and shaggy, trudged on, while mutual hand-waves were kept up until the old Hudson's Bay Post dropped out of sight, and the buckboard with its lightsome load of hearts, deliriously happy, jogged on over the uneven trail.

She was 'all the rage' that winter at the provincial capital. The men called her a 'deuced fine little woman.' The ladies said she was 'just the sweetest wildflower.' Whereas she was really but an ordinary, pale, dark girl who spoke slowly and with a strong accent, who danced fairly well, sang acceptably, and never stirred outside the door without her husband.

Charlie was proud of her; he was proud that she had 'taken' so well among his friends, proud that she bore herself so complacently in the drawing-rooms of the wives of pompous Government officials, but doubly proud of her almost abject devotion to him. If ever human being was worshipped that being was Charlie McDonald; it could scarcely have been otherwise, for the almost godlike strength of his passion for that little wife of his would have mastered and melted a far more invincible citadel than an already affectionate woman's heart.

Favourites socially, McDonald and his wife went everywhere. In fashionable circles she was 'new' – a potent charm to acquire popularity, and the little velvet-clad figure was always the centre of interest among all the women in the room. She always dressed in velvet. No woman in Canada, has she but the faintest dash of native blood in her veins, but loves velvets and silks. As beef to the Englishman, wine to the Frenchman, fads to the Yankee, so are velvet and silk to the Indian girl, be she wild as prairie grass, be she on the borders of civilization, or, having stepped within its boundary, mounted the steps of culture even under its superficial heights.

'Such a dolling little appil blossom,' said the wife of a local M.P., who brushed up her etiquette and English once a year at Ottawa. 'Does she always laugh so sweetly, and gobble you up with those great big grey eyes of hers, when you are togetheah at home, Mr McDonald? If so, I should think youah pooah brothah would feel himself terribly *de trop*.'

He laughed lightly. 'Yes, Mrs Stuart, there are not two of Christie; she is the same at home and abroad, and as for Joe, he doesn't mind us a bit; he's no end fond of her.'

'I'm very glad he is. I always fancied he did not care for her, d'you know.'

If ever a blunt woman existed it was Mrs Stuart. She really meant nothing, but her remark bothered Charlie. He was fond of his brother, and jealous for Christie's popularity. So that night when he and Joe were having a pipe he said: 'I've never asked you yet what you thought of her, Joe.' A brief pause, then Joe spoke. 'I'm glad she loves you.'

'Why?'

'Because that girl has but two possibilities regarding humanity – love or hate.'

'Humph! Does she love or hate *you*?'

'Ask her.'

'You talk bosh. If she hated you, you'd get out. If she loved you I'd *make* you get out.'

Joe McDonald whistled a little, then laughed. 'Now that we are on the subject, I might as well ask – honestly, old man, wouldn't you and Christie prefer keeping house alone to having me always around?'

'Nonsense, sheer nonsense. Why, thunder, man, Christie's no end fond of you, and as for me – you surely don't want assurances from me?'

'No, but I often think a young couple –'

'Young couple be blowed! After a while when they want you and your old surveying chains, and spindle-legged tripod telescope kickshaws, farther west, I venture to say the little woman will cry her eyes out – won't you, Christie?' This last in a higher tone, as through clouds of tobacco smoke he caught sight of his wife passing the doorway.

She entered. 'Oh, no, I would not cry; I never do cry, but I would be heart-sore to lose you, Joe, and apart from that' – a little wickedly – 'you may come in handy for an exchange some day, as Charlie does always say when he hoards up duplicate relics.'

'Are Charlie and I duplicates?'

'Well – not exactly' – her head a little to one side, and eyeing them both merrily, while she slipped softly on to the arm of her husband's chair – 'but, in the event of Charlie's failing me' – everyone laughed then. The 'some day' that she spoke of was nearer than they thought. It came about in this wise.

There was a dance at the Lieutenant-Governor's, and the world and his wife were there. The nobs were in great feather that night, particularly the women, who flaunted about in new gowns and much splendour. Christie McDonald had a new gown also, but wore it with the utmost unconcern, and if she heard any of the flattering remarks made about her she at least appeared to disregard them.

'I never dreamed you could wear blue so splendidly,' said Captain Logan, as they sat out a dance together.

'Indeed she can, though,' interposed Mrs Stuart, halting in one of her gracious sweeps down the room with her husband's private secretary.

'Don't shout so, captain. I can hear every sentence you uttah – of course Mrs McDonald can wear blue – she has a morning gown of cadet blue that she is a picture in.'

'You are both very kind,' said Christie. 'I like blue; it is the colour of

all the Hudson's Bay posts, and the factor's residence is always deco-
rated in blue.'

'Is it really? How interesting – do tell us some more of your old home,
Mrs McDonald; you so seldom speak of your life at the post, and we fel-
lows so often wish to hear of it all,' said Logan eagerly.

'Why do you not ask me of it, then?'

'Well – er, I'm sure I don't know; I'm fully interested in the Ind – in
your people – your mother's people, I mean, but it always seems so per-
sonal, I suppose; and–a–a–'

'Perhaps you are, like all other white people, afraid to mention my
nationality to me.'

The captain winced, and Mrs Stuart laughed uneasily. Joe McDonald
was not far off, and he was listening, and chuckling, and saying to him-
self, 'That's you, Christie, lay 'em out; it won't hurt 'em to know how
they appear once in a while.'

'Well, Captain Logan' she was saying, 'what is it you would like to hear
– of my people, or my parents, or myself?'

'All, all, my dear,' cried Mrs Stuart clamorously. 'I'll speak for him –
tell us of yourself and your mother – your father is delightful, I am sure
– but then he is only an ordinary Englishman, not half as interesting as a
foreigner, or – or, perhaps I should say, a native.'

Christie laughed. 'Yes,' she said, 'my father often teases my mother
now about how very native she was when he married her; then, how
could she have been otherwise? She did not know a word of English,
and there was not another English-speaking person besides my father
and his two companions within sixty miles.'

'Two companions, eh? one a Catholic priest and the other a wine
merchant, I suppose, and with your father in the Hudson's Bay, they
were good representatives of the pioneers in the New World,' remarked
Logan, waggishly.

'Oh, no, they were all Hudson's Bay men. There were no rumsellers
and no missionaries in that part of the country then.'

Mrs Stuart looked puzzled. 'No *missionaries*?' she repeated with an
odd intonation.

Christie's insight was quick. There was a peculiar expression of inter-
rogation in the eyes of her listeners, and the girl's blood leapt angrily up
into her temples as she said hurriedly, 'I know what you mean; I know what
you are thinking. You are wondering how my parents were married –'

'Well – er, my dear, it seems peculiar – if there was no priest, and no
magistrate, why – a –' Mrs Stuart paused awkwardly.

'The marriage was performed by Indian rites,' said Christie.

'Oh, do tell me about it; is the ceremony very interesting and quaint –
are your chieftains anything like Buddhist priests?' It was Logan who
spoke.

'Why, no,' said the girl in amazement at that gentleman's ignorance.
'There is no ceremony at all, save a feast. The two people just agree to
live only with and for each other, and the man takes his wife to his
home, just as you do. There is no ritual to bind them; they need none;
an Indian's word was his law in those days, you know.'

Mrs Stuart stepped backwards. 'Ah!' was all she said. Logan removed
his eye-glass and stared blankly at Christie. 'And did McDonald marry
you in this singular fashion?' he questioned.

'Oh, no, we were married by Father O'Leary. Why do you ask?'

'Because if he had, I'd have blown his brains out to-morrow.'

Mrs Stuart's partner, who had hitherto been silent, coughed and
began to twirl his cuff stud nervously, but nobody took any notice of
him. Christie had risen, slowly, ominously – risen, with the dignity and
pride of an empress.

'Captain Logan,' she said, 'what do you dare to say to me? What do
you dare to mean? Do you presume to think it would not have been law-
ful for Charlie to marry me according to my people's rites? Do you for
one instant dare to question that my parents were not as legally –'

'Don't, dear, don't,' interrupted Mrs Stuart hurriedly; 'it is bad
enough now, goodness knows; don't make –' Then she broke off blindly.
Christie's eyes glared at the mumbling woman, at her uneasy partner, at
the horrified captain. Then they rested on the McDonald brothers, who
stood within earshot, Joe's face scarlet, her husband's white as ashes,
with something in his eyes she had never seen before. It was Joe who
saved the situation. Stepping quickly across towards his sister-in-law, he
offered her his arm, saying, 'The next dance is ours, I think, Christie.'

Then Logan pulled himself together, and attempted to carry Mrs Stu-
art off for the waltz, but for once in her life that lady had lost her head.
'It is shocking!' she said, 'outrageously shocking! I wonder if they told
Mr McDonald before he married her!' Then looking hurriedly round,
she too saw the young husband's face and knew that they had not.

'Humph! deuced nice kettle of fish – poor old Charlie has always
thought so much of honourable birth.'

Logan thought he spoke in an undertone, but 'poor old Charlie' heard
him. He followed his wife and brother across the room. 'Joe,' he said, 'will
you see that a trap is called?' Then to Christie, 'Joe will see that you get
home all right.' He wheeled on his heel then and left the ballroom.

Joe *did* see.

He tucked a poor, shivering, pallid little woman into a cab, and wound her bare throat up in the scarlet velvet cloak that was hanging uselessly over her arm. She crouched down beside him, saying, 'I am so cold, Joe; I am so cold,' but she did not seem to know enough to wrap herself up. Joe felt all through this long drive that nothing this side of Heaven would be so good as to die, and he was glad when the poor little voice at his elbow said, 'What is he so angry at, Joe?'

'I don't know exactly, dear,' he said gently, 'but I think it was what you said about this Indian marriage.'

'But why should I not have said it? Is there anything wrong about it?' she asked pitifully.

'Nothing, that I can see – there was no other way; but Charlie is very angry, and you must be brave and forgiving with him, Christie, dear.'

'But I did never see him like that before, did you?'

'Once.'

'When?'

'Oh, at college, one day, a boy tore his prayer-book in half, and threw it into the grate, just to be mean, you know. Our mother had given it to him at his confirmation.'

'And did he look so?'

'About, but it all blew over in a day – Charlie's tempers are short and brisk. Just don't take any notice of him; run off to bed, and he'll have forgotten it by the morning.'

They reached home at last. Christie said goodnight quietly, going directly to her room. Joe went to his room also, filled a pipe and smoked for an hour. Across the passage he could hear her slippered feet pacing up and down, up and down the length of her apartment. There was something panther-like in those restless footfalls, a meaning velvetyness that made him shiver, and again he wished he were dead – or elsewhere.

After a time the hall door opened, and someone came upstairs, along the passage, and to the little woman's room. As he entered, she turned and faced him.

'Christie,' he said harshly, 'do you know what you have done?'

'Yes,' taking a step nearer him, her whole soul springing up into her eyes, 'I have angered you, Charlie, and –'

'Angered me? You have disgraced me; and, moreover, you have disgraced yourself and both your parents.'

'*Disgraced?*'

'Yes, *disgraced*; you have literally declared to the whole city that your

father and mother were never married, and that you are the child of –
what shall we call it – love? certainly not legality.'

Across the hallway sat Joe McDonald, his blood freezing; but it leapt
into every vein like fire at the awful anguish in the little voice that cried
simply, 'Oh! Charlie!'

'How could you do it, how could you do it, Christie, without shame
either for yourself or for me, let alone your parents?'

The voice was like an angry demon's – not a trace was there in it of
the yellow-haired, blue-eyed, laughing-lipped boy who had driven away
so gaily to the dance five hours before.

'Shame? Why should I be ashamed of the rites of my people any more
than you should be ashamed of the customs of yours – of a marriage
more sacred and holy than half of your white man's mockeries?'

It was the voice of another nature in the girl – the love and the plead-
ing were dead in it.

'Do you mean to tell me, Charlie – you who have studied my race and
their laws for years – do you mean to tell me that, because there was no
priest and no magistrate, my mother was not married? Do you mean to
say that all my forefathers, for hundreds of years back, have been ille-
gally born? If so, you blacken my ancestry beyond – beyond – beyond all
reason.'

'No, Christie, I would not be so brutal as that; but your father and
mother live in more civilized times. Father O'Leary has been at the post
for nearly twenty years. Why was not your father straight enough to have
the ceremony performed when he *did* get the chance?'

The girl turned upon him with the face of a fury. 'Do you suppose,'
she almost hissed, 'that my mother would be married according to your
white rites after she had been five years a wife, and I had been born in
the meantime? *No*, a thousand times I say, *no*. When the priest came with
his notions of Christianizing, and talked to them of re-marriage by the
Church, my mother arose and said, "Never – never – I have never had
but this one husband; he has had none but me for wife, and to have you
re-marry us would be to say as much to the whole world as that we had
never been married before.* You go away; *I* do not ask that *your* people
be re-married; talk not so to me. I *am* married, and you or the Church
cannot do or undo it.'

'Your father was a fool not to insist upon the law, and so was the
priest.'

---

* Fact [Johnson's note].

'Law? *My* people have *no* priest, and my nation cringes not to law. Our priest is purity, and our law is honour. Priest? Was there a *priest* at the most holy marriage known to humanity – that stainless marriage whose offspring is the God you white men told my pagan mother of?'

'Christie – you are *worse* than blasphemous; such a profane remark shows how little you understand the sanctity of the Christian faith –'

'I know what I *do* understand; it is that you are hating me because I told some of the beautiful customs of my people to Mrs Stuart and those men.'

'Pooh! who cares for them? It is not them; the trouble is they won't keep their mouths shut. Logan's a cad and will toss the whole tale about at the club before to-morrow night; and as for the Stuart woman, I'd like to know how I'm going to take you to Ottawa for presentation and the opening, while she is blabbing the whole miserable scandal in every drawing-room, and I'll be pointed out as a romantic fool, and you as worse; I can't understand why your father didn't tell me before we were married; I at least might have warned you to never mention it.' Something of recklessness rang up through his voice, just as the panther-likeness crept up from her footsteps and couched itself in hers. She spoke in tones quiet, soft, deadly.

'Before we were married! Oh! Charlie, would it have – made – any – difference?'

'God knows,' he said, throwing himself into a chair, his blonde hair rumpled and wet. It was the only boyish thing about him now.

She walked towards him, then halted in the centre of the room. 'Charlie McDonald,' she said, and it was as if a stone had spoken, 'look up.' He raised his head, startled by her tone. There was a threat in her eyes that, had his rage been less courageous, his pride less bitterly wounded, would have cowed him.

'There was no such time as that before our marriage, for we *are not married now.* Stop,' she said, outstretching her palms against him as he sprang to his feet, 'I tell you we are not married. Why should I recognize the rites of your nation when you do not acknowledge the rites of mine? According to your own words, my parents should have gone through your church ceremony as well as through an Indian contract; according to my words, we should go through an Indian contract as well as through a church marriage. If their union is illegal, so is ours. If you think my father is living in dishonour with my mother, my people will think I am living in dishonour with you. How do I know when another nation will come and conquer you as you white men conquered us? And they will have another marriage rite to perform, and they will tell us another truth, that you are not my husband, that you are but disgracing and dishonouring me, that you are keeping me here, not as your wife, but as your – your *squaw.*'

The terrible word had never passed her lips before, and the blood stained her face to her very temples. She snatched off her wedding ring and tossed it across the room, saying scornfully, 'That thing is as empty to me as the Indian rites to you.'

He caught her by the wrists; his small white teeth were locked tightly, his blue eyes blazed into hers.

'Christine, do you dare to doubt my honour towards you? *you*, whom I should have died for; do you *dare* to think I have kept you here, not as my wife, but –'

'Oh, God! You are hurting me; you are breaking my arm,' she gasped.

The door was flung open, and Joe McDonald's sinewy hands clinched like vices on his brother's shoulders.

'Charlie, you're mad, mad as the devil. Let go of her this minute.'

The girl staggered backwards as the iron fingers loosed her wrists. 'Oh, Joe,' she cried, 'I am not his wife, and he says I am born – nameless.'

'Here,' said Joe, shoving his brother towards the door. 'Go downstairs till you can collect your senses. If ever a being acted like an infernal fool, you're the man.'

The young husband looked from one to the other, dazed by his wife's insult, abandoned to a fit of ridiculously childish temper. Blind as he was with passion, he remembered long afterwards seeing them standing there, his brother's face darkened with a scowl of anger – his wife, clad in the mockery of her ball dress, her scarlet velvet cloak half covering her bare brown neck and arms, her eyes like flames of fire, her face like a piece of sculptured greystone.

Without a word he flung himself furiously from the room, and immediately afterwards they heard the heavy hall door bang behind him.

'Can I do anything for you, Christie?' asked her brother-in-law calmly.

'No, thank you – unless – I think I would like a drink of water, please.'

He brought her up a goblet filled with wine; her hand did not even tremble as she took it. As for Joe, a demon arose in his soul as he noticed she kept her wrists covered.

'Do you think he will come back?' she said.

'Oh, yes, of course; he'll be all right in the morning. Now go to bed like a good little girl, and – and, I say, Christie, you can call me if you want anything; I'll be right here, you know.'

'Thank you, Joe; you are kind – and good.'

He returned then to his apartment. His pipe was out, but he picked up a newspaper instead, threw himself into an armchair, and in a half-hour was in the land of dreams.

When Charlie came home in the morning, after a six-mile walk into the country and back again, his foolish anger was dead and buried. Logan's 'Poor old Charlie' did not ring so distinctly in his ears. Mrs Stuart's horrified expression had faded considerably from his recollection. He thought only of that surprisingly tall, dark girl, whose eyes looked like coals, whose voice pierced him like a flint-tipped arrow. Ah, well, they would never quarrel again like that, he told himself. She loved him so, and would forgive him after he had talked quietly to her, and told her what an ass he was. She was simple-minded and awfully ignorant to pitch those old Indian laws at him in her fury, but he could not blame her. Oh, no, he could not for one moment blame her. He had been terribly severe and unreasonable, and the horrid McDonald temper had got the better of him; and he loved her so. Oh! he loved her so! She would surely feel that, and forgive him, and – He went straight to his wife's room. The blue velvet evening dress lay on the chair into which he had thrown himself when he doomed his life's happiness by those two words, 'God knows.' A bunch of dead daffodils and her slippers were on the floor, everything – but Christie.

He went to his brother's bedroom door.

'Joe,' he called, rapping nervously thereon; 'Joe, wake up; where's Christie, d'you know?'

'Good Lord, no,' gasped that youth, springing out of his armchair and opening the door. As he did so a note fell from off the handle. Charlie's face blanched to his very hair while Joe read aloud, his voice weakening at every word:

'DEAR OLD JOE – I went into your room at daylight to get that picture of the Post on your bookshelves. I hope you do not mind, but I kissed your hair while you slept; it was so curly, and yellow, and soft, just like his. Good-bye, Joe.

CHRISTIE.'

And when Joe looked into his brother's face and saw the anguish settle in those laughing blue eyes, the despair that drove the dimples away from that almost girlish mouth; when he realized that this boy was but four-and-twenty years old, and that all his future was perhaps darkened and shadowed for ever, a great, deep sorrow arose in his heart, and he forgot all things, all but the agony that rang up through the voice of the fair, handsome lad as he staggered forward, crying, 'Oh! Joe – what shall I do – what shall I do?

———— • ————

It was months and months before he found her, but during all that time he had never known a hopeless moment; discouraged he often was, but despondent, never. The sunniness of his ever-boyish heart radiated with a warmth that would have flooded a much deeper gloom than that which settled within his eager young life. Suffer? ah! yes, he suffered, not with locked teeth and stony stoicism, not with the master-ful self-command, the reserve, the conquered bitterness of the still-water sort of nature, that is supposed to run to such depths. He tried to be bright, and his sweet old boyish self. He would laugh sometimes in a pitiful, pathetic fashion. He took to petting dogs, looking into their large, solemn eyes with his wistful, questioning blue ones; he would kiss them, as women sometimes do, and call them 'dear old fel-low,' in tones that had tears; and once in the course of his travels, while at a little way-station, he discovered a huge St Bernard impris-oned by some mischance in an empty freight car; the animal was nearly dead from starvation, and it seemed to salve his own sick heart to rescue back the dog's life. Nobody claimed the big starving crea-ture, the train hands knew nothing of its owner, and gladly handed it over to its deliverer. 'Hudson,' he called it, and afterwards when Joe McDonald would relate the story of his brother's life he invariably ter-minated it with, 'And I really believe that big lumbering brute saved him.' From what, he was never known to say.

But all things end, and he heard of her at last. She had never returned to the Post, as he at first thought she would, but had gone to the little town of B—, in Ontario, where she was making her living at embroidery and plain sewing.

The September sun had set redly when at last he reached the outskirts of the town, opened up the wicket gate, and walked up the weedy, unkept path leading to the cottage where she lodged.

Even through the twilight, he could see her there, leaning on the rail of the verandah – oddly enough she had about her shoulders the scarlet velvet cloak she wore when he had flung himself so madly from the room that night.

The moment the lad saw her his heart swelled with a sudden heat, burning moisture leapt into his eyes, and clogged his long, boyish lashes. He bounded up the steps – 'Christie,' he said, and the word scorched his lips like audible flame.

She turned to him, and for a second stood magnetized by his passionately wistful face; her peculiar greyish eyes seemed to drink the very life of his unquenchable love, though the tears that suddenly sprang into his seemed to absorb every pulse in his body through those hungry, pleading eyes of his that had, oh! so often, been blinded by her kisses when once her whole world lay in their blue depths.

'You will come back to me, Christie, my wife? My wife, you will let me love you again?'

She gave a singular little gasp, and shook her head. 'Don't, oh! don't,' he cried piteously. 'You will come to me, dear? it is all such a bitter mistake – I did not understand. Oh! Christie, I did not understand, and you'll forgive me, and love me again, won't you – won't you?'

'No,' said the girl with quick, indrawn breath.

He dashed the back of his hand across his wet eyelids. His lips were growing numb, and he bungled over the monosyllable 'Why?'

'I do not like you,' she answered quietly.

'God! Oh! God, what is there left?'

She did not appear to hear the heart-break in his voice; she stood like one wrapped in sombre thought; no blaze, no tear, nothing in her eyes; no hardness, no tenderness about her mouth. The wind was blowing her cloak aside, and the only visible human life in her whole body was once when he spoke the muscles of her brown arm seemed to contract.

'But, darling, you are mine – *mine* – we are husband and wife! Oh, heaven, you *must* love me, you *must* come to me again.'

'You cannot *make* me come,' said the icy voice, 'neither church, nor law, nor even' – and the voice softened – 'nor even love can make a slave of a red girl.'

'Heaven forbid it,' he faltered. 'No, Christie, I will never claim you without your love. What reunion would that be? But, oh, Christie, you are lying to me, you are lying to yourself, you are lying to heaven.'

She did not move. If only he could touch her he felt as sure of her yielding as he felt sure there was a hereafter. The memory of times when he had but to lay his hand on her hair to call a most passionate response from her filled his heart with a torture that choked all words before they reached his lips; at the thought of those days he forgot she was unapproachable, forgot how forbidding were her eyes, how stony her lips. Flinging himself forward, his knee on the chair at her side, his face pressed hardly in the folds of the cloak on her shoulder, he clasped his arms about her with a boyish petulance, saying, 'Christie, Christie, my little girl wife, I love you, I love you, and you are killing me.'

She quivered from head to foot as his fair, wavy hair brushed her neck, his despairing face sank lower until his cheek, hot as fire, rested on the cool, olive flesh of her arm. A warm moisture oozed up through her skin, and as he felt its glow he looked up. Her teeth, white and cold, were locked over her under lip, and her eyes were as grey stones.

Not murderers alone know the agony of a death sentence.

'Is it all useless? all useless, dear?' he said, with lips starving for hers.

'All useless,' she repeated. 'I have no love for you now. You forfeited me and my heart months ago, when you said *those two words*.'

His arms fell away from her wearily, he arose mechanically, he placed his little grey checked cap on the back of his yellow curls, the old-time laughter was dead in the blue eyes that now looked scared and haunted, the boyishness and the dimples crept away for ever from the lips that quivered like a child's; he turned from her, but she had looked once into his face as the Law Giver must have looked at the land of Canaan outspread at his feet. She watched him go down the long path and through the picket gate, she watched the big yellowish dog that had waited for him lumber up to its feet – stretch – then follow him. She was conscious of but two things, the vengeful lie in her soul, and a little space on her arm that his wet lashes had brushed.

———••———

It was hours afterwards when he reached his room. He had said nothing, done nothing – what use were words or deeds? Old Jimmy Robinson was right; she had 'balked' sure enough.

What a bare, hotelish room it was! He tossed off his coat and sat for ten minutes looking blankly at the sputtering gas jet. Then his whole life, desolate as a desert, loomed up before him with appalling distinctness. Throwing himself on the floor beside his bed, with clasped hands and arms outstretched on the white counterpane, he sobbed, he sobbed. 'Oh! God, dear God, I thought you loved me; I thought you'd let me have her again, but you must be tired of me, tired of loving me, too. I've nothing left now, nothing! it doesn't seem that I even have you to-night.'

He lifted his face then, for his dog, big and clumsy and yellow, was licking at his sleeve.

THE IROQUOIS WOMEN OF CANADA

By One of Them

To the majority of English speaking people, an Indian is an Indian, an inadequate sort of person possessing a red brown skin, nomadic habits, and an inability for public affairs. That the various tribes and nations of the great Red population of America, differ as much one from another, as do the white races of Europe, is a thought that seldom occurs to those disinterested in the native of the western continent. Now, the average Englishman would take some offence if any one were unable to discriminate between him and a Turk – though both are 'white;' and yet the ordinary individual seems surprised that a Sioux would turn up his nose if mistaken for a Sarcee, or an Iroquois be eternally offended if you confounded him with a Micmac.

Francis Parkman, that ablest and most delightful historian of the age, that accurate and truthful chronicler of North American Indian tribes, customs, legends and histories, concedes readily to the Iroquois all the glories of race, bravery and lineage that this most arrogant and haughty nation lay claim to even in the present day. In his phylogenetic and unbiased treatment of the various tribes of red men, Parkman declares the undeniable fact, which has been for many decades asserted by historians, explorers, voyagers and traders, that for physical strength, intelligence, mental acquirement, morality and bloodthirstiness, the Iroquois stand far in advance of any Indian tribe in America. The constitutional government of this race has since the time of its founder, Hiawatha (a period of about four centuries), had an uninterrupted existence, without hindrance from internal political strife; has stood the test of ages, and wars and invasions and subjection from mightier foreign powers. This people stand undemolished and undemoralized to-day, right in the heart of Canada, where the lands granted a century ago in recognition of their loyal services to the Imperial Government, are still known as the 'Six Nations' Indian reserve of the Grand River.

That the women of this Iroquois race are superior in many ways to their less fortunate sisters throughout Canada, is hardly necessary to state. Women who have had in the yesterdays a noble and pure-blooded ancestry, who look out on the to-morrows with minds open to educational acquirements; women whose grandmothers were the mothers of fighting men, whose daughters will be the mothers of men elbowing their way to the front ranks in the great professional and political arena in Canada; women whose thrift and care and morality will count for their nation, when that nation is just at its turn of tide toward civilization and advancement, are not the women to sit with idle hands and brains, caring not for the glories of yesterday, nor the conquests of to-morrow.

The Iroquois woman of to-day is one who recognizes the responsibilities of her position, and who makes serious and earnest efforts to possess and master whatever advantages may drift her way. She has already acquired the arts of cookery, of needlework, of house-wifeliness, and one has but to attend the annual Industrial Exhibition on the Indian reserve, an Institution that is open to all Indians in Canada, who desire to compete for prizes, to convince themselves by very material arguments that the Iroquois woman is behind her white sister in nothing pertaining to the larder, the dairy or the linen press. She bakes the loveliest, lightest wheaten bread, of which, by the way, her men folk complain loudly, declaring that she forces them to eat this new-fangled food to the absolute exclusion of their time-honoured corn bread, to which the national palate ever clings; her rolls of yellow butter are faultlessly sweet and firm, her sealed fruits are a pleasure to see as well as taste, in fact, in this latter industry she excels herself, outdoing frequently her white competitors at the neighbouring city of Brantford, where the 'southern fair' of Ontario is held annually. Her patch-work quilts, her baby garments, her underwear, her knitted mittens and stockings, her embroidery and fancy work are features of the exhibition that call for even much masculine attention, and yet while you gaze, and admire, and marvel at her accomplishments, she is probably standing beside you, her placid, brown face apparently quite unintelligent, her brown, deft hands devoid of gloves, her slight but sturdy figure clad in the regulation Iroquois fashion, a short broadcloth petticoat, bordered with its own vari-coloured self-edge, over this a bright calico 'short-dress' and plain round waist, her neatly braided black hair tied under a red bandanna handkerchief, her feet encased in coarse leather shoes, her only ornaments a necklace of green or yellow glass beads and a pair of gilt earrings.

Beside her is her daughter, who has long since discarded the broadcloth petticoat, the ill-shapen short dress, the picturesque head gear. Miss Iroquois has most likely arrayed herself in a very becoming stuff gown, made in modern style. She wears gloves and a straw hat, decorated with bright ribbon and a few pretty flowers. She is altogether like the daughter of one of Canada's prosperous farmers, save for her dark colourless skin, her extremely retiring manner and her pretty, tripping accent when she condescends to address you in English. Then, too, she has not been idly reared, for although the elder woman may have made the patchwork, and the butter rolls, the girl is probably 'out at service,' or teaches one of the district schools. Then, too, if she is a member of one of the fifty-two noble families, who compose the Iroquois Government, she has this divine right in addition to woman's great right of motherhood – the divine right of transmitting the title, if she in the direct line of lineage, for the Chief's title is inherited through the mother, not the father, which fact is a powerful contradiction to the widespread error, that Indian men look down upon and belittle their women. Add to this the privilege, which titled Iroquois women possess, of speaking in the great council of their nation, and note the deference with which the old chiefs listen to these speeches, when some one woman, more daring than her sisters, sees the necessity of stepping into public affairs – then I think the reader will admit that not all civilized races honour their women as highly as do the stern old chiefs, warriors and braves of the Six Nations' Indians.

AS IT WAS IN THE BEGINNING

They account for it by the fact that I am a Redskin, but I am something else, too – I am a woman.

I remember the first time I saw him. He came up the trail with some Hudson's Bay trappers, and they stopped at the door of my father's tepee. He seemed even then, fourteen years ago, an old man; his hair seemed just as thin and white, his hands just as trembling and fleshless as they were a month since, when I saw him for what I pray his God is the last time.

My father sat in the tepee, polishing buffalo horns and smoking; my mother, wrapped in her blanket, crouched over her quill-work, on the buffalo-skin at his side; I was lounging at the doorway, idling, watching, as I always watched, the thin, distant line of sky and prairie; wondering, as I always wondered, what lay beyond it. Then he came, this gentle old man with his white hair and thin, pale face. He wore a long black coat, which I now know was the sign of his office, and he carried a black leather-covered book, which, in all the years I have known him, I have never seen him without.

The trappers explained to my father who he was, the Great Teacher, the heart's Medicine Man, the 'Blackcoat' we had heard of, who brought peace where there was war, and the magic of whose black book brought greater things than all the Happy Hunting Grounds of our ancestors.

He told us many things that day, for he could speak the Cree tongue, and my father listened, and listened, and when at last they left us, my father said for him to come and sit within the tepee again.

He came, all the time he came, and my father welcomed him, but my mother always sat in silence at work with the quills; my mother never liked the Great 'Blackcoat.'

His stories fascinated me. I used to listen intently to the tale of the strange new place he called 'heaven,' of the gold crown, of the white dress, of the great music; and then he would tell of that other strange place – hell. My father and I hated it; we feared it, we dreamt of it, we trembled at it. Oh, if the 'Blackcoat' would only cease to talk of it! Now I know he saw its effect upon us, and he used it as a whip to lash us into his new religion, but even then my mother must have known, for each time he left the tepee she would watch him going slowly away across the prairie; then when he was disappearing into the far horizon she would laugh scornfully, and say:

'If the white man made this Blackcoat's hell, let him go to it. It is for the man who found it first. No hell for Indians, just Happy Hunting Grounds. Blackcoat can't scare me.'

And then, after weeks had passed, one day as he stood at the tepee door he laid his white, old hand on my head and said to my father: 'Give me this little girl, chief. Let me take her to the mission school; let me keep her, and teach her of the great God and His eternal heaven. She will grow to be a noble woman, and return perhaps to bring her people to the Christ.'

My mother's eyes snapped. 'No,' she said. It was the first word she ever spoke to the 'Blackcoat.' My father sat and smoked. At the end of a half-hour he said: 'I am an old man, Blackcoat. I shall not leave the God of my fathers. I like not your strange God's ways – all of them. I like not His two new places for me when I am dead. Take the child, Blackcoat, and save her from hell.'

The first grief of my life was when we reached the mission. They took my buckskin dress off, saying I was now a little Christian girl and must dress like all the white people at the mission. Oh, how I hated that stiff new calico dress and those leather shoes! But, little as I was, I said nothing, only thought of the time when I should be grown, and do as my mother did, and wear the buckskins and the blanket.

My next serious grief was when I began to speak the English, that they forbade me to use any Cree words whatever. The rule of the school was that any child heard using its native tongue must get a slight punishment. I never understood it, I cannot understand it now, why the use of my dear Cree tongue could be a matter for correction or an action deserving punishment.

She was strict, the matron of the school, but only justly so, for she had a heart and a face like her brother's, the 'Blackcoat.' I had long since ceased to call him that. The trappers at the post called him 'St Paul,' because, they told me, of his self-sacrificing life, his kindly deeds, his rarely beautiful old face; so I, too, called him 'St Paul,' though oftener 'Father Paul,' though he never liked the latter title, for he was a Protestant. But as I was his pet, his darling of the whole school, he let me speak of him as I would, knowing it was but my heart speaking in love. His sister was a widow, and mother to a laughing yellow-haired little boy of about my own age, who was my constant playmate and who taught me much of English in his own childish way. I used to be fond of this child, just as I was fond of his mother and of his uncle, my 'Father Paul,' but as my girlhood passed away, as womanhood came upon me, I got strangely wearied of them all; I longed, oh, God, how I longed for the old wild life! It came with my womanhood, with my years.

What mattered it to me now that they had taught me all their ways? – their tricks of dress, their reading, their writing, their books. What mattered it that 'Father Paul' loved me, that the traders at the post called me pretty, that I was a pet of all, from the factor to the poorest trapper in the service? I wanted my own people, my own old life, my blood called out for it, but they always said I must not return to my father's tepee. I heard them talk amongst themselves of keeping me away from pagan influences; they told each other that if I returned to the prairies, the tepees, I would degenerate, slip back to paganism, as other girls had done; marry, perhaps, with a pagan – and all their years of labour and teaching would be lost.

I said nothing, but I waited. And then one night the feeling overcame me. I was in the Hudson's Bay store when an Indian came in from the north with a large pack of buckskin. As they unrolled it a dash of its insinuating odour filled the store. I went over and leaned above the skins a second, then buried my face in them, swallowing, drinking the fragrance of them, that went to my head like wine. Oh, the wild wonder of that wood-smoked tan, the subtlety of it, the untamed smell of it! I drank it into my lungs, my innermost being was saturated with it, till my mind reeled and my heart seemed twisted with a physical agony. My childhood recollections rushed upon me, devoured me. I left the store in a strange, calm frenzy, and going rapidly to the mission house I confronted my Father Paul and demanded to be allowed to go 'home,' if only for a day. He received the request with the same refusal and the same gentle sigh that I had so often been greeted with, but this time the desire, the smoke-tan, the heart-ache, never lessened.

Night after night I would steal away by myself and go to the border of the village to watch the sun set in the foothills, to gaze at the far line of sky and prairie, to long and long for my father's lodge. And Laurence – always Laurence – my fair-haired, laughing, child playmate, would come calling and calling for me: 'Esther, where are you? We miss you; come in, Esther, come in with me.' And if I did not turn at once to him and follow, he would come and place his strong hands on my shoulders and laugh into my eyes and say, 'Truant, truant, Esther; can't *we* make you happy?'

My old child playmate had vanished years ago. He was a tall, slender young man now, handsome as a young chief, but with laughing blue eyes, and always those yellow curls about his temples. He was my solace in my half-exile, my comrade, my brother, until one night it was, 'Esther, Esther, can't *I* make you happy?'

I did not answer him; only looked out across the plains and thought of the tepees. He came close, close. He locked his arms about me, and with my face pressed up to his throat he stood silent. I felt the blood from my heart sweep to my very finger-tips. I loved him. O God, how I loved him! In a wild, blind instant it all came, just because he held me so and was whispering brokenly, 'Don't leave me, don't leave me, Esther; *my* Esther, my child-love, my playmate, my girl-comrade, my little Cree sweetheart, will you go away to your people, or stay, stay for me, for my arms, as I have you now?'

No more, no more the tepees; no more the wild stretch of prairie, the intoxicating fragrance of the smoke-tanned buckskin; no more the bed of buffalo hide, the soft, silent moccasin; no more the dark faces of my people, the dulcet cadence of the sweet Cree tongue – only this man, this fair, proud, tender man who held me in his arms, in his heart. My soul prayed his great white God, in that moment, that He let me have only this. It was twilight when we re-entered the mission gate. We were both excited, feverish. Father Paul was reading evening prayers in the large room beyond the hallway; his soft, saint-like voice stole beyond the doors, like a benediction upon us. I went noiselessly upstairs to my own room and sat there undisturbed for hours.

The clock downstairs struck one, startling me from my dreams of happiness, and at the same moment a flash of light attracted me. My room was in an angle of the building, and my window looked almost directly down into those of Father Paul's study, into which at that instant he was entering, carrying a lamp. 'Why, Laurence,' I heard him exclaim, 'what are you doing here? I thought, my boy, you were in bed hours ago.'

'No, uncle, not in bed, but in dreamland,' replied Laurence, arising from the window, where evidently he, too, had spent the night hours as I had done.

Father Paul fumbled about a moment, found his large black book, which for once he seemed to have got separated from, and was turning to leave, when the curious circumstance of Laurence being there at so unusual an hour seemed to strike him anew. 'Better go to sleep, my son,' he said simply, then added curiously, 'Has anything occurred to keep you up?'

Then Laurence spoke: 'No, uncle, only – only, I'm happy, that's all.'

Father Paul stood irresolute. Then: 'It is – ?'

'Esther,' said Laurence quietly, but he was at the old man's side, his hand was on the bent old shoulder, his eyes proud and appealing.

Father Paul set the lamp on the table, but, as usual, one hand held that black book, the great text of his life. His face was paler than I had ever seen it – graver.

'Tell me of it,' he requested.

I leaned far out of my window and watched them both. I listened with my very heart, for Laurence was telling him of me, of his love, of the new-found joy of that night.

'You have said nothing of marriage to her?' asked Father Paul.

'Well – no; but she surely understands that –'

'Did you speak of *marriage*?' repeated Father Paul, with a harsh ring in his voice that was new to me.

'No, uncle, but –'

'Very well, then; very well.'

There was a brief silence. Laurence stood staring at the old man as though he were a stranger; he watched him push a large chair up to the table, slowly seat himself; then mechanically following his movements, he dropped onto a lounge. The old man's head bent low, but his eyes were bright and strangely fascinating. He began:

'Laurence, my boy, your future is the dearest thing to me of all earthly interests. Why, you *can't* marry this girl – no, no, sit, sit until I have finished,' he added, with raised voice, as Laurence sprang up, remonstrating. 'I have long since decided that you marry well; for instance, the Hudson's Bay factor's daughter.'

Laurence broke into a fresh, rollicking laugh. 'What, uncle,' he said, 'little Ida McIntosh? Marry that little yellow-haired fluff ball, that kitten, that pretty little dolly?'

'Stop,' said Father Paul. Then, with a low, soft persuasiveness, 'She is *white*, Laurence.'

My lover started. 'Why, uncle, what do you mean?' he faltered.

'Only this, my son: poor Esther comes of uncertain blood; would it do for you – the missionary's nephew, and adopted son, you might say – to marry the daughter of a pagan Indian? Her mother is hopelessly uncivilized; her father has a dash of French somewhere – half-breed, you know, my boy, half-breed.' Then, with still lower tone and half-shut, crafty eyes, he added: 'The blood is a bad, bad mixture, *you* know that; you know, too, that I am very fond of the girl, poor dear Esther. I have tried to separate her from evil pagan influences; she is the daughter of the Church; I want her to have no other parent; but you never can tell what lurks in *a caged animal that has once been wild*. My whole heart is with the Indian people, my son; my whole heart, my whole life, has been devoted to bringing them to Christ, *but it is a different thing to marry with one of them.*'

His small old eyes were riveted on Laurence like a hawk's on a rat. My heart lay like ice in my bosom.

Laurence, speechless and white, stared at him breathlessly.

'Go away somewhere,' the old man was urging; 'to Winnipeg, Toronto, Montreal; forget her, then come back to Ida McIntosh. A union of the Church and the Hudson's Bay will mean great things, and may ultimately result in my life's ambition, the civilization of this entire tribe, that we have worked so long to bring to God.'

I listened, sitting like one frozen. Could those words have been uttered by my venerable teacher, by him whom I revered as I would one of the saints in his own black book? Ah, there was no mistaking it. My white father, my life-long friend who pretended to love me, to care for my happiness, was urging the man I worshipped to forget me, to marry with the factor's daughter – because of what? Of my red skin; my good, old, honest pagan mother; my confiding French-Indian father. In a second all the care, the hollow love he had given me since my childhood, were as things that never existed. I hated that old mission priest as I hated his white man's hell. I hated his long, white hair; I hated his thin, white hands; I hated his body, his soul, his voice, his black book – oh, how I hated the very atmosphere of him!

Laurence sat motionless, his face buried in his hands, but the old man continued, 'No, no; not the child of that pagan mother; you can't trust her, my son. What would you do with a wife who might any day break from you to return to her prairies and her buckskins? *You can't trust her.*' His eyes grew smaller, more glittering, more fascinating then, and leaning with an odd, secret sort of movement towards Laurence, he almost whispered, 'Think of her silent ways, her noiseless step; the girl glides about like an apparition; her quick fingers, her wild longings – I don't know why, but with all my fondness for her, she reminds me sometimes of a strange – snake.'

Laurence shuddered, lifted his face, and said hoarsely: 'You're right, uncle; perhaps I'd better not; I'll go away, I'll forget her, and then – well, then – yes, you are right, it *is* a different thing to marry one of them.' The old man arose. His feeble fingers still clasped his black book; his soft white hair clung about his forehead like that of an Apostle; his eyes lost their peering, crafty expression; his bent shoulders resumed the dignity of a minister of the living God; he was the picture of what the traders called him – 'St Paul.'

'Good-night, son,' he said.

'Good-night, uncle, and thank you for bringing me to myself.'

They were the last words I ever heard uttered by either that old archfiend or his weak, miserable kinsman. Father Paul turned and left the room. I watched his withered hand – the hand I had so often felt resting on my head in holy benedictions – clasp the door-knob, turn it slowly, then, with bowed head and his pale face wrapped in thought, he left the room – left it with the mad venom of my hate pursuing him like the very Evil One he taught me of.

What were his years of kindness and care now? What did I care for his God, his heaven, his hell? He had robbed me of my native faith, of my parents, of my people, of this last, this life of love that would have made a great, good woman of me. God! how I hated him!

I crept to the closet in my dark little room. I felt for a bundle I had not looked at for years – yes, it was there, the buckskin dress I had worn as a little child when they brought me to the mission. I tucked it under my arm and descended the stairs noiselessly. I would look into the study and speak good-bye to Laurence; then I would –

I pushed open the door. He was lying on the couch where a short time previously he had sat, white and speechless, listening to Father Paul, I moved towards him softly. God in heaven, he was already asleep. As I bent over him the fullness of his perfect beauty impressed me for the first time; his slender form, his curving mouth that almost laughed even in sleep, his fair, tossed hair, his smooth strong-pulsing throat. God! how I loved him!

Then there arose the picture of the factor's daughter. I hated her. I hated her baby face, her yellow hair, her whitish skin. 'She shall not marry him,' my soul said. 'I will kill him first – kill his beautiful body, his lying, false heart.' Something in my heart seemed to speak; it said over and over again, 'Kill him, kill him; she will never have him then. Kill him. It will break Father Paul's heart and blight his life. He has killed the best of you, of your womanhood; kill *his* best, his pride, his hope – his sister's son, his nephew Laurence.' But how? how?

What had that terrible old man said I was like? A *strange snake*. A snake? The idea wound itself about me like the very coils of a serpent. What was this in the beaded bag of my buckskin dress? this little thing rolled in tan that my mother had given me at parting with the words, 'Don't touch much, but some time maybe you want it!' Oh! I knew well enough what it was – a small flint arrow-head dipped in the venom of some *strange snake*.

I knelt beside him and laid my hot lips on his hand. I worshipped him, oh, how, how I worshipped him! Then again the vision of *her* baby face, *her* yellow hair – I scratched his wrist twice with the arrow-tip. A single drop of red blood oozed up; he stirred. I turned the lamp down and slipped out of the room – out of the house.

I dream nightly of the horrors of the white man's hell. Why did they teach me of it, only to fling me into it?

Last night as I crouched beside my mother on the buffalo-hide, Dan Henderson, the trapper, came in to smoke with my father. He said old Father Paul was bowed with grief, that with my disappearance I was suspected, but that there was no proof. Was it not merely a snake bite?

They account for it by the fact that I am a Redskin.

They seem to have forgotten I am a woman.

A PAGAN IN ST PAUL'S CATHEDRAL

Iroquois Poetess' Impressions in London's Cathedral

It is a far cry from a wigwam to Westminster, from a prairie trail to the Tower Bridge, and London looks a strange place to the Red Indian whose eyes still see the myriad forest trees, even as they gaze across the Strand, and whose feet still feel the clinging moccasin even among the scores of clicking heels that hurry along the thoroughfares of this camping-ground of the paleface.

So this is the place where dwells the Great White Father, ruler of many lands, lodges, and tribes, in the hollow of whose hands is the peace that rests between the once hostile red man and white. They call him the King of England, but to us, the powerful Iroquois nation of the north, he is always the 'Great White Father.' For once he came to us in our far-off Canadian reserves, and with his own hand fastened decorations and medals on the buckskin coats of our oldest chiefs, just because they and their fathers used their tomahawks in battle in the cause of England.

So I, one of his loyal allies, have come to see his camp, known to the white man as London, his council which the whites call his Parliament, where his sachems and chiefs make the laws of his tribes, and to see his wigwam, known to the palefaces as Buckingham Palace, but to the red man as the 'Tepee of the Great White Father.' And this is what I see:

What the Indian Sees

Lifting toward the sky are vast buildings of stone, not the same kind of stone from which my forefathers fashioned their carven pipes and corn-pounders, but a greyer, grimier rock that would not take the polish we give by fingers dipped in sturgeon oil, and long days of friction with fine sand and deer-hide.

I stand outside the great palace wigwam, the huge council-house by the river. My seeing eyes may mark them, but my heart's eyes are looking beyond all this wonderment, back to the land I have left behind me. I picture the tepees by the far Saskatchewan; there the tent poles, too, are lifting skyward, and the smoke ascending through them from the smouldering fires within curls softly on the summer air. Against the blurred sweep of horizon other camps etch their outlines, other bands of red

men with their herds of wild cattle have sought the river lands. I hear
the untamed hoofs thundering up the prairie trail.

But the prairie sounds are slipping away, and my ears catch other
voices that rise above the ceaseless throb about me – voices that are
clear, high, and calling; they float across the city like the music of a thou-
sand birds of passage beating their wings through the night, crying and
murmuring plaintively as they journey northward. They are the voices of
St Paul's calling, calling me – St Paul's where the paleface worships the
Great Spirit, and through whose portals he hopes to reach the happy
hunting grounds.

The Great Spirit

As I entered its doorways it seemed to me to be the everlasting abiding-
place of the white man's Great Spirit.

The music brooded everywhere. It beat in my ears like the far-off
cadences of the Sault Ste Marie rapids, that rise and leap and throb –
like a storm hurling through the fir forest – like the distant rising of an
Indian war-song; it swept up those mighty archways until the grey dome
above me faded, and in its place the stars came out to look down, not on
these paleface kneeling worshippers, but on a band of stalwart, sinewy,
copper-coloured devotees, my own people in my own land, who also
assembled to do honour to the Manitou of all nations.

The deep-throated organ and the boys' voices were gone; I heard
instead the melancholy incantations of our own pagan religionists. The
beautiful dignity of our great sacrificial rites seemed to settle about me,
to enwrap me in its garment of solemnity and primitive stateliness.

Beat of the Drum

The atmosphere pulsed with the beat of the Indian drum, the eerie
penetrations of the turtle rattle that set the time of the dancers' feet.
Dance? It is not a dance, that marvellously slow, serpentine-like figure
with the soft swish, swish of moccasined feet, and the faint jingling of
elks'-teeth bracelets, keeping rhythm with every footfall. It is not a
dance, but an invocation of motion. Why may we not worship with the
graceful movement of our feet? The paleface worships by moving his
lips and tongue; the difference is but slight.

The altar-lights of St Paul's glowed for me no more. In their place
flared the camp fires of the Onondaga 'long-house,' and the resinous

scent of the burning pine drifted across the fetid London air. I saw the tall, copper-skinned fire-keeper of the Iroquois council enter, the circle of light flung fitfully against the black surrounding woods. I have seen their white bishops, but none so regal, so august as he. His garb of fringed buckskin and ermine was no more grotesque than the vestments worn by the white preachers in high places; he did not carry a book or a shining golden symbol, but from his splendid shoulders was suspended a pure white lifeless dog.

Into the red flame the strong hands gently lowered it, scores of reverent, blanketed figures stood silent, awed, for it is the highest, holiest festival of the year. Then the wild, strange chant arose – the great pagan ritual was being intoned by the fire-keeper, his weird, monotonous tones voicing this formula:

'The Great Spirit desires no human sacrifice, but we, His children, must give to Him that which is nearest our hearts and nearest our lives. Only the spotless and stainless can enter into His presence, only that which is purified by fire. So do we offer to Him this spotless, innocent animal – this white dog – a member of our household, a co-habitant of our wigwam, and on the smoke that arises from the purging fires will arise also the thanksgivings of all those who desire that the Great Spirit in His happy hunting grounds will forever smoke His pipe of peace, for peace is between Him and His children for all time.'

The mournful voice ceases. Again the hollow pulsing of the Indian drum, the purring, flexible step of cushioned feet. I lift my head, which has been bowed on the chair before me. It is St Paul's after all – and the clear boy-voices rise above the rich echoes of the organ.

THE LODGE OF THE LAW-MAKERS

Contrasts Between the Parliaments of the White Man and the Red

The Paleface is a man of many moods; what he approves to-day he will disapprove to-morrow.

He is never content to let his mighty men rule for more than four or five years, after which time he wearies of their council fires, their law-giving, and their treaties with other tribes; he wants new chiefs, warriors, and braves, and he secures them by the voice and vote of the nation.

We of the ancient Iroquois race can but little understand this strange mode of government. We and our fathers, and their fathers before them, have always been pleased with our own Parliament, which has never varied through the generations – save when death leaves one seat empty, and another chief in the line of lineage steps forward to fill the vacancy.

But to more fully learn the wisdom of the white man's superior civilisation, I followed the wide crowded trail that leads to his council-house. I knew I would find it on the banks of a river, for any trails, even in my own country, whether they are beaten by man, horse, or buffalo, lead always to the edge of a stream.

As I neared the place I knew it for the abode of the wise men of this nation, for the voice of power and diplomacy, and tactics and skilful intrigue, thundered out from the white man's strange timepiece set in the carven square tower that rises majestic and inviolate as the tallest pine in the undiscovered wilderness of the West; and as the mountain tornado thrashes through the topmost branches, waking them to murmuring voices that dominate all other sounds of the forest, so do the tongues of these mighty men beneath the tower proclaim their dominion over all the wilderness of mankind in these island kingdoms of the East.

The Debate

Old men and young were debating with great spirit. Their speech was not so pleasant, or so diplomatic, or so fraught with symbols, as is the speech of our Indian rulers; the law-making for the nation is not pleasant councilling; therefore, we say, use the speech that may breed dissension as one would use the stone war-club. We hide and wrap the stone in vari-coloured beads and brilliantly stained moose-hair; it is then more acceptable to the eye and the touch, but the weapon and the force are there nevertheless. The white man's speech shows the grim baldness of the stone alone – no adornment, no colouring to render it less aggressive; but his tongue is arrow-headed, fleet, and direct, and where he aims is the spot he strikes.

Do the white law-makers in this great council-house on the Thames river know that there exists within my own Indian race the oldest constitutional government of America – a free Commonwealth older than any in Europe, save that of this ancient England and the land of the crags and cañons which they call Switzerland?

Hiawatha's Work

And this Commonwealth, which dominated the vast continent of North America even after the white traders set their feet on our territory, was devised and framed through the brain of the young Onondaga diplomat, Hiawatha, who, conceiving an idea for a universal peace, called together the representative chiefs of all the hostile tribes. It mattered not that war and bloodshed had existed for many decades between the tribes that these envoys represented, the words of Hiawatha were as oil.

The council fires burned ceaselessly, the council pipes were filled and smoked endlessly, until the fifty chiefs in conclave all ratified the policy under discussion. And thus was framed the constitution of a government that was to live through the ages, that does exist in absolute authority to-day, where the chiefs who are the lineal descendants of those fifty noble families still meet, and direct the affairs of their people with no less wisdom and judgment than is displayed by these Palefaces here beneath the square tower by the Thames.

Our fifty titles are not necessarily borne by the eldest sons of the noble families, for he may be greatly lacking in the qualities that make a statesman. Is not his second, or, maybe his youngest brother, of as noble birth as he? Why not then, put him in the high places, to let him use the brain and mind that, perhaps, his elder brother lacks? This is the Iroquois policy, and we practice it; but the white man knows little of the intricate workings of our inflexible league, for we are a silent people. Will the white man who considers us a savage, unenlightened race wonder if I told him that the fate of 'Senate' lies in the hands of the women of our tribes?

The Daughters

I have heard that the daughters of this vast city cry out for a voice in the Parliament of this land. There is no need for an Iroquois woman to clamour for recognition in our councils; she has had it for upwards of four centuries. The highest title known to us is that of 'chief matron.' It is borne by the oldest woman of each of the noble families.

From her cradle-board she is taught to judge men and their intellectual qualities, their aptness for public life, and their integrity, so that when he who bears the title leaves his seat in council to join the league-makers in the happy hunting grounds she can use her wisdom and her learning in nominating his fittest successor. She must bestow the title upon one of his kinsmen, one of the blood royal so that the heritage is unbroken, so, perhaps, she passes by the inadequate eldest son and nominates the capable younger one. Thus is the council given the best of the brain and blood of the nation.

The old and powerful chiefs-in-council never attempt to question her decision; her appointment is final, and at the 'condoling council,' when he is installed, and his title conferred as he first takes his seat, the chief matron may, if she desires, enter the council-house and publicly make an address to the chief braves, and warriors assembled, and she is listened to not only with attention, but with respect.

There are fifty matrons possessing this right in the Iroquois Confederacy. I have not yet heard of fifty white women even among those of noble birth who may speak and be listened to in the lodge of the lawmakers here.

WE-HRO'S SACRIFICE

A Story of a Boy and a Dog

We-hro was a small Onondaga Indian boy, a good-looking, black-eyed little chap with as pagan a heart as ever beat under a copper-coloured skin. His father and grandfathers were pagans. His ancestors for a thousand years back, and yet a thousand years back of that, had been pagans, and We-hro, with the pride of his religion and his race, would not have turned from the faith of his fathers for all the world. But the world, as he knew it, consisted entirely of the Great Indian Reserve, that lay on the banks of the beautiful Grand River, sixty miles west of the great Canadian city of Toronto.

Now, the boys that read this tale must not confuse a pagan with a heathen. The heathen nations that worship idols are terribly pitied and despised by the pagan Indians, who are worshippers of 'The Great Spirit,' a kind and loving God, who, they say, will reward them by giving them happy hunting grounds to live in after they die; that is, if they live good, honest, upright lives in this world.

We-hro would have scowled blackly if anyone had dared to name him a heathen. He thoroughly ignored the little Delaware boys, whose fathers worshipped idols fifty years ago, and on all the feast days and dance days he would accompany his parents to the 'Longhouse' (which was their church), and take his little part in the religious festivities. He could remember well as a tiny child being carried in his mother's blanket 'pick-a-back,' while she dropped into the soft swinging movement of the dance, for We-hro's people did not worship their 'Great Spirit' with hymns of praise and lowly prayers, the way the Christian Indians did. We-hro's people worshipped their God by dancing beautiful, soft, dignified steps, with no noisy clicking heels to annoy one, but only the velvety shuffle of the moccasined feet, the weird beat of the Indian drums, the mournful chanting of the old chiefs, keeping time with the throb of their devoted hearts.

Then, when he grew too big to be carried, he was allowed to clasp his mother's hand, and himself learn the pretty steps, following his father, who danced ahead, dressed in full costume of scarlet cloth and buckskin, with gay beads and bear claws about his neck, and wonderful carven silver ornaments, massive and solid, decorating his shirt and leggings. We-hro loved the tawny fringes and the hammered silver quite as much as a white lady loves diamonds and pearls; he loved to see his father's face painted in fierce reds, yellows and blacks, but most of all he loved the unvarying *chuck-a, chuck-a, chuck-a* of the great mud-turtle rattles that the 'musicians' skilfully beat upon the benches before them. Oh, he was a thorough little pagan, was We-hro! His loves and his hates were as decided as his comical but stately step in the dance of his ancestors' religion. Those were great days for the small Onondaga boy. His father taught him to shape axe-handles, to curve lacrosse sticks, to weave their deer-sinew netting, to tan skins, to plant corn, to model arrows and – most difficult of all – to 'feather' them, to 'season' bows, to chop trees, to burn, hollow, fashion and 'man' a dugout canoe, to use the paddle, to gauge the wind and current of that treacherous Grand River, to learn wild cries to decoy bird and beast for food. Oh, little pagan We-hro had his life filled to overflowing with much that the civilized white boy would give all his dimes and dollars to know.

And it was then that the great day came, the marvellous day when We-hro discovered his *second self*, his playmate, his loyal, unselfish, loving friend – his underbred, unwashed, hungry, vagabond dog, born white and spotless, but begrimed by contact with the world, the mud, and the white man's hovel.

It happened this way:

We-hro was cleaning his father's dugout canoe, after a night of fish spearing. The soot, the scales, the fire ashes, the mud – all had to be 'swabbed' out at the river's brink by means of much water and an Indian 'slat' broom. We-hro was up to his little ears in work, when suddenly, above him, on the river road, he heard the coarse voice and thundering whipfalls of a man urging and beating his horse – a white man, for no Indian used such language, no Indian beat an animal that served him. We-hro looked up. Stuck in the mud of the river road was a huge wagon, grain-filled. The driver, purple of face, was whaling the poor team, and shouting to a cringing little drab-white dog, of fox-terrier lineage, to 'Get out of there or I'll – !'

The horses were dragging and tugging. The little dog, terrified, was sneaking off with tail between its hind legs. Then the brutal driver's whip came down, curling its lash about the dog's thin body, forcing from the little speechless brute a howl of agony. Then We-hro spoke – spoke in all the English he knew.

'Bad! bad! You die some day – you! You hurt that dog. White man's God, he no like you. Indian's Great Spirit, he not let you shoot in happy hunting grounds. You die some day – you bad!'

'Well, if I am bad I'm no pagan Indian Hottentot like you!' yelled the angry driver. 'Take the dog, and begone!'

'Me no Hottentot,' said We-hro, slowly. 'Me Onondaga, all right. Me take dog;' and from that hour the poor little white cur and the copper-coloured little boy were friends for all time.

———•———

The Superintendent of Indian Affairs was taking his periodical drive about the Reserve when he chanced to meet old 'Ten-Canoes,' We-hro's father.

The superintendent was a very important person. He was a great white gentleman, who lived in the city of Brantford, fifteen miles away. He was a kindly, handsome man, who loved and honoured every Indian on the Grand River Reserve. He had a genial smile, a warm hand-shake, so when he stopped his horse and greeted the old pagan, Ten-Canoes smiled too.

'Ah, Ten-Canoes!' cried the superintendent, 'a great man told me he was coming to see your people – a big man, none less than Great Black-Coat, the bishop of the Anglican Church. He thinks you are a bad lot, because you are pagans; he wonders why it is that you have never turned Christian. Some of the missionaries have told him you pagans are no good, so the great man wants to come and see for himself. He wants to see some of your religious dances – the "Dance of the White Dog," if you will have him; he wants to see if it is really *bad*.'

Ten-Canoes laughed. 'I welcome him,' he said, earnestly, 'Welcome the "Great Black-Coat." I honour him, though I do not think as he does. He is a good man, a just man; I welcome him, bid him come.'

Thus was his lordship, the Bishop, invited to see the great pagan Onondaga 'Festival of the White Dog.'

But what was *this* that happened?

Never yet had a February moon waned but that the powerful Onondaga tribe had offered the burnt 'Sacrifice of the White Dog,' that most devout of all native rites. But now, search as they might, not a single spotlessly white dog could be found. No other animal would do. It was the law of this great Indian tribe that no other burnt sacrifice could possibly be offered than the strangled body of a white dog.

We-hro heard all the great chiefs talking of it all. He listened to plans for searching the entire Reserve for a dog, and the following morning he arose at dawn, took his own pet dog down to the river and washed him as he had seen white men wash their sheep. Then out of the water dashed the gay little animal, yelping and barking in play, rolling in the snow, tearing madly about, and finally rushing off towards the log house which was We-hro's home, and scratching at the door to get in by the warm fire to dry his shaggy coat. Oh! what an ache that coat caused in We-hro's heart. From a dull drab grey the dog's hair had washed pure white, not a spot or a blemish on it, and in an agony of grief the little pagan boy realized that through his own action he had endangered the life of his dog friend; that should his father and his father's friends see that small white terrier, they would take it away for the nation's sacrifice.

Stumbling and panting and breathless, We-hro hurried after his pet, and, seizing the dog in his arms, he wrapped his own shabby coat about the trembling, half-dry creature, and carried him to where the cedars grew thick at the back of the house. Crouched in their shadows he hugged his treasured companion, thinking with horror of the hour when the blow would surely fall. For days the boy kept his dog in the shelter of the cedars, tied up tightly with an old rope, and sleeping in a warm raccoon skin, which We-hro smuggled away from his own simple bed. The dog contented himself with what little food We-hro managed to carry to him, but the hiding could not keep up forever, and one dark, dreaded day Wehro's father came into the house and sat smoking in silence for many minutes. When at last he spoke, he said:

'We-hro, your dog is known to me. I have seen him, white as the snow that fell last night. It is the law that someone must always suffer for the good of the people. We-hro, would you have the great "Black-Coat," the great white preacher, come to see our beautiful ceremony, and would you have the great Onondaga tribe fail to show the white man how we worship our ancient Great Spirit? Would you have us fail to burn the sacrifice? Or will you give your white dog for the honour of our people?'

The world is full of heroes, but at that moment it held none greater than the little pagan boy, who crushed down his grief and battled back his tears as he answered:

'Father, you are old and honoured and wise. For you and for my people alone would I give the dog.'

At last the wonderful Dance Day arrived. His lordship, the Bishop of the Anglican Church, drove down from the city of Brantford; with him the Superintendent of Indian Affairs, and a man who understood both the English and the Onondaga languages. Long before they reached the 'Longhouse' they could hear the wild beat of the drum, could count the beats of the dance rattles, could distinguish the half-sad chant of the worshippers. The kind face of the great bishop was very grave. It pained his gentle old heart to know that this great tribe of Indians were pagans – savages, as he thought – but when he entered that plain log building that the Onondagas held as their church, he took off his hat with the beautiful reverence all great men pay to other great men's religion, and he stood bareheaded while old Ten-Canoes chanted forth this speech:

'Oh, brothers of mine! We welcome the white man's friend, the great "Black-Coat," to this, our solemn worship. We offer to the red man's God – the Great Spirit – a burnt offering. We do not think that anything save what is pure and faithful and without blemish can go into the sight of the Great Spirit. Therefore do we offer this dog, pure as we hope our spirits are, that the God of the red man may accept it with our devotion, knowing that we, too, would gladly be as spotless as this sacrifice.'

Then was a dog carried in dead, and beautifully decorated with wampum, beads and porcupine embroidery. Oh! so mercifully dead and out of pain, gently strangled by reverent fingers, for an Indian is never unkind to an animal. And far over in a corner of the room was a little brown figure, twisted with agony, choking back the sobs and tears – for was he not taught that tears were for babies alone, and not for boys that grew up into warriors?

'Oh, my dog! my dog!' he muttered. 'They have taken you away from me, but it was for the honour of my father and of my own people.'

The great Anglican bishop turned at that moment, and, catching the sight of suffering on little We-hro's face, said aloud to the man who spoke both languages:

'That little boy over there seems in torture. Can I do anything for him, do you think?'

'That little boy,' replied the man who spoke both languages, 'is the son of the great Onondaga chief. No white dog could be found for this ceremony but his. This dog was his pet, but for the honour of his father and of his tribe he has given up his pet as a sacrifice.'

For a moment the great Anglican bishop was blinded by his own tears. Then he walked slowly across the wide log building and laid his white hand tenderly on the head of the little Onondaga boy. His kindly old eyes closed, and his lips moved – noiselessly, for a space, then he said aloud:

'Oh, that the white boys of my great city church knew and practised half as much of self-denial as has this little pagan Indian lad, who has given up his heart's dearest because his father and the honour of his people required it.'

MOTHERS OF A GREAT RED RACE

There exists to-day no more splendid specimens of vigorous womanhood than those found among the mothers of the great Iroquois Indian nation of Canada. Semi-civilization has not yet obliterated the grand physique, the silent courage, the beautiful, old-fashioned womanliness that have their chief pride in giving warrior sons and gentle daughters to the nation. The Indian mother has not yet joined the ranks of 'new women.' The grace of motherhood is to her a primitive glory. She has been reared to consider it her right and privilege; and just because her entire life from babyhood to old age is so replete with the freedom of forest life, with occupations in the open air, with absence of worry and useless strivings for lesser things, she may well be greeted as one of the ideal mothers of our day. There are no women in the world fonder of children than the daughters of the warlike Iroquois. Every little one that comes to the red mother's arms is welcomed royally, and the practice of adopting children of some less favoured family may almost be termed a national habit. I have never heard of a single instance of an Iroquois child being sent to any 'Home' or 'Orphanage.' Somebody's wigwam door is always thrown open for the little, copper-coloured waif to enter; some Indian mother's arms can always find time to cradle the un-sheltered baby and lay it to sleep beside her own little, brown family, no matter how many the number. The entire upbringing of an Iroquois maiden is so foreign to that of her white sisters, that the contrast is sufficiently glaring to give rise to discussion as to the merits of 'savagery' or civilization for our womankind. The Indian mother is exempt from unceasing war which the white mother wages – the war against unnatural foods, unreasonable apparel and unhealthy hours and environment which are a menace to the frail little bodies of the majority of white children. No worry enters into the wigwam to fret the placid red mother, to upset her nerves, to irritate her temper and thereby to warp her baby's upbringing. The needs of both mother and child are simple. They fit into their forest surroundings as a dulcet poem adjusts itself to music, and their lives are one harmonious whole with the primal elements of the great outdoors. Nothing complex or artificial interferes with the Indian mother's training of her child. It is true that the nations makes greater demands upon her regarding the native laws of hereditary titles, etiquette and food-getting. These she must teach her boys and girls, before the former are consigned to their father's, or, more often, to their grandfather's tutelage in the sterner craft of hunting, trapping, national sports, the council fire, or the warpath.

Frequently the slender, young, copper-coloured Iroquois girl is a mother at sixteen. Her husband has been chosen for her by her very wise father, who has been approached by the young lover's father with the proposition that the marriage would be a suitable one. The two old men smoke together for many hours, talk the matter over, then lay the proposal before the girl. If she favours the suitor, she accepts shyly, but she always has the privilege of saying no. A marriage is never forced, although sometimes it is urged, particularly when a chief's title is to be considered, for it is through the mother that the title is inherited, and an eligible marriage is, therefore, to be commended. This almost unknown fact, that the fifty-two titles which compose the senate of the famous Iroquois council are transmitted, not through the paternal but the maternal side, places the Iroquois mother as the foremost woman, the paramount and most vital mother on the American continent. Her importance and influence are openly acknowledged by every man of her tribe, be he chief, brave or warrior. Perhaps she herself is 'noble,' inheriting from her maternal ancestors that rare and distinctive honour of being 'chief matron' of her clan – that beautiful, dignified title which descends from mother to daughter, and has done so for many ages; that living, breathing contradiction to the common idea that Indian men look down upon women, and treat the mothers of their children as mere property. There is not a feminine influence known to civilization that means to this nation what the title, 'chief matron,' means to the Iroquois. The mother who wears it is a power in her tribe that can and does make itself felt in the nation's 'parliament,' and it is to her astute discernment, her ability to estimate the man best fitted for public life, that the Indian council owes the integrity of most of its members; for it is she who nominates the succeeding chief when death leaves the chair empty in the council house. To be sure, he must be in the direct 'blood' line inheriting the title, but not necessarily the 'eldest son,' and oftentimes, if the seeming rightful heir or his brothers are, to her discriminating judgement, not qualified or capable to bear such responsibilities, she will nominate an uncle or cousin, though always keeping within the strictest confines of blood inheritance to the title.

The 'parliament' cannot question her decision nor overthrow her nominee. They must accept her choice, for, if the slightest discussion arises, she may, and, indeed, oftentimes has claimed, the privilege of stepping into the council and voicing her own arguments in defense of the man she has appointed; for, extraordinary as it may seem, the 'chief matron' has the right to speak in the assembled council of the Six Great Nations of the Iroquois. And, more than that, her words and views are listened to by the grave old chiefs with a deference that is but a prelude to assent, for there is no record of failure to carry 'the house' when a chief matron voices her arguments. A well-known instance, remembered still on the Grand River Indian Reserve, is that when the writer's grandmother, who was chief matron of the Mohawks, had nominated a chief to whom the council took exception on the ground that he was the official tribal interpreter in the house, the quiet but determined old Indian mother arose and took her place on the platform, confronting the assembly of Iroquois chiefs, and, after a bitter, scathing, ironical speech, in which she reprimanded the entire council for about forty minutes, she clapped her argument with the threat that, unless they accepted her nominee she would annul the title forever, thus weakening by one the Mohawk portion of the council and shattering a constitution that had existed for centuries. The wise old chiefs, knowing the power of that matron, discreetly withdrew their objection, order was restored, and the new chief was installed.

But the marrow of this entire incident lies in the fact that the chief matron had nominated her second son, one whose ability she well knew fitted him for the nation's public affairs. She had other sons, uncles, cousins, but she would prefer to destroy forever her family title to nobility, rather than show a lack of faith in that son's efficiency. Her reward came in the years that followed, when the entire tribe proclaimed him their head chief. But that Iroquois mother was ready and willing to cast aside her ancient family title, to abolish its very existence, rather than show a shadow of doubt of the integrity and honour of her son. Truly the red Indian mother is a Spartan mother also. No wonder that she gives birth to warrior sons. But even apart from these affairs of 'state,' the duties of the Iroquois mother are onerous, and begin when her little, brown baby is but a few days old. With her own hands she places his tiny body on a cradle board, straightening his limbs, placing his feet with heel beside heel, toes straight and even, all to be wrapped around with bands of gayly adorned cloth – the patterns worked by careful fingers with moose hair, porcupine quills and varicoloured beads – which encase him like a little mummy. On the wooden loop that arches above his head, she suspends trinkets – ermine tails, tinkling elks' teeth, gay ribbons and beads, all of which divert his attention in waking hours. Should housewifely duties demand much of her attention, she hangs the cradle board by this wooden loop to the wall in winter, and to the down-bending tree branches in summer, where he swings contentedly with every motion of the breeze. Not only do his cradle-board days mean safety to himself and absolute freedom to his mother, but every hour he spends strapped to his primitive couch is strengthening his limbs, fortifying them against 'bow-legged' or 'knock-kneed' deformity, training his feet to keep a straight line, neither 'toeing' in or out. Every hour is teaching him self-control of muscles, members and features – such an essential qualification of Indian manhood.

Before the little, copper-coloured baby is many weeks old, his mother always carries him to some of the great religious dances or festivals of his tribe, so his religious training is begun long before he can take even the smallest active part in the 'services.' He is usually lifted to his mother's shoulders and carried pick-a back. An adroit twist to her blanket forms an easy pocket wherein he hangs rather than sits, his little black eyes watching with fascinated delight the gorgeous trappings of the worshippers, the brilliant colours, the shining silver and bead ornaments; his alert little ears catching every jingle of the clinking bracelets and necklets of bears' claws and elks' teeth worn by the dancers, who circle about the length of the old 'long house.' The men, in their festive paint and feathers, lead, the magnificent abandon and agility of their dancing being as the footfall of one man, so perfect is the time they keep to the wild beat of the turtle rattles, the eerie throb of the Indian drum, the monotonous, melancholy chant of the 'musicians.' Then follow the women, with an odd, swinging movement of limbs that is grace and dignity combined, and the young red mother steps into the circle to give her tiny baby its first introduction to the solemn worship of the Great Spirit, who, in the far Happy Hunting Grounds, watches over his Indian children while they offer to him their simple but sincere forest homage.

But the little redskin baby does not remain small enough to be carried into the dances. With his second year comes the privilege of walking demurely into the circle, his wee hand clinging tightly to his mother's, his small, moccasined feet stumbling into step and rhythm. The very first day that he masters the slightest resemblance to a dance, he receives the reward of being taken among the men, even though his father must needs steady his baby feet and occasionally lift his tiny body to a great, bronze, naked shoulder to give the faithful devotee breathing space and rest.

But if the baby treasure is a girl, she will always remain with the women. She will be clad precisely like her mother and grandmother from the day she is able to take her first step – a broadcloth petticoat, bordered at the rim by its own varicoloured selvage; above it a calico 'short dress,' ornamented with many and valuable silver brooches beaten from coin by the native silversmiths of her tribe; a gay handkerchief folded smoothly about her head and knotted beneath her chin; a heavy string of blue or green beads about her neck; and soft, pliable, easy moccasins encasing her feet. Her very occupations will be those of her elders; her baby habits, tastes, pastimes and customs are modelled upon those of her mother, of whom she is a grave little miniature, and to whom she gives the most absolute obedience – a virtue that both she and her little redskin brother have inherited through countless generations that have been born and bred to revere age as a greater honour than even the blood-royal birthright of a chieftain's title or the flaming eagle plume of the warrior.

MOTHER OF THE MOTHERLESS

We had put in a bad night of it, boarding the train at the station of a small prairie town about four in the morning. In the double seat behind us was a family consisting of a weary-looking woman, a serious-faced man and three small, pretty girl children, the youngest about three years of age. From time to time this little girl whimpered and fretted, occasionally breaking into a positive storm of weeping. The passengers seemed just to get settled, just lulled to that heavy slumber that assails one before daybreak – particularly when one has been up all night – when this irrepressible youngster would break forth anew, awaking the entire carful of wearied travellers, who would fidget, yawn and scowl, then make one more attempt to recover their broken sleep. This sort of thing went on for two hours, then dawn broke along the row of windows facing eastward, and the child, now fully awake herself, cried with fresh energy.

'I'd hate to be the mother of that child, and be as unpopular as she is in this car,' declared my companion, audibly. The woman winced, but said nothing.

Then I bethought me of an old and very deadly insult that in similar cases I had once or twice flung at a mother who would allow her child to make twenty people miserable, while she invariably took things complacently. So I said with *malice prepense* and in far-reaching tones, 'Don't get irritable. The child is sick. *Anyone* with half an eye could see it is terribly delicate. It's *sick.*' At this the weary-faced woman leaned across the back of my seat and said sweetly:

'No, she's not sick. But we buried her father yesterday and her mother last week, and she's – lonesome.'

Instantly every erstwhile grumbling commercial traveller in that car was on his feet. My companion, with all the kindliness and humanizing sympathy of his heart, swung out of his seat, and, with hat in hand, was making for the forward car to hunt up 'Newsy,' with his basket of fruit and candies. I slipped quietly into the seat beside the children, for, at mention of their recent grief, the two other children began to wipe their eyes. By this time a drummer had extracted a package of salted peanuts from his coat pocket, and was sheepishly offering it to the wee girl. I took the child into my arms, showing her my rings and trinkets, and in awe of such things, and of a stranger's proximity, she ceased her sobs. My companion returned with 'Newsy' at his heels. Oranges, candies, prize packages, were literally loaded into the small laps, comic papers, picture postal cards – anything, everything that money could buy on that train. The little girls began to be interested, then to smile, then to eat, and finally to play. My companion sat on the arm of the seat near the solemn-faced man.

'Now, girlies,' he said, 'just dig in and have a good time.' Then to the man and woman: 'I never felt so mean in all my life. I'm *so* sorry I complained. Poor little people! It certainly is hard luck, and are they quite homeless?'

'Not while he and I live,' said the woman. 'We've taken these three for our own.'

'Then you have no children?' I asked.

'Oh, bless your heart, we have six!' she replied, smilingly.

Then I extracted from her this most unusual story:

Her husband had been telegraphed for to go to Saskatchewan, some five hundred miles distant. His brother and sister-in-law were both laid low with typhoid fever, and their family of two grown boys, a girl of seventeen, and these three little ones were in great distress and unable to do the nursing required. When this dire message came to the farmhouse in far-off Manitoba, the wife immediately declared her intention of accompanying him.

'It was a woman's care they needed in that afflicted home,' she said sweetly, 'and I just made up my mind the farm and our own children could take care of themselves. I could picture those two poor things lying ill, with a houseful of inexperienced children, no nurse, no housekeeper, no cook. So I packed up and came, and I've been thankful ever since. I never saw people in such a plight; but all we could do did not count – nothing availed. The mother died almost immediately. The father followed in a few days. We buried them side by side out on the prairie. They had not long been West from Ontario; the farm was not all paid for. *He* got the two grown boys places as harvest hands. The oldest daughter went out to service at a clergyman's house in Regina, and these three were left. Now if they had been boys, I *might* have hesitated, but one *couldn't* leave these little girls to face the world and strangers alone, or to go back to *his* relatives in Ontario, so they are mine now – aren't you, dears?' she finished, cuddling her arms about the tiny orphans with the most exquisite motherliness I have ever witnessed.

'We haven't got much of our own,' she continued, 'just starting to make our way out here in the West, but bless us, we'll never miss what these will eat!'

Dear, homely, golden-hearted mother that she was! In the conversation that followed I gathered that she had never even seen the dead parents of these babies before she entered the afflicted house. These very children were her husband's nieces, no relatives of hers whatever, but that counted to her as nothing.

Her husband had long ago lost his solemn look. As soon as the childish griefs were lifted, his kindly, weather-tanned, honest face beamed in unison. I think every baby tear fell on his sorrowing heart, and now every baby smile reflected itself in his quiet, humorous eyes.

Before leaving the train, I got their names and address; such people are too rare to lose sight of.

That was four years ago, and with my life crowded with incident and travel, they had almost escaped my memory, but last September when chance took me to a small town in Manitoba, that good woman drove in seven miles to see me. She came to the hotel, and to my room. 'Do you know me?' she smiled out at once. I should have known her at the Antipodes, but my joy at again having the honour of clasping hands with her was checked by the black gown, the black hat, the black wrap she wore.

She saw my questioning look, and a moment afterwards had told me, bravely and brightly as ever, that the kind, honest husband with the twinkling, half-humorous eyes had gone before us all; but she had brought me a photograph of the three little girls – 'my littlest girls,' as she called them. They had grown taller, prettier, sweeter, were all attending school and happy as the day is long.

'But now that your dear right arm has gone, can you afford to maintain these little strangers –nieces of your dead husband?' I asked, tenderly, for she had casually mentioned bad harvests and losses.

'Why bless you! I'll never miss what they eat,' she replied. The selfsame words she had used four years ago, when her husband was beside her to fight the great battle of life in the uncertain Northwest. 'And I couldn't let these little girls go elsewhere, dear little motherless things!' she concluded.

I did not agree with the latter part of her remark. They were not 'motherless.'

So we said good-by. I watched her drive up the long, straggling street, turn to the trail, and head for the prairie's rim, and I thought Manitoba a blessed province to contain within its borders this noble, courageous woman, this mother to the motherless.

THE LEGEND OF THE TWO SISTERS

You can see them from the heights, from the pleasure grounds, from the gay thoroughfares, from the great hotel windows – those twin peaks of the twin mountains that lift their pearly summits across the inlet which washes with its ceaseless tides the margins of Vancouver, the beautiful city which is called 'The Sunset Gateway' of the Dominion of Canada. Sometimes the smoke of forest fires blurs these twin peaks, until they swim in a purple atmosphere too beautiful for words to paint. Sometimes the slanting rains festoon their grey and gauzy veils about the crests, and the peaks fade into inadequate outlines of soft shadows, melting, melting, forever melting, into the distances. But for most days of the year, the sun circles the twin glories with a sweep of gold, the moon washes them with a torrent of silver, and they stand immovable through sun and shadow, smiling on one side above the waters of the restless Pacific, on the other, above the depths and eternal silence of the Capilano Cañon.

Throughout the British Empire these peaks are known as 'The Lions of Vancouver.' Their striking resemblance to Landseer's Lions at the base of Nelson's Monument in Trafalgar Square, London, has won them this name. But the Indians of the coast know nothing of the white man's appellation, and you must indeed get near to the heart of some ancient Klootchman[1] before she will consent to tell you the Legend of the Twin Sisters.

———•◆•———

We had been driving for some time, the handsome chief of the Capilanos sitting in the front seat of the light surrey, his slim, silent young daughter beside him, I in the back seat, and at my side the quaint old Indian mother, who, from time to time, told me the traditions of her people, in the half-halting broken English that is never so beautiful as when it slips from an Indian tongue. At our feet were baskets of exquisite weavery, all her handiwork, and that of her young daughter sitting before us. With housewifely care she had stowed these away before starting for the drive, for it was berry time, and she had no thought of leaving such precious muck-a-muck[2] for the foxes and birds, when her children and grandchildren had willing mouths to be filled. The chief was an excellent provider, but 'Why not add to the store?' she remarked simply. 'One must not be wasteful of these precious, God-given wild

---

1 In the Chinook tongue, in general usage as a trade language on the Pacific Coast, 'Klootchman' means woman, and is a word used with great respect among the Indian tribes [Johnson's note].

2 Chinook for food [Johnson's note].

things.' So the baskets reposed nearby, ready to be filled when opportunity afforded.

The trail wound about the foot of a cluster of mountains, following a riotous stream called the Capilano River, which brawled and quarrelled, whispered and laughed among its rocks and boulders, tumbling headlong one moment, the next circling into a deep, transparent pool where leaping salmon and shy mountain trout glinted in the sunshine.

'So many things belong to this river,' said the Klootchman in her pretty, stammering English, which I must eliminate if I am to make this story lucid. So I must keep to the everyday phrases, and my readers must be the losers of her fascinating expressions; but after all, it was her wonderful eyes and gestures that really made the tale, and what use to attempt a description of these? It is impossible.

'Yes, the river holds many secrets,' she continued, 'secrets of strong men's battles and many tragedies, but the mountains hold the secrets of an Indian mother's heart, and those are the greatest secrets of all things.'

Her voice fell to a whisper, but her speaking eyes swept the distant summits with an understanding far subtler than sight. I did not offer a reply, for I knew that in her own good time the Klootchman would catch the mood of the mountains and impart to me some of their lore. The silence was long. Once or twice she swept effective gestures that were filled with meaning. She wished me to notice the crags and ledges, haunts of the mountain sheep and wild goats, a winging hawk, a leaping trout, the crimsoning o-lil-lies (Chinook for berries). Then as if from dreams she suddenly awoke.

'You will want to know the secret that is held in the mountains, the secret of the Indian mother's heart?' she asked.

I nodded. I could see she liked that wordless reply, for she placed her narrow brown hand on my arm, nor did she remove it during her entire recital of

The Legend of the Two Sisters

'You see them – those two peaks – towering forever and ever in that high place? Those are the Chief's Daughters, that every Indian mother loves. You see them, but you may not know – you who have come from the Land of Morning, the Land of Sunrise – for you have different customs, different traditions, from those of our people in the Sunset Land. I say you may not know that when our daughters step from childhood into the great world of womanhood, when the fitness for motherhood crowns them, we coast Indians of the sunset country regard this occasion as one of extreme rejoicing, great honour and unspeakable gladness. The being who possesses the possibility of some day becoming a mother receives much honour in most nations, but to us, the Sunset Tribes of Redmen, she is almost sacred. So, when our girls reach womanhood, we make it a great occasion. The parents usually give a feast that lasts many days. The entire tribe is bidden to this festival. More than that, when a great Tyee (Chinook for chief) celebrates for his daughter, sometimes the tribes from far up the coast, from the far North, from inland, from the mountain passes, and the Cariboo Country, are bidden as guests to the feast. During these feast days the girl is placed in a high seat, an exalted position, for is she not marriageable? and does not marriage mean motherhood? and is not motherhood the most exalted position in the world? So we place the girl on a high elevation, for she must know and realize her responsibility, she must recognize that she is the greatest factor in the world, and she must sit in a high place as becomes her heritage as a woman, therefore as a possible mother, for this is the law of our people – we of the Sunset Tribes.

It was years ago, hundreds of years – yes, thousands of years (the sweet old Klootchman pronounced it 'Tousen off yea-rs.' It was the only sentence of her quaint, broken English I was ever able to actually capture) – yes, more than thousands of years ago that the great Tyee of our tribe had two daughters, young, lovable, and oh! very beautiful. They grew to womanhood the same time, and a mighty feast was to be given, such a feast as the Coast had never yet seen. The only shadow on the joy of it all was *war,* for the tribe of the great Tyee was at war with the Upper Coast Indians – those who lived north of what is now named by the white men the Port of Prince Rupert.

'Giant war canoes fretted the entire coast line, war parties paddled their way up and down, war songs broke the silences of the nights, strife, hatred, vengeance festered everywhere, like sores on the surface of the earth. But the great Tyee snatched a week away from bloodshed and battle, for he must make this feast in his daughters' honour, nor permit any mere enemy to come between him and the traditions of his race and household. So he turned deaf ears to their war songs, he ignored their insulting paddle-dips, which encroached within his own coast waters, and he prepared, as a great Tyee should, to celebrate in honour of his daughters.

'But five suns before the feast these two maidens came to him, hand within hand. "Some day we may mother a man-child," they said, "a man-child who may grow to be just such a great Tyee as you are, oh, our father, and for this honour that may some day be ours, we have come to crave a favour of you."

'"What favour, children of mine, and of your mother? It is yours for the asking, this day," he answered.

"Will you, for our sakes, invite the hostile tribe, the tribe you war upon, to our feast?" they asked.

"To a peaceful feast, a feast in the honour of women?" he exclaimed.

"So we would have it," they replied.

"And so shall it be," he declared. "I can deny you nothing this day, and sometime your sons may be born to bless this peace you have asked, and to bless their mothers' sire for giving it."

'Then he turned to the young men of the tribe and said, "Build fires this night on all the coast headlines, fires of welcome. Go forth in your canoes, face the north, and greet the enemy, and tell them that I, the Tyee of the Capilanos, bid them join me for a feast in honour of my two daughters."

'And when the Northern tribes got that invitation they flocked down the coast to this feast of a great Peace. They brought their women and their children, they brought game and fish and o-lil-lie, as gifts. Never was such a Potlatch (a gift feast), never was such joyousness, such long, glad days, such soft, sweet nights. The war canoes were emptied of deadly weapons and filled with the daily catch of salmon. The hostile war songs ceased, and in their place were heard laughter and singing, and the play-games of the children of two tribes which had been until now ancient enemies, and a great and lasting brotherhood was sealed between them. The war songs were ended forever.'

The Klootchman's voice fell very low, and the last words were almost whispered.

'And what of the two sweet daughters of the great Tyee?' I asked, slipping my hand in hers.

'They are there,' she said, pointing to the twin peaks which rose far above us. 'The Great Spirit made them immortal. They will always be there in that high place. Their offspring now rule these tribes, for were not Peace and Brotherhood born of them? And there the two Sisters have stood these thousands of years, and will stand for thousands of years to come, guarding the Peace of the Pacific coast, and the serenity of the Capilano Cañon.'

THE SILVER CRAFT OF THE MOHAWKS:
THE PROTECTIVE TOTEM

The red Indian races have always been workers in metals, and the earliest records show that in their most primitive savagery they compelled the earth as well as the forest to yield them material whereby they might gain a living. Flint arrowheads were the main weapons of bringing down big game for food but these were frequently supplanted by arrowheads of beaten copper. Silver was seldom used except for ornamentation, but so deep a meaning was always attached to the 'white metal,' as many tribes called it, that it finally became of the greatest importance, and ornaments made of it and worn by chiefs and warriors marked their standing and position in the tribe as decidedly as the eagle plume of power, or the string of scalps of conquest.

Since the white man came with his silver coin the Indians have almost ceased to work the virgin metal into totems or ornaments. For two hundred years they have hammered, bent, beaten, and melted the already refined coin to suit their own uses. Certain men among the Mohawks have made a life trade of silver craft. The father works at it until he is an old, old man, his son follows in the same business, and his grandson begins to learn the trade while he is yet a very little boy. One family has worked at it for so many generations that their surname is now legally 'Silversmith.' There is 'Old John' Silversmith, 'Young John' Silversmith and little 'Alick' Silversmith – three generations bearing a name that has been earned honestly and creditably because of splendid workmanship and fine industry.

Among the Mohawks' 'brooches' are the particular ornaments to be manufactured by the slim agile fingers of the silversmiths. Bracelets, head-bands and earrings are worn by men as well as women. But the silver brooch with its unusual fastening is the one thing that must never be omitted from your costume if you make any pretense at all to distinction among your fellow-men. The designs of these brooches are so ancient that they are now of great historical value and a matter of not only family pride but tribal tradition.

The foremost national design of the Mohawk brooches is without question the heart. In almost every one of the scores of curious and beautiful patterns the heart can be traced. If carefully examined, every brooch reveals some suggestion of this heart. Added to this a large percentage of the brooches display the form of an owl, or something that suggests the bird – its eyes, its claws, its 'horns,' the shape of its body – and one of the first lessons an Indian boy who desires to learn silver craft is, to design his own patterns, which, however fantastic he may make them, must reveal a heart or an owl cunningly 'woven' through the bolder pattern. If he can succeed in combining the two, he is regarded as indeed an expert. The Mohawks hold that the heart means the strength of life of all races and nations, but the owl belongs to their own particular people. It is the guardian of their council fires; it watches over the smouldering embers through the night hours, for its extraordinary eyes see better in the dark than in the daylight; and it wards evil and strife and meanness from approaching the great affairs of the nation. It protects the lawmakers from thinking of themselves instead of the people, it guards the counselors from doing things for their own personal benefit instead of for the lasting good of the nation. Its keen sight can discover evil coming out of the dark, and it stands between that evil and the chiefs and braves and warriors, so that the council fire may always burn in a clear, clean, sinless, pure flame.

It is called the 'Protective Totem,' or the 'Guardian Owl.' Our illustration [No. 1] gives one of the most ancient designs of silver brooches. It is called the 'Wolf of the Council Fire,' the Wolf 'Clan' and Totem being the most aristocratic in the Mohawk tribe. In dissecting this brooch one can unearth many a 'buried treasure.' The space in the centre represents the Council Fire, the bars immediately enclosing it stand for the fire-keepers, the outside bars are the chiefs, and the edges of semicircles, or scallops indicate the braves and warriors arrayed in war paint ready to do and die in defense of their ancient government. In Illustration No. 2 a suggestion of the wolf's head can be seen. No. 3 shows the horned owl; the centre of the owl's breast. where its heart is supposed to

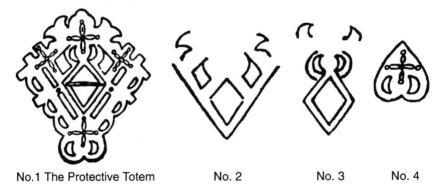

No.1 The Protective Totem   No. 2   No. 3   No. 4

be, is also the exact position of the Council Fire. The owl's ever watchful eyes peer out immediately above it. The whole is based on an inverted heart (No. 4). If the reader will cut out these drawings he will find they fit exactly one over the other, yet with all its apparent simplicity the brooch is teeming with design and meaning. The identical brooch from which the writer made these sketches was beaten from coin many years before the American Revolution, when the Mohawks lived in the Mohawk Valley in New York State. In that war they sided with the Mother Country, and fought for King George against the Colonists. During these stormy years the Mohawks, following the custom of their ancestors, buried their treasure for safe-keeping. Pounds and pounds of these solid silver brooches were hidden in the earth near Niagara Falls, and when the United States declared their Independence, these red-skinned loyalists exhumed their valuables and brought them into Canada, which was still the king's domain, and where immense grants of lands were given them as a reward for adhering to 'The Crown.' This brooch was one of the 'buried' many which the Mohawks treasure to-day as other natives treasure jewels. Perhaps the most beautiful thing about this particular brooch is the fact that a boy need not wait to grow up into a warrior before he can have the right to make or wear it. He has not got to be the son of a chief, or to win his eagle plume, or to be known as a mighty hunter, before he pins this significant emblem on his buckskin shirt or his soft turban. He may be young, poor, unsuccessful, untitled, but with Mohawk blood in his veins he has as much right to wear this great national badge as has the most powerful chief of his tribe.

FROM THE CHILD'S VIEWPOINT

In Two Chapters

Chapter I

There are people who hold that the mother's teaching will have a lasting influence upon the entire after life of a child. How, then, must we account for a family of, say, six children, all reared in the same environment, all taught the same codes of Christian morals and civilized etiquette, and with the same educational advantages, producing five worthy citizens and one black sheep? It is an odd thing, but invariably the black sheep shows his blackness from his very babyhood. His mother's influence, which has been exerted over him with just as much love and earnestness as upon his brothers and sisters, has either never taken root, or has slipped from his life as a bird moults its feathers. We must, therefore, conclude that his individual oddities have never been studied; that he has been praised or punished in precisely the same way as have the other five in the family, with little regard to the fact that he is somebody apart and must be handled differently. Fortunately my mother bore no 'black sheep,' but this system of training her family of four in exactly the same fashion, regardless of their various dispositions, was something that I must acknowledge that she did. But it was an excellent training nevertheless; and, after years of life before the public, years of homelessness, of living in hotels, and drifting from ocean to ocean many times, I am sometimes amazed to feel the potent influence of my mother's teaching, astonished to find the habits she formed in me *still* habits, although my life is as different from hers, my present as opposite in every detail from my childhood's past, as midnight from high noon.

I often wonder why a mother seems to forget her own lost babyhood, and her feelings and impressions as a child. Does Nature provide her with some subtle veil that hangs between her and her lost infancy? Perhaps it was because my mother's childhood was an unhappy one that *she* never forgot her early years, and used to manage her own children from the standpoint of her sad recollections of her girlhood.

She was abnormally sensitive, prone to melancholy or extreme jollity, and, according to her own statement, was high tempered; but I can never recollect having seen her more than 'irritated' or 'annoyed.' She had conquered her temper very early in life – completely subdued it. Early, too, in our infancy she looked for those traits in us, expected them, recognized them and grappled with them. I can remember once going to her as a very little child of four, or perhaps five, and saying, desolately, 'Mamma, I feel as if I have no friends in the world; as if I was forgotten.' I know now how that remark, which had its birth in prenatal melancholy, must have distressed her, but she only laughed, and said, 'I know what will bring back the friends; run hard from the hall down to the barn gate six times, and take Rover with you.' Poor little mother! She stood on the step and counted the 'runs'! 'No, no! That is only five times! Once more, dear!' And I raced up and down, my dog barking and dancing at my heels, once again, then dropped, laughing and breathless, at her feet, my little legs too tired for my little heart to remember its 'blues.' 'Oh, mamma, my friends are all back again!' I laughed. 'Of course,' she replied. 'A good romp with Rover will always bring them back.' It was my first lesson in conquering self by means of substituting action.

But an inherited sensitiveness was a perfect bane in our childhood. We were all shy, which mother conquered in us by having us assume a dignity far beyond our years. We learned from her to disguise our wretched bashfulness with a peculiar, cold reserve, that made our schoolfellows call us 'stuck-up,' and our neighbours' children mock us as 'proudy,' but it saw us through the exigencies of life, and serves me to this very day. A long public career has never lessened this inherited shyness, but the mask of reserve and dignity learned from my mother has stood me in excellent stead.

But, as sensitive children, we never could tolerate teasing, and, worse yet, we are not good at taking it even as grown-ups. I often wish my mother had instilled into us some sense of humour. I have learned the blessing of humour through a hard school. Had it been taught me from the cradle, I would have been better armed for life's battle. I wish every mother would teach her children that the tragedies of childish disappointments of school days, of facing the world, are often merely pranks played by circumstance or fortune; that, looked at in the right light, they are only things to be laughed at and forgotten. The wounds would be less deep, and, in many instances, the scars would be effaced altogether. Humour, laughter, joys, they are splendid weapons, but I fought for these swords and guns, and it took me years to win them.

I think the strongest habit formed by my mother's teaching which I have retained is an abhorrence of wasting food. We were never allowed to be fastidious as children. The slice of bread or cake, the apple or orange nearest us in the dish, was the one we must take. It would have been an unforgivable breach of etiquette for us to reach beyond the adjacent slices to secure a brown crust if we wanted it, and even yet it causes me annoyance when I see children eyeing dishes of celery or plates of cookies, then selecting the best, with never a reproof from their mother. We had many poor people about us, and mother often used to say, 'If you want to throw your pocket money away, do so; even your ribbons, if you would prefer to go without them; but food must never be wasted while others are hungry.'

I have lived in hotels for sixteen years, and I cannot yet find it in my heart to order a single dish that I do not eat; a slice of buttered toast wasted, that I cannot eat, hurts me as much as if I saw little, starving faces looking at me, and little, blue lips saying, 'Give it to me; I am so hungry.'

I remember spending a delightful afternoon with Max O'Rell in Montreal, and, in the course of conversation, he remarked, 'Oh, this America, this Canada! It is appalling! The waste of food! Your fashionable men and women go into a hotel dining-room and order salads and baked meats and rissoles. They know they cannot eat them all; they nibble, just nibble a little at each, and leave it, while outside there are hungry children. No one does that in France, not even the most wealthy.' Then I told him of my mother's training, and he said, 'And you will never forget it; you will never waste food.' And I never have.

The next strongest habit retained from mother's inculcating is a horror of idleness. When I was little, my father being considered 'well off,' we always had plenty of servants for our simple country needs – an Indian nurse, a white cook, and a stableman. As we had also a governess, school hours started at half-past nine. Between that time and the breakfast hour there was a period of perhaps thirty minutes wherein mother insisted that the boys should bring in wood and kindling for the cook's use, and we girls should do some simple bit of household work. My sister's duty was to clean the lamps, my own to sweep the stairs. How endless those stairs were! I can count them yet – nineteen horrors, with mahogany coloured velvet carpet, so difficult to dust, a strip of linen in the centre, so gloriously easy to slide over, and broad, polished brass rods, perfect demons for holding the 'fluff' from the velvet. With my dustpan and whisk broom, I would toil halfway down the endless flight, then sit amidships with woebegone face, and wonder why Milly the nurse, or Jane the cook, or even mother herself, could not do this labour. Then I would hear a voice calling, 'Come, chicken, mamma knows you have only half finished; work away like a little woman; school will begin in ten minutes.' Then I would get to my stiff little legs again, and reattack those stairs that stretched down behind me with infinite length. I must admit that I have thoroughly hated dusting down stairs ever since, but I know the work rendered me more capable in after years, more considerate of servants, for mother's excuse in making us do the work was, 'It is something whereby you can help Milly and Jane.' On the same principle, I was never allowed to throw threads or scraps on the floor, as 'it gives so much work to Jane.' Perhaps it was mother's way of making me tidy; but at all events, to this day I always leave a hotel room just as I find it, so far as scraps, papers, etc., are concerned. It costs me no effort, thanks to mother's consideration for her own maids. Next to these and other habits formed in extreme youth, I think the likes and dislikes engendered by mother's teaching have remained longest and strongest in my tastes of to-day. In my childhood's home not a coarse or vulgar word was ever allowed to be spoken, no story of questionable colour was ever told or repeated. I have frequently heard my mother say that, in all her married life, our father never made a single remark or spoke the smallest word to her that he could not have uttered in a room-ful of ladies and gentlemen. This hatred of vulgarity, taught me very early by both my parents, has never lessened. I think, in fact, it strengthens with the years. When I was sent to a public school in a distant city, the only admonition my mother gave me was, 'Never allow the girls to talk of vulgar things in your presence.' I attended the school for three years, and I think it speaks pretty well for the scholars in that Canadian school when I say that, during all that time, I never heard one remark that I felt like resenting from the standard of my mother's teaching. There was one 'coarse' girl – coarse in habit, speech, using distressingly 'low' phrases and words – but she only shocked our ears, not our modesty. I have read columns in recent years about the impurity in speech and action in public schools to-day, but I never saw or heard a hint of it in my own school days. Some people to whom I have told the above, argue that, owing to my guarded home life and upbringing, I could not have recognized the depravity even when it revealed itself in the school; but I disagree with them, for even children who are carefully reared have human instincts and intuitions that would discern the venom of the serpent of depravity. I do not think the rattle of that snake would have escaped me, unharmed and babyishly ignorant as I was, for I was sent away to school at the age of fourteen, a perfect know-nothing so far as the world was concerned. But of this matter I shall speak further in chapter two.

Other and minor customs learned at my mother's knees I frequently become aware that I am yet following, almost unconsciously. As children we were not allowed candy, with the exception of five 'sugar sticks' at Christmas, and five on the Queen's Birthday. Those five were divided among four of us. Each had one stick, and the following day, to ease this dissipation, the remaining stick was broken into four equal pieces and distributed accordingly. I have never yet formed the 'candy habit.' Even as a schoolgirl I never spent my pocket money in sweets. I can recall purchasing chocolates but once as a girl, and have never touched candies at dinner parties, entertainments, or where other girls are 'treating' or making them at home, except upon rare occasions when politeness absolutely demanded it. My parents were both 'teeth cranks,' consequently we four possess teeth that are marvels to every dentist who sees them.

Chapter II

I remember once, some years ago, when a young friend of mine, a boy of eighteen, was going to New York on a newspaper assignment, I was having a grave little talk with him before he said good-by.

'I shall try and avoid the pitfalls,' he said, earnestly.

'But,' I urged, anxiously, 'one hardly knows how much a boy of your age has learned about pitfalls.'

He looked very directly at me. I shall never forget the clarity of his eyes. 'Don't be anxious. I have had a good father,' he replied, simply.

Then I knew that his father was one of the few who had forestalled outside knowledge coming to his boy, who had done his duty, who was, in fact, a real father. And now I arrive at the vexed question as to how much the modern mother imparts to her young daughter of the knowledge of things that must inevitably be learned, either within the home or outside its loving doors. Innumerable periodicals and papers are crying out for the daughter to learn what concerns her own self, sex, and probability of marriage and motherhood, from her own mother's lips. I cannot possibly imagine my mother imparting to me one iota of information that could not be given in the presence of my father and brothers. Her naturally shrinking nature would have made it a torture and an agony to speak of the essentially untalked-of things, even to her daughters. Since I have been out in the world, I frequently wonder if this temperamental delicacy of hers ever reproached her; if she ever really struggled against the seal that shyness placed on her lips. I once heard her say to a woman who was rather free of speech:

'You are quite right; I don't think I enjoy the company of married ladies – always. They are so apt to talk of things that single women taboo.'

The remark was a little keynote to her disposition that nothing else can ever strike. I believe in my heart that she found it *impossible* to 'enlighten' her girls, so she buried her failure to do so beneath a peculiar training that has served us in place of aural knowledge. She began, as she did in all things, with our earliest infancy. As the tiniest toddler, I was taught to shake hands gravely with both men and boys. Only elderly men friends of my father's were ever allowed to toss me up in the air and kiss me or ride me on their shoulders. 'My little girl does not kiss gentlemen; she does not care to,' mother would say, laughingly, to would-be playfellows who were visiting at our home when I was yet too small to really distinguish men from women guests. Kissing games were never tolerated – in fact, were positively forbidden – and I was always admonished with the statement that any boy who tried to kiss me was paying me anything but a compliment – in truth, was offering me an insult by his freedom. The summer I was eight years old some jolly schoolboys and girls from the city came to spend the holidays with their aunt, a neighbour of ours. One day, while we were all romping together, a laughing-eyed boy of nine or ten suddenly developed a teasing tendency. 'I'll kiss all you girls and make you cry!' he shouted, waving his arms like a windmill, and rushing toward the biggest girl, who took to her heels, screaming with laughter, and calling back:

'Georgie, peorgie, pudding and pie.
Kiss the girls and make them cry.'

Of course he caught her, kissing her a half-dozen times; then he chased and captured several others, and finally made a rush for where I stood, my little back fortified against a tree trunk, my face sullen and sulky. 'Run; he'll catch you,' shouted the others, but I never stirred, only stood and glowered at him, and, with all the indignation my eight years could muster, I shouted at him, 'Don't you dare insult me, sir!' The 'sir' was added to chill him, and it did. He left me alone. My mother's substitute for imparting 'worldly' knowledge had begun to tell at a very early age.

As I grew older, mother's insistent 'Never under any circumstances allow a gentleman to take liberties with you; never allow him to lay a finger on your hand. It is only ill-bred girls that allow boys to touch them. It is not aristocratic' was oft repeated. I was never given any other reason for keeping myself to myself; never told that these 'liberties' may result in evil; in fact, did not know what 'evil' was. It was this fear, I think, that any man or boy might regard me as 'plebeian,' rather than any knowledge of the thin edge of vice, that made me follow her teaching when I left home, for I was sent to a public school ten miles away, and lived in a city boarding-house with five men law students, clerks, etc., and an old gentleman and his three unmarried daughters, who were friends of my parents. I was sent out into the city world without the slightest knowledge of life or evil, of sin or danger. I knew as little as a baby. My mother knew I had every evening to myself, every day after four o'clock, that young men boarded in the same house; but the one coat-of-mail which she clasped about me when she left me in the city was, 'Allow no liberties; it is not aristocratic.' Consequently, I was a very lonely, isolated girl of fourteen, away from home for the first time, for I carried this creed with me

as far as women were concerned as well as men, and even women don't
care for a chilling, haughty, reserved young miss, who is continually on
the lookout to snub them for approaching intimacy. Since I have known
our world better, I often wonder how mother dared let me go in my
childishness and ignorance, but she did, and I remained the same 'aris-
tocrat' that her prayers were doubtless begging of God that I should be.

This horror of being regarded as 'plebeian,' grew with the years into a
second nature. Mother must have known it would, but with still greater
guardianship, she always conducted our conversation away from senti-
mentality as far as the opposite sex was concerned. As children and
young ladies we were not permitted to talk of 'beaux,' 'fellows,''spoon-
ing,' etc.; and when young gentlemen began coming to the house to see
us, we were expected to have music, or chess, or checkers, or perhaps to
show them the grounds, the views, the grape arbours, etc., but there was
no 'mooning' about in hammocks or stealing away into remote corners.
We had every liberty at home and no restrictions; we could go riding on
horseback, or canoeing alone with gentlemen, but there seemed some
subtle, unvoiced limitation hedging us in – the peculiar shyness that
shrank from 'lovemaking.' Marriage, for us, either boys or girls, mother
never talked of. I think the greatest annoyance I ever saw her give way to
was once, when the family doctor was paying a social visit to our house,
and began, after his usual habit, to talk to us girls about marriage.
Mother interrupted quite fretfully, 'Doctor, you never step into this
house but you begin that foolish topic. You seem never to talk of any-
thing but love and marriage, love and marriage.' So it may well be seen
that mother was no 'managing, match-making mamma.'

After we four were well grown up and advancing along slowly into the
years, my eldest brother said to me, one day, that mother had been at
fault in this one thing: that she should have talked to us of the nobility,
the beauty of love, the honour of marriage, instead of choking our
human tendency, which occasionally drifted toward the world-old incli-
nations. I exclaimed, with horror, that it was almost sacrilege to think
mother at fault in anything, and he replied, gravely, 'I know; it seems so,
but mother never encouraged the thought of marriage in any of us. The
chances are that, when she goes from us, we will all be waifs and strays. I
wish she had not regarded talking of love and sweethearts as "foolish."
We should all probably have married, which is far the better thing for
men and women in this world.'

This brother died at the age of forty, unmarried. My surviving
brother, sister and myself are all unmarried, living homeless lives in

hotels and boarding-houses. Each of us is alone, for our various pursuits in life necessitate our going far afield. Was mother at fault in this one particular? I do not know, but I think her dislike of 'sentimental' talk was merely the outcome of her way of keeping us from evil while young, for she always held the opinion that, to talk of things, either good or detrimental, was only accustoming the ear to that which the conscience or the habit of a person would afterwards follow or adopt. Oft-repeated sentiments are apt to lose their horror, and I think she had the idea that, if we talked much of love and marriage, we would drift unconsciously into 'love sick' girls, or worse still, 'beau hunters.'

Perhaps much of the foregoing will not be read with approval by some mothers, whose methods of bringing up their children differ widely and radically from these few hints of my mother's system, but I am writing this from a daughter's standpoint, and I recognize more clearly every day that the things which are helping me out in the world are the things I learned almost in the cradle.

The only thing I ever acquired apart from my mother's teaching, that I have found helpful, is Humour, but I have touched upon that before. One helpful thing I have been most grateful for is the fact that the instant we were spoken to, or called, we must not allow one second to elapse before jumping to perform the service. 'Wait a minute' was a forbidden reply, even to our brothers and sisters. Instantaneous obedience came to us as naturally as breathing. I now find not the slightest difficulty in dropping on the second any occupation I may be at, and doing whatever service is required of me. The habit has remained all through my life, and where others must be taken into consideration, it prevents endless friction – and, in eliminating friction from our daily life, we have practically ousted the serpent from Eden. But there are scores of minor things which influence my present life that I cannot touch upon in the space of these brief papers. Such simple things as changing one's entire dress before the evening meal, which I was made to do in childhood, of having my underwear fresh and in the pink of condition at all times, of personal tidiness, of the care of books, of returning borrowed articles, of giving up my place to others rather than 'fight for my rights' – these things are all strong habits even now. Some people will not agree with this last. It is an age of 'sticking up for one's self,' but mother's philosophy was, 'If I lose my place by the selfish crowding of others, I at least have the higher satisfaction of knowing that I have not been the selfish one.'

All these things have been untold mainstays in my life. I have never drifted very far from any of them, for they are my mother's teachings, I have found that they are good, and I would not exchange those principles that she imparted in my baby soul for anything that the world can give.

THE SIWASH ROCK

Unique, and so distinct from its surroundings as to suggest rather the handicraft of man than a whim of Nature, it looms up at the entrance to the Narrows, a symmetrical column of solid grey stone. There are no similar formations within the range of vision, or indeed within many a day's paddle up and down the coast. Amongst all the wonders, the natural beauties that encircle Vancouver, the marvels of mountains, shaped into crouching lions and brooding beavers, the yawning canyons, the stupendous forest firs and cedars, Siwash Rock stands as distinct, as individual, as if dropped from another sphere.

I saw it first in the slanting light of a redly setting August sun; the little tuft of green shrubbery that crests its summit was black against the crimson of sea and sky, and its colossal base of grey stone gleamed like flaming polished granite.

My old tillicum lifted his paddle-blade to point towards it. 'You know the story?' he asked. I shook my head (experience has taught me his love of silent replies, his moods of legend-telling). For a time we paddled slowly; the rock detached itself from its background of forest and shore, and it stood forth like a sentinel – erect, enduring, eternal.

'Do you think it stands straight – like a man?' he asked.

'Yes, like some noble-spirited, upright warrior,' I replied.

'It is a man,' he said, 'and a warrior man, too; a man who fought for everything that was noble and upright.'

'What do you regard as everything that is noble and upright, Chief?' I asked, curious as to his ideas. I shall not forget his reply; it was but two words – astounding, amazing words. He said simply:

'Clean fatherhood.'

Through my mind raced tumultuous recollections of numberless articles in yet numberless magazines, all dealing with the recent 'fad' of motherhood, but I had to hear from the lips of a Squamish Indian chief the only treatise on the nobility of 'clean fatherhood' that I have yet unearthed. And this treatise has been an Indian legend for centuries; and, lest they forget how all-important these two little words must ever be, Siwash Rock stands to remind them, set there by the Deity as a monument to one who kept his own life clean, that cleanliness might be the heritage of the generations to come.

It was 'thousands of years ago' (all Indian legends begin in extremely remote times) that a handsome boy chief journeyed in his canoe to the upper coast for the shy little northern girl whom he brought home as his wife. Boy though he was, the young chief had proved himself to be an excellent warrior, a fearless hunter, and an upright, courageous man among men. His tribe loved him, his enemies respected him, and the base and mean and cowardly feared him.

The customs and traditions of his ancestors were a positive religion to him, the sayings and the advices of the old people were his creed. He was conservative in every rite and ritual of his race. He fought his tribal enemies like the savage that he was. He sang his war songs, danced his war dances, slew his foes, but the little girl-wife from the north he treated with the deference that he gave his own mother, for was she not to be the mother of his warrior son?

The year rolled around, weeks merged into months, winter into spring, and one glorious summer at daybreak he wakened to her voice calling him. She stood beside him, smiling.

'It will be to-day,' she said proudly.

He sprang from his couch of wolf-skins and looked out upon the coming day; the promise of what it would bring him seemed breathing through all his forest world. He took her very gently by the hand and led her through the tangle of wilderness down to the water's edge, where the beauty spot we moderns call Stanley Park bends about Prospect Point – 'I must swim,' he told her.

'I must swim, too,' she smiled, with the perfect understanding of two beings who are mated. For, to them, the old Indian custom was law – the custom that the parents of a coming child must swim until their flesh is so clear and clean that a wild animal cannot scent their proximity. If the wild creatures of the forests have no fear of them, then, and only then, are they fit to become parents, and to scent a human is in itself a fearsome thing to all wild creatures.

So those two plunged into the waters of the Narrows as the grey dawn slipped up the eastern skies and all the forest awoke to the life of a new, glad day. Presently he took her ashore, and smilingly she crept away under the giant trees. 'I must be alone,' she said, 'but come to me at sunrise: you will not find me alone then.' He smiled also, and plunged back into the sea. He must swim, swim, swim through this hour when his fatherhood was coming upon him. It was the law that he must be clean, spotlessly clean, so that when his child looked out upon the world it would have the chance to live its own life clean. If he did not swim hour upon hour his child would come to an unclean father. He must give his child a chance in life; he must not hamper it by his own uncleanliness at its birth. It was the tribal law – the law of vicarious purity.

As he swam joyously to and fro, a canoe bearing four men headed up the Narrows. These men were giants in stature, and the stroke of their paddles made huge eddies that boiled like the seething tides.

'Out from our course!' they cried as his lithe, copper-coloured body arose and fell with his splendid stroke. He laughed at them, giants though they were, and answered that he could not cease his swimming at their demand.

'But you shall cease!' they commanded. 'We are the men of the Sagalie Tyee, and we command you ashore out of our way!' (I find in all these Coast Indian legends that the Deity is represented by four men, usually paddling an immense canoe.)

He ceased swimming, and, lifting his head, defied them. 'I shall not stop, nor yet go ashore,' he declared, striking out once more to the middle of the channel.

'Do you dare disobey us,' they cried – 'we, the men of the Sagalie Tyee? We can turn you into a fish, or a tree, or a stone for this; do you dare disobey the Great Tyee?'

'I dare anything for the cleanliness and purity of my coming child. I dare even the Sagalie Tyee Himself, but my child must be born to a spotless life.'

The four men were astounded. They consulted together, lighted their pipes, and sat in council. Never had they, the men of the Sagalie Tyee, been defied before. Now, for the sake of a little unborn child, they were ignored, disobeyed, almost despised. The lithe young copper-coloured body still disported itself in the cool waters; superstition held that should their canoe, or even their paddle-blades, touch a human being, their marvellous power would be lost. The handsome young chief swam directly in their course. They dared not run him down; if so, they would become as other men. While they yet counselled what to do, there floated from out the forest a faint, strange, compelling sound. They listened, and the young chief ceased his stroke as he listened also. The faint sound drifted out across the waters once more. It was the cry of a little, little child. Then one of the four men, he that steered the canoe, the strongest and tallest of them all, arose, and, standing erect, stretched out his arms towards the rising sun and chanted, not a curse on the young chief's disobedience, but a promise of everlasting days and freedom from death.

'Because you have defied all things that come in your path we promise this to you,' he chanted: 'you have defied what interferes with your child's chance for a clean life, you have lived as you wish your son to live, you have defied us when we would have stopped your swimming and hampered your child's future. You have placed that child's future before all things, and for this the Sagalie Tyee commands us to make you forever a pattern for your tribe. You shall never die, but you shall stand through all the thousands of years to come, where all eyes can see you. You shall live, live as an indestructible monument to Clean Fatherhood.'

The four men lifted their paddles and the handsome young chief swam inshore; as his feet touched the line where sea and land met he was transformed into stone.

Then the four men said, 'His wife and child must ever be near him; they shall not die, but live also.'

And they, too, were turned into stone. If you penetrate the hollows in the woods near Siwash Rock you will find a large rock and a smaller one beside it. They are the shy little bridewife from the north, with her hour-old baby beside her. And from the uttermost parts of the world vessels come daily throbbing and sailing up the Narrows. From far trans-Pacific ports, from the frozen North, from the lands of the Southern Cross, they pass and repass the living rock that was there before their hulls were shaped, that will be there when their very names are forgotten, when their crews and their captains have taken their long last voyage, when their merchandise has rotted, and their owners are known no more. But the tall, grey column of stone will still be there – a monument to one man's fidelity to a generation yet unborn – and will endure from everlasting to everlasting.

THE POTLATCH*

Young Ta-la-pus sat on the highest point of rock that lifted itself on the coast at the edge of his father's Reserve. At his feet stretched the Straits of Georgia, and far across the mists of the salt Pacific waters he watched the sun rise seemingly out of the mainland that someone had told him stretched eastward thousands of miles, where another ocean, called the Atlantic, washed its far-off shore, for Ta-la-pus lived on Vancouver Island, and all his little life had been spent in wishing and longing to set his small, moccasined feet on that vast mainland that the old men talked of, and the young men visited year in and year out. But never yet had he been taken across the wide, blue Straits, for he was only eleven years old, and he had two very big brothers who always accompanied their father, old chief Mowitch, on his journeyings, for they were good fishermen, and could help in the salmon catch, and bring good *chicamin* (money) home to buy supplies for the winter. Sometimes these big brothers would tease him and say, 'What can you expect? Your name is Ta-la-pus, which means a prairie wolf. What has a prairie wolf to do with crossing great waters? He cannot swim, as some other animals can. Our parents gave us better names, "Chet-woot," the bear, who swims well, and "Lapool," the water fowl, whose home is on the waters, whose feet are webbed, and who floats even while he sleeps. No, our young brother, Ta-la-pus, the prairie wolf, was never meant to cross the great salt Straits.'

Then little Ta-la-pus would creep away to his lonely rock, trying to still the ache in his heart, and forcing back the tears from his eyes. Prairie wolves must not cry like little girl babies – and sometimes when his heart was sorest, a clear, dazzlingly bright day would dawn, and far, far off he could see the blur of the mainland coast, resting on the sea like an enormous island. Then he would tell himself that, no matter what his name was, some day he would cross to that great, far country, whose snow-

---

* 'Potlatch' is a Chinook word meaning 'a gift.' Among the Indian tribes of British
  Columbia it is used as the accepted name of a great feast which some Indian, who is
  exceedingly well off, gives to scores of guests. He entertains them for days, sometimes
  weeks, together, presenting them with innumerable blankets and much money, for it is
  part of the Indian code of honour that, when one has great possessions, he must divide
  them with his less fortunate tribesmen. The gifts of money usually take the form of
  ten-dollar bank notes, and are bestowed broadcast upon any man, woman or child who
  pleases the host by either dancing the tribal dances very beautifully, or else originates an
  attractive dance of their own [Johnson's note].

crowned mountain peaks he could just see merging into the distant clouds.

Then, late in the summer, there came one marvellous night, when his father and brothers returned from the sock-eye salmon fishing, with news that set the entire Indian village talking far into the early morning. A great Squamish chief on the mainland was going to give a Potlatch. He had been preparing for it for weeks. He had enjoyed a very fortunate fishing season, was a generous-hearted man, and was prepared to spend ten thousand dollars[1] in gifts and entertainment for his friends and all the poor of the various neighbouring tribes.

Chief Mowitch and all his family were invited, and great rejoicing and anticipation were enjoyed over their salmon suppers that night.

'You and the boys go,' said his wife. 'Perhaps you will be lucky and bring home *chicamin* and blankets. The old men say the winter will be cold. Grey geese were going south yesterday, three weeks earlier than last year. Yes, we will need blankets when the *ollallies* (berries) are ripe in October. I shall stay at home, until the babies are older. Yes, you and the boys go.'

'Yes,' responded the chief. "It would never do for us to miss a great Squamish Potlatch. We must go.'

Then the elder son, Chet-woot, spoke joyously:

'And, mama,[2] we may bring back great riches, and even if the cold does come while we are away, our little brother Ta-la-pus, will care for you and the babies. He'll carry water and bring all the wood for your warmth.'

The father looked smilingly at Ta-la-pus, but the boy's eyes, great and dark, and hungry for the far mainland, for the great feasts he had heard so much of, were fastened in begging, pleading seriousness on his father's face. Suddenly a whim seized the old chief's fancy.

'Ta-la-pus,' he said, 'you look as if you would like to go too. Do you want to take part in the Potlatch?'

Instantly Chet-woot objected. 'Papa, he could never go, he's too young. They may ask him to dance for them. He can't dance. Then perhaps they would never ask us."

The chief scowled. He was ruler in his own lodge, and allowed no interference from anyone.

---

1 Fact. This amount has frequently been given away [Johnson's note].

2 The Chinook for father and mother is 'papa' and 'mama,' adopted from the English language [Johnson's note].

'Besides,' continued Chet-woot, 'there would be no one to fetch wood for mama and the babies.'

'Yes, there would be someone,' said the chief, his eyes snapping fiercely. '*You* would be here to help your mama.'

'I,' exclaimed the young man. 'But how can I, when I shall be at the Potlatch? I go to *all* the Potlatches.'

'So much more reason that you stay home this once and care for your mama and baby sisters, and you *shall* stay. Lapool and little Ta-la-pus will go with me. It is time the boy saw something of the other tribes. Yes, I'll take Lapool and Ta-la-pus, and there is no change to my word when it is once spoken.'

Chet-woot sat like one stunned, but an Indian son knows better than to argue with his father. But the great, dark eyes of little Ta-la-pus glowed like embers of fire, his young heart leaped joyously. At last, at last, he was to set foot in the country of his dreams – the far, blue, mountain-circled mainland.

All that week his mother worked day and night on a fine new native costume for him to wear on the great occasion. There were trousers of buckskin fringed down each side, a shirt of buckskin, beaded and beautified by shell ornaments, a necklace of the bones of a rare fish, strung together like little beads on deer sinew, earrings of pink and green pearl from the inner part of the shells of a bivalve, neat moccasins, and solid silver, carven bracelets.

She was working on a headdress, consisting of a single red fox-tail and eagle feathers, when he came and stood beside her.

'Mama,' he said, 'there is a prairie wolf skin you cover the babies with while they sleep. Would you let me have it this once, if they would not be cold without it?'

'They will never be cold,' she smiled, 'for I can use an extra blanket over them. I only use it because I started to when you were the only baby I had, and it was your name, so I covered you with it at night.'

'And I want to cover myself with it now,' he explained, 'its head as my headdress, its front paws about my neck, its thick fur and tail trailing behind me as I dance.'

'So you are going to dance, my little Ta-la-pus?' she answered proudly. 'But how is that, when you do not yet know our great tribal dances?'

'I have made one of my own, and a song, too,' he said, shyly.

She caught him to her, smoothing the hair back from his dark forehead. 'That is right,' she half whispered, for she felt he did not want anyone but herself to know his boyish secret. 'Always make things for yourself, don't depend on others, try what you can do alone. Yes, you may take the skin of the prairie wolf. I will give it to you for all time – it is yours.'

That night his father also laid in his hands a gift. It was a soft, pliable belt, woven of the white, peeled roots of the cedar, dyed brilliantly, and worked into a magnificent design.

'Your great-grandmother made it,' said the chief. 'Wear it on your first journey into the larger world than this island, and do nothing in all your life that would make her regret, were she alive, to see it round your waist.'

So little Ta-la-pus set forth with his father and brother, well equipped for the great Potlatch, and the meeting of many from half a score of tribes.

They crossed the Straits on a white man's steamer, a wonderful sight to Ta-la-pus, who had never been aboard any larger boat than his father's fishing smack and their own high-bowed, gracefully-curved canoe. In and out among the islands of the great gulf the steamer wound, bringing them nearer, ever nearer to the mainland. Misty and shadowy, Vancouver Island dropped astern, until at last they steamed into harbour, where a crowd of happy-faced Squamish Indians greeted them, stowed them away in canoes, paddled a bit up coast, then sighted the great, glancing fires that were lighting up the grey of oncoming night – fires of celebration and welcome to all the scores of guests who were to partake of the lavish hospitality of the great Squamish chief.

As he stepped from the great canoe, Ta-la-pus thought he felt a strange thrill pass through the soles of his feet. They had touched the mainland of the vast continent of North America for the first time; his feet seemed to become sensitive, soft, furry, cushioned like those of a wild animal. Then, all at once, a strange inspiration seized him. Why not try to make his footsteps 'pad' like the noiseless paws of a prairie wolf? 'pad' in the little dance he had invented, instead of 'shuffling' in his moccasins, as all the grown men did? He made up his mind that when he was alone in his tent he would practise it, but just now the great Squamish chief was coming towards them with outstretched greeting hands, and presently he was patting little Ta-la-pus on the shoulder, and saying, 'Oh, ho, my good Tillicum Mowitch, I am glad you have brought this boy. I have a son of the same size. They will play together, and perhaps this Tenas Tyee (Little Chief) will dance for me some night.'

'My brother does not dance our tribal dances,' began Lapool, but Ta-la-pus spoke up bravely.

'Thank you, O Great Tyee (Chief), I shall dance when you ask me.'

His father and brother both stared at him in amazement. Then Chief Mowitch laughed, and said, 'If he says he will dance, he will do it. He never promises what he cannot do, but I did not know he could do the steps. Ah! he is a little *hoolool* (mouse), this boy of mine; he keeps very quiet, and does not boast what he can do.'

Little Ta-la-pus was wonderfully encouraged by his father's notice of him and his words of praise. Never before had he seemed so close to manhood, for, being the youngest boy of the family, he had but little companionship with any at home except his mother and the little sisters that now seemed so far behind him in their island home. All that evening the old chiefs and the stalwart young braves were gravely shaking hands with his father, his brother Lapool, and himself, welcoming them to the great festival and saying pleasant things about peace and brotherhood prevailing between the various tribes instead of war and bloodshed, as in the olden times. It was late when the great supper of boiled salmon was over, and the immense bonfires began to blaze on the shore where the falling tides of the Pacific left the beaches dry and pebbly. The young men stretched themselves on the cool sands, and the old men lighted their peace pipes, and talked of the days when they hunted the mountain sheep and black bear on these very heights overlooking the sea. Ta-la-pus listened to everything. He could learn so much from the older men, and hour by hour he gained confidence. No more he thought of his dance with fear and shyness, for all these people were kindly and hospitable even to a boy of eleven. At midnight there was another feast, this time of clams, and luscious crabs, with much steaming black tea. Then came the great Squamish chief, saying more welcoming words, and inviting his guests to begin their tribal dances. Ta-la-pus never forgot the brilliant sight that he looked on for the next few hours. Scores of young men and women went through the most graceful figures of beautiful dances, their shell ornaments jingling merrily in perfect time to each twist and turn of their bodies. The wild music from the beat of Indian drums and shell rattles arose weirdly, half sadly, drifting up the mountain heights, until it lost itself in the timber line of giant firs that crested the summits. The red blaze from the camp fires flitted and flickered across the supple figures that circled around, in and out between the three hundred canoes beached on the sands, and the smoke-tipped tents and log lodges beyond the reach of tide water. Above it all a million stars shone down from the cloudless heavens of a perfect British Columbian night. After a while little Ta-la-pus fell asleep, and when he awoke, dawn was just breaking. Someone had covered him with a beautiful, white, new blanket, and as his young eyes opened they looked straight into the kindly face of the great Squamish chief.

'We are all aweary, Tenas Tyee, (Little Chief),' he said. 'The dancers are tired, and we shall all sleep until the sun reaches midday, but my guests cry for one more dance before sunrise. Will you dance for us, oh, little Ta-la-pus?'

The boy sprang up, every muscle and sinew and nerve on the alert. The moment of his triumph or failure had come.

'You have made me, even a boy like me, very welcome, O Great Tyee,' he said, standing erect as an arrow, with his slender, dark chin raised manfully. 'I have eaten of your *kloshe muck-a-muck* (very good food), and it has made my heart and my feet very *skookum* (strong). I shall do my best to dance and please you.' The boy was already dressed in the brilliant buckskin costume his mother had spent so many hours in making, and his precious wolfskin was flung over his arm. The great Squamish chief now took him by the hand and led him towards the blazing fires round which the tired dancers, the old men and women, sat in huge circles where the chill of dawn could not penetrate.

'One more dance, then we sleep,' said the chief to the great circle of spectators. 'This Tenas Tyee will do his best to amuse us.'

Then Ta-la-pus felt the chief's hand unclasp, and he realized that he was standing absolutely alone before a great crowd of strangers, and that every eye was upon him.

'Oh, my brother,' he whispered, smoothing the prairie wolf skin, 'help me to be like you, help me to be worthy of your name.' Then he pulled the wolf's head over his own, twisted the fore legs about his throat, and stepped into the great circle of sand between the crouching multitude and the fires.

Stealthily he began to pick his way in the full red flare from the flames. He heard many voices whispering, 'Tenas,' 'Tenas,' meaning 'He is little, he is young,' but his step only grew more stealthy, until he 'padded' into a strange, silent trot in exact imitation of a prairie wolf. As he swung the second time round the fires, his young voice arose, in a thin, wild, wonderful barking tone, so weird and wolf-like that half the spectators leaped upto their knees, or feet, the better to watch and listen. Another moment, and he was putting his chant into words.

'They call me Ta-la-pus, the prairie-wolf,
   And wild and free am I.

I cannot swim like Eh-ko-lie, the whale,
   Nor like the eagle, Chack-chack, can I fly.

'I cannot talk as does the great Tyee,
   Nor like the o-tel-agh[3] shine in the sky.
I am but Ta-la-pus, the prairie-wolf,
   And wild and free am I'

With every word, every step, he became more like the wolf he was describing. Across his chanting and his 'padding' in the sand came murmurs from the crowd. He could hear 'Tenas, tenas,' 'To-ke-tie Tenas' (pretty boy), 'Skookum-tanse,' (good strong dance). Then at last, 'Ow,' 'Ow,' meaning 'Our young brother.' On and on went Ta-la-pus. The wolf feeling crept into his legs, his soft young feet, his clutching fingers, his wonderful dark eyes that now gleamed red and lustrous in the firelight. He was as one inspired, giving a beautiful and marvellous portrait of the wild vagabonds of the plains. For fully ten minutes he circled and sang, then suddenly crouched on his haunches, then, lifting his head, he turned to the east, his young throat voiced one long, strange note, wolf-like he howled to the rising sun, which at that moment looked over the crest of the mountains, its first golden shaft falling full upon his face.

His chant and his strange wolf-dance were ended. Then one loud clamour arose from the crowd. 'Tenas Tyee,' 'Tenas Tyee,' they shouted, and Ta-la-pus knew that he had not failed. But the great Squamish chief was beside him.

'Tillicums,'[4] he said, facing the crowd, 'this boy has danced no tribal dance learned from his people or his parents. This is his own dance, which he has made to deserve his name. He shall get the first gifts of our great Potlatch. Go,' he added, to one of the young men 'bring ten dollars of the white man's *chicamin* (money) and ten new blankets as white as that snow on the mountain top.'

The crowd was delighted. They approved the boy and rejoiced to see the real Potlatch was begun. When the blankets were piled up beside him they reached to the top of Ta-la-pus' head. Then the chief put ten dollars in the boy's hand with the simple words, 'I am glad to give it. You won it well, my Tenas Tyee.'

That was the beginning of a great week of games, feasting and tribal

---

3 Sun [Johnson's note].
4 'Friends, my people' [Johnson's note].

dances, but not a night passed but the participants called for the wild
'wolf-dance' of the little boy from the island. When the Potlatch was
over, old Chief Mowitch and Lapool and Ta-la-pus returned to Vancou-
ver Island, but no more the boy sat alone on the isolated rock, watching
the mainland through a mist of yearning. He had set foot in the wider
world, he had won his name, and now honoured it, instead of hating it
as in the old days when his brothers taunted him, for the great Squa-
mish chief, in bidding good-bye to him, had said:

'Little Ta-la-pus, remember a name means much to a man. You
despised your name, but you have made it great and honourable by your
own act, your own courage. Keep that name honourable, little Ta-la-pus;
it will be worth far more to you than many blankets or much of the
white man's *chicamin.*'

HOOLOOL OF THE TOTEM POLES

A Story of the North Pacific Coast

The upcoast people called her 'Hoolool,' which means 'The Mouse' in
the Chinook tongue. For was she not silent as the small, grey creature
that depended on its own bright eyes and busy little feet to secure a
living?

The fishermen and prospectors had almost forgotten the time when
she had not lived alone with her little son 'Tenas,' for although Big Joe,
her husband, had been dead but four years, time travels slowly north of
Queen Charlotte Sound, and four years on the 'Upper Coast' drag
themselves more leisurely than twelve at the mouth of the Fraser River.
Big Joe had left her but three precious possessions – 'Tenas,' their boy,
the warm roomy firwood house of the thrifty Pacific Coast Indian build,
and the great Totem Pole that loomed outside at its northwestern cor-
ner like a guardian of her welfare and the undeniable hallmark of their
child's honourable ancestry and unblemished lineage.

After Big Joe died Hoolool would have been anchorless without that
Totem Pole. Its extraordinary carving, its crude but clever colouring, its
massed figures of animals, birds and humans, all designed and carved
out of the solid trunk of a single tree, meant a thousand times more to
her than it did to the travellers who, in their great 'Klondike rush,'
thronged the decks of the northern-bound steamboats; than it did even

to those curio-hunters who despoil the Indian lodges of their ancient wares, leaving their white man's coin in lieu of old silver bracelets and rare carvings in black slate or finely-woven cedar-root baskets.

Many times was she offered money for it, but Hoolool would merely shake her head, and, with a half smile, turn away, giving no reason for her refusal. 'The woman is like a mouse,' those would-be purchasers would say, so 'Hoolool' she became, even to her little son, who called her the quaint word as a white child would call its mother a pet name; and she in turn called the little boy 'Tenas,' which means 'Youngness' – the young spring, the young day, the young moon – and he was all these blessed things to her. But all the old-timers knew well why she would never part with the Totem Pole.

'No use to coax her,' they would tell the curio-hunters. 'It is to her what your family crest is to you. Would you sell your *crest*?'

So year after year the greedy-eyed collectors would go away empty-handed, their coin in their pockets, and Hoolool's silent refusal in their memories. Yet how terribly she really needed their money she alone knew. To be sure, she had her own firewood in the forest that crept almost to her door, and in good seasons the salmon fishing was a great help. She caught and smoked and dried this precious food, stowing it away for use through the long winter months; but life was a continual struggle, and Tenas was yet too young to help her in the battle.

Sometimes when the silver coins were very, very scarce, when her shoulders ached with the cold, and her lips longed for tea and her mouth for bread, when the smoked salmon revolted her, and her thin garments grew thinner, she would go out and stand gazing at the Totem Pole, and think of the great pile of coin that the last 'collector' had offered for it – a pile of coin that would fill all her needs until Tenas was old enough to help her, to take his father's place at the hunting, the fishing, and above all, in the logging camps up the coast.

'I would sell it to-day if they came,' she would murmur. 'I would not be strong enough to refuse, to say no.'

Then Tenas, knowing her desperate thoughts, would slip, mouse-like, beside her and say:

'Hoolool, you are looking with love on our great Totem Pole – with love, as you always do. It means that I shall be a great man some day, does it not, Hoolool?'

Then the treachery of her thoughts would roll across her heart like a crushing weight, and she knew that no thirst for tea, no hunger for flour-bread, no shivering in thin garments, would ever drive her to part with it. For the grotesque, carven thing was the very birthright of her boy. Every figure, hewn with infinite patience by his sire's, his grand-sire's, his great-grandsire's hands meant the very history from which sprang the source of red blood in his young veins, the birth of each gen-eration, its deeds of valor, its achievements, its honours, its undeniable right to the family name.

Should Tenas grow to youth, manhood, old age, and have no Totem Pole to point to as a credential of being the honourable son of a long line of honourable sons? Never! She would suffer in silence, like the lit-tle grey, hungry Hoolool that scampered across the bare floors of her firwood shack in the chill night hours, but her boy must have his birth-right. And so the great pole stood unmoved, baring its grinning figures to the storms, the suns, the grey rains of the Pacific Coast, but by its very presence it was keeping these tempests from entering the heart of the lonely woman at its feet.

It was the year that spring came unusually early, weeks earlier than the oldest Indian recalled its ever having come before. March brought the wild geese honking northward, and great flocks of snow-white swans came daily out of the southern horizon to sail overhead and lose them-selves along the Upper Coast, for it was mating and nesting time, and the heat of the south had driven them early from its broad lagoons.

Every evening Tenas would roll himself in his blanket bed, while he chatted about the migrating birds, and longed for the time when he would be a great hunter, able to shoot the game as they flitted south-ward with their large families in September.

'*Then,* Hoolool, we will have something better to eat than the smoked salmon,' he would say.

'Yes, little loved one,' she would reply, 'and you are growing so fast, so big, that the time will not be long now before you can hunt down the wild birds for your Hoolool to eat, eh, little Spring Eyes? But now you must go to sleep; perhaps you will dream of the great flocks of the fat, young, grey geese you are to get us for food.'

'I'll tell you if I do; I'll tell you in the morning if I dream of the little geese,' he would reply, his voice trailing away into dreamland as his eyes blinked themselves to sleep.

'Hoolool, I *did* dream last night,' he told her one early April day, when he awoke dewy-eyed and bird-like from a long night's rest. 'But it was not of the bands of grey geese; it was of our great Totem Pole.'

'Did it speak to you in your dreams, little April Eyes?' she asked, play-fully.

'No-o,' he hesitated, 'it did not really speak, but it showed me something strange. Do you think it will come true, Hoolool?' His dark, questioning eyes were pathetic in appeal. He *did* want it to come true.

'Tell your Hoolool,' she replied indulgently, 'and perhaps she can decide if the dream will come true.'

'You know how I longed to dream of the great flocks of young geese flying southward in September,' he said, longingly, his little thin elbows propped each on one of her knees, his small, dark chin in his hands, his wonderful eyes shadowy with the fairy dreams of childhood. 'But the flocks I saw were not flying grey geese, that make such fat eating, but around the foot of our Totem Pole I saw flocks and flocks of little tenas Totem Poles, hundreds of them. They were not *half* as high as I am. They were just baby ones you could take in your hand, Hoolool. Could you take my knife the trader gave me and make me one just like our big one? Only make it little, young – oh, *very* tenas – that I can carry it about with me. I'll paint it. Will you make me one, Hoolool?'

The woman sat still, a peculiar stillness that came of half fear, half unutterable relief, and wholly of inspiration. Then she caught up the boy, and her arms clung about him as if they would never release him.

'I know little of the white man's God,' she murmured, 'except that He is good, but I know that the Great Tyee (god) of the West is surely good. One of them has sent you this dream, my little April Eyes.'

'Perhaps the Great Tyee and the white man's God are the same,' the child said, innocent of expressing a wonderful truth. '*You* have two names –'Marna' (mother, in the Chinook) and 'Hoolool' – yet you are the same. Maybe it's that way with the two Great Tyees, the white man's and ours. But why should they send me dreams of flocks of baby Totem Poles?'

'Because Hoolool will make *you* one to-day, and then flocks and flocks of tenas poles for the men with the silver coins. I cannot sell them our great one, but I can make many small ones like it. Oh! they will buy the little totems, and the great one will stand as the pride of your manhood and the honour of your old age.' Her voice rang with the hope of the future, the confidence of years of difficulty overcome.

Before many hours had passed, she and the child had scoured the nearby edges of the forest for woods that were dried, seasoned, and yet solid. They had carried armfuls back to the fir shack, and the work of carving had begun. The woman sat by the fire hour after hour – the fire that burned in primitive fashion in the centre of the shack, stoveless and hearthless, its ascending smoke curling up through an aperture in the roof, its red flames flickering and fading, leaping and lighting the work that even her unaccustomed fingers developed with wonderful accuracy in miniature of the Totem Pole at the northwest corner outside. By nightfall it was completed, and by the fitful firelight Tenas painted and stained its huddled figures in the black, orange, crimson and green that tribal custom made law. The warmth of the burning cedar knots dried the paints and pigments, until their acrid fragrance filled the little room, and the child's eyelids drooped sleepily, and in a delightful happiness he once more snuggled into his blanket bed, the baby Totem Pole hugged to his little heart. But his mother sat far into the night, her busy fingers at work on the realization of her child's dream. She was determined to fashion his dream-flock of 'young' totems which would bring to them both more of fat eating than many bands of grey geese flying southward. The night wore on, and she left her task only to rebuild the fire and to cover with an extra blanket the little form of her sleeping boy. Finally she, too, slept, but briefly, for daybreak found her again at her quaint occupation, and the following nightfall brought no change. A week drifted by, and one morning, far down the Sound, the whistle of a coming steamer startled both boy and woman into brisk action. The little flock of Totem Poles now numbered nine, and hastily gathering them together in one of her cherished cedar-root baskets she clasped the child's hand, and they made their way to the landing-stage.

When she returned an hour later, her basket was empty, and her kerchief filled with silver coins.

On the deck of the steamer one of the ship's officers was talking to a little group of delighted tourists who were comparing their miniature purchases with the giant Totem Pole in the distance.

'You *are* lucky,' said the officer. 'I know people who have tried for years to buy the big Pole from her, but it was always "No" with her – just a shake of her head, you might as well try to buy the moon. It's for that little boy of hers she's keeping it, though she could have sold it for hundreds of good dollars twenty times over.'

That all happened eleven years ago, and last summer when I journeyed far north of Queen Charlotte Sound, as the steamer reached a certain landing I saw a giant Totem Pole with a well-built frame house at its base. It was standing considerably away from the shore, but its newness was apparent, for on its roof, busily engaged at shingling, was an agile Indian youth of some seventeen years.

'That youngster built that house all by himself,' volunteered one of the ship's officers at my elbow. 'He is a born carpenter, and gets all the work he can do. He has supported his mother in comfort for two years, and he isn't full grown yet.'

'Who is he?' I asked, with keen interest.

'His name is Tenas,' replied the officer. 'His mother is a splendid woman. 'Hoolool,' they call her. She is quite the best carver of Totem Poles on the North Coast.'

THE SHAGGANAPPI

When 'Fire-Flint' Larocque said good-bye to his parents, up in the Red River Valley, and started forth for his first term in an Eastern college, he knew that the next few years would be a fight to the very teeth. If he could have called himself 'Indian' or 'White' he would have known where he stood in the great world of Eastern advancement, but he was neither one nor the other – but here he was born to be a thing apart, with no nationality in all the world to claim as a blood heritage. All his young life he had been accustomed to hear his parents and himself referred to as 'half-breeds,' until one day, when the Governor-General of all Canada paid a visit to the Indian school, and the principal, with an air of pride, presented 'Fire-Flint' to His Excellency, with 'This is our head pupil, the most diligent boy in the school. He is Trapper Larocque's son.'

'Oh? What tribe does he belong to?' asked the Governor, as he clasped the boy's hand genially.

'Oh, Fire-Flint belongs to no tribe; he is a halfbreed,' explained the principal.

'What an odd term!' said the Governor, with a perplexed wrinkle across his brows; then, 'I imagine you mean a half-blood, not breed.' His voice was chilly and his eyes a little cold as he looked rather haughtily at the principal. 'I do not like the word "breed" applied to human beings. It is a term for cattle and not men,' he continued. Then, addressing 'Fire-Flint,' he asked, 'Who are your parents, my boy?'

'My father is half French and half Cree; my mother about three-quarters Cree; her grandfather was French,' replied the boy, while his whole loyal young heart reached out towards this great man, who was lifting him out of the depths of obscurity. Then His Excellency's hands rested with a peculiar half fatherly, half brotherly touch on the shoulders of the slim lad before him.

'Then you have blood in your veins that the whole world might envy,' he said slowly. 'The blood of old France and the blood of a great aboriginal race that is the offshoot of no other race in the world. The Indian blood is a thing of itself, unmixed for thousands of years, a blood that is distinct and exclusive. Few white people can claim such a lineage. Boy, try and remember that as you come of Red Indian blood, dashed with that of the first great soldiers, settlers and pioneers in this vast Dominion, that you have one of the proudest places and heritages in the world; you are a Canadian in the greatest sense of that great word. When you go out into the world will you remember that, Fire-Flint?' His Excellency's voice ceased, but his thin, pale, aristocratic fingers still rested on the boy's shoulders, his eyes still shone with that peculiar brotherly light.

'I shall remember, sir,' replied Fire-Flint, while his homeless young heart was fast creating for itself the foothold amongst the great nations of the earth. The principal of the school stood awkwardly, hoping that all this attention would not spoil his head pupil; but he never knew that boy in all the five years he had instructed him, as His Excellency, Lord Mortimer, knew him in that five minutes' chat.

'No,' said the Governor, again turning to the principal, 'I certainly do not like that term "half-breed." Most of the people of the continent of America are of mixed nationality – how few are pure English or Scotch or Irish – or indeed of any particular race? Yet the white people of mixed nations are never called half-breeds. Why not? It would be quite reasonable to use the term regarding them.' Then, once again addressing Fire-Flint, he asked, 'I suppose all the traders use this term in speaking of your parents and of you?'

'Of my parents, yes, sir,' replied the boy.

'And you?' questioned His Excellency, kindly.

'They call me the "Shagganappi,"' answered Fire-Flint.

'I am afraid that is beyond me, my boy,' smiled His Excellency. 'Won't you tell me what it means?' The boy smiled responsively.

'It is a buckskin, a colour; a shagganappi cayuse is a buckskin colour. They say I look that way.'

'Ah, I understand,' replied His Excellency, as his eyes rested on the dark cream brown tint of the boy's face. 'Well, it is a good name; buckskin is a thing essential to white people and to Indians alike, from the Red River to the Rockies. And the cayuse – well, the horse is the noblest animal known to man. So try to be worthy of the nickname, my boy. Live to be essential to your people – like the buckskin, to be noble – like the horse. And now good-bye, Shagganappi, and remember that you are the real Canadian.'

Another handclasp and Lord Mortimer was walking away with the principal at his side, who was saying, 'Your Excellency, you have greatly encouraged that boy; I think he always felt terribly that he was a half-bree – half-blood. He would have loved to claim either all Cree or all French ancestry.'

'He is a fine lad and I like him,' returned Lord Mortimer, rather shortly, for he felt a little impatient with the principal, who could so easily have lightened the boy's heart from the very first year he had entered the school, by fostering within him pride of the two great races that blended within his veins into that one mighty nation called Canadian.

But that day proved the beginning of a new life for Fire-Flint; Lord Mortimer had called him Shagganappi in a half playful way, had said the name meant good and great things. No more did the little half-blood despise his own unusually tinted skin, no more did he hate that dash of grey in his brown eyes that bespoke 'white blood,' no more did he deplore the lack of proper colouring that would have meant the heritage of pure Indian blood. He was content to fight it out, through all his life to come, as 'The Shagganappi,' and when the time came for him to go to the great Eastern college in Ontario he went with his mind made up that no boy living was going to shoulder him into a corner or out-do him in the race for attainment.

———•———

'Hello, fellows, there is an Indian blown in from the North-West. Cracker-jack of a looking chap,' announced 'Cop' Billings to his room-mates late one morning as he burst into the room after his early mile run to find them with yet ten minutes to spare before the 'rising bell.'

'Shut up, and let a fellow sleep,' growled 'Sandy,' from his bed in the corner.

'Indian?' exclaimed young Locke, sitting bolt upright; 'this ain't a Redskin school; he's got to get put out, or I'm a deader.'

'You'll be a deader if you try to put him out,' sneered Cop Billings; 'first place he's got an arm like braided whipcord, and he's got a chin – hanged determined swat-you-in-the-face sort of chin – not a boiled-fish sort of jaw like yours,' and he glared at the unfortunate Locke with sneering disapproval.

'Where'd you see him?' ventured little chunky Johnny Miller, getting into his clothes.

'Saw him in the library as I passed. The Head called me in and –'

'Stow it! stow it!' they all yelled; then Locke jeered, 'The Head is never up at six-thirty – we are not rabbits.'

'Just where you get left; the Head was up at five-thirty and went to the station to meet mister Indian.'

'Well, I'll be jing-banged,' exclaimed Sandy, nearly awake; 'what's the meaning of it all?'

'Meaning's just this, my son,' replied Cop, getting out of his limited running togs into something more respectable, 'that if you chumps guessed all day you'd never strike just how the Indian came to this school. Who do you suppose wrote to the Head recommending him to take the Redskin, and kind of insinuating that the college would do well to treat him properly? None other than His Excellency Lord Mortimer, Governor General of "this Canada of ours." Now, Locke, will you act good and pretty, and take your bread and milk like a nice little tootsy-wootsy and allow the Indian to stay?'

'Whew!' bellowed Locke, 'I guess I'm it, fellows.'

'Just found it out, eh?' answered Cop; then, as the first bell clanged throughout the building and hustling was in order, he proceeded to explain that as he passed the library door on his way to the baths, Professor Warwick called him in and introduced him to the tall, lithe Westerner, who had wonderfully easy manners, a skin like a tan-coloured glove, and whose English was more attractive than marred by a strong accent that sounded 'Frenchy.'

'When he found that I was heading for the baths he asked to come too,' rattled Cop; 'been on the train over three days and nights coming from Winnipeg; said he felt grimy, so I took him along. Jingo, you should see his clothes – silk socks, silk shirt, top-coat lined with mink, an otter collar – must have cost hundreds.' Says I, "Well, pal, your governor must be well fixed." Says he, "My father is a trapper and trades with the Hudson's Bay Company. He trapped all these minks, and my other clothes – oh, we buy those at the H.B.C. in Winnipeg." Wouldn't that phase you, fellows? But I forgot his clothes when I saw him strip. Jiminy Christmas! I never saw such a body. I'm in bully training, but I'm a cow compared to "Shag."'

'What a rum name!' said Locke, still a little resentful.

'Found out all about that, too,' went on Cop. 'Seems he has a whole string of names to choose from. Heard him tell the Head that his first name is "Fire-Flint," and his last name is "Larocque." Seemed to kind of take the Head where he is weakest.

'"If you don't like it," says the Indian, with a dead-quiet, plumb-straight look at the Head, "you may call me what the people up along the Red River call me; I'm known there as the Shagganappi – Shag, if you want to cut off part of the word. The other boys may call me Shag if they want to." Say, fellows, I liked him right there and then. He may chum up with me all he likes, for all his silk socks and shirts.'

'What did the head say?' asked little Johnnie Miller.

'Said he liked the name Shag,' replied Cop. '"Then I'm Shag to you, sir, and the others here," speaks up his Indian nibs. Then he and I struck for the tubs, then they took him to get his room, and I came up here.'

As Cop finished speaking the chapel bell sounded and all four boys scrambled down to prayers. As they entered the little sanctuary, one of the masters, standing irresolute near the door, beckoned to Cop. 'Billings,' he whispered, 'Will you please go and ask Larocque if he cares to come to prayers? He's in room 17; you met him this morning, I believe.'

'Certainly, sir,' replied Cop, dashing up the nearest stairway.

'Entrez,' replied an even voice to Cop's unusually respectful knock. Then the voice rapidly corrected itself, 'Enter, come in,' it said in English.

'How about prayers?' asked Cop. 'Perhaps you're tired and don't care to come?'

'I'll go,' replied the Indian, and followed noiselessly where Billings led the way.

They entered just as Professor Warwick was beginning prayers, and although the eighty or so boys present were fairly exemplary, none could resist furtive looks at the newcomer, who walked up the little aisle beside Billings with a peculiarly silent dignity and half-indifference that could not possibly be assumed. How most of them envied him that manner! They recalled their own shyness and strangeness on the first day of their arrival; how they stumbled over their own feet that first morning at prayers; how they hated being stared at and spoken of as 'the new boy.' How could this Indian come among them as if he had been born and bred in their midst? But they never knew that Larocque's wonderful self-possession was the outcome of his momentary real indifference; his thoughts were far away from the little college chapel, for the last time he had knelt in a sanctuary was at the old, old cathedral at St Boniface, whose twin towers arose under the blue of a Manitoba sky, whose foundations stood where the historic Red and Assiniboine rivers meet, about whose bells one of America's sweetest singers, Whittier, had written lines that have endeared his name to every worshipper that bends the knee in that prairie sanctuary. The lines were drifting through his mind now. They were the first words of English poetry he had learned to memorize:

'Is it the clang of the wild geese?
  Is it the Indian's yell,
That lends to the call of the north wind
  The tones of a far-off bell?

'The voyageur smiles as he listens
  To the sound that grows apace.
Well he knows the vesper ringing
  Of the bells of St Boniface.

'The bells of the Roman mission –
  That call from their turrets twain
To the boatman on the river,
  To the hunter on the plain.'

'To the hunter on the plain,' said Shag's thoughts, over and over. Perhaps the hunter was his trapper father, who with noiseless step and wary eye was this very moment stalking some precious fur-bearing animal, whose pelt would bring a good price at the great Hudson's Bay trading-post; a price that would go toward keeping his son at this Eastern college for many terms. Shag's grey-brown eyes grew dreamy. He saw the vast prairies sweeping away into the West, and his father, a mere speck on the horizon, the ever present gun, the silent moccasin, the scarlet sash, the muffled step, all proclaiming 'the hunter on the plain.'

The prayers were ended and Shag found that he was not really watching his father coming up some prairie trail, but that before him was a different type of man, Professor Warwick, whose studious eyes now required glasses to see through, and whose hand was white and silken in its touch – how hopelessly lost this little man would be should circumstances turn him forth to gain his livelihood at hunting and trapping. Old Larocque himself would hardly be more incongruous teaching in this college. It was this thought that made Shag smile as he rose from his knees, with the echoes of the bells of St Boniface haunting his heart.

Then the chapel emptied, each boy on breakfast bent. 'Cop' Billings still remained at the Indian's elbow, but at the door one or two of the masters stopped to greet the new arrival, and a tall, remarkably handsome lad waited, apparently to speak. He was a boy that anyone would pick from a crowd of fifty – straight, well built, with fine, strong, thin hands, and a face with contradictory eyes, for they twinkled and danced as if nothing so serious as thoughtfulness ever disturbed them. As the two boys approached him he stepped impulsively forward extending his hand to Shag with the words, 'May I shake hands with you and say hello?'

'Thank you,' replied Shag; 'the way you boys are treating me makes me feel less strange.'

'Oh, no one feels strange here,' laughed the handsome boy. 'You must try and like us. So you're from Manitoba, are you?'

'Yes, Red River,' answered Shag.

'Father's been up there, and grandfather, too,' said the other, falling in step with the two boys on their way to the dining-room. 'Come up to my ranch some time soon – to-night if you like. Cop will bring you,' he added with a parting nod, as he left them for his own table at the other side of the room.

Cop stared hard at his companion. 'Thunderation!' he blurted, 'but you're the lucky kid!'

'Yes?' questioned Shag. 'Never mind the luck, but tell me who that chap is; he's very nice; I like him.'

'Like him!' almost yelled Cop; 'I should think you would like him! Why, he's the "Pop"!'

'"Pop"? What's that?' said Shag, with a puzzled air.

'Popular, the most popular boy in college – head in everything – clubs, classes, sports. Everybody is dippy over him from the Head right down to 'Infant' Innis, that little geezer in shorts across the table, who is only eleven last birthday. Even Dirty Dick, the gardener, is batty about him; and here he's put himself out to shake your fin, and ask you up to his room – thing he's only done twice since he entered college. You are lucky, kid!'

'Does he think a lot of himself?' asked Shag with some suspicion.

'He? Not much! Just the bulliest old pal in the world. Why, he wouldn't be the 'pop' if he threw on side,' asserted Cop loyally.

'You haven't told me who he is yet,' said Shag.

'Oh, I forgot,' apologized Cop. 'It seems so funny that everybody shouldn't know. Why, he's Harry Bennington. You must have heard of Sir George Bennington, big railroad man. Queen Victoria knighted him for some big scoop he made for Canada or the Colonies or something. Well, Hal's his son; but do you suppose that his dad's title makes any difference to Hal? Not much! But Hal's handshake will make a big difference to you in this college, I'll tell you that, Shag. You're made, that's what you are – just made; even Lord Mortimer back of you couldn't give you the place among the crowd here that Hal Bennington's grip did to-day.'

Shag did not reply; he was looking across the room at Sir George Bennington's son. He knew the name of the wealthy man whom Queen Victoria had honoured, knew it well. His father, Trapper Larocque, had met Sir George in the old pioneer days of the railroad in the North-West. There was a little story about Sir George, well known in the Red River Valley; Trapper Larocque knew it, the Hudson's Bay Company knew it, Shag knew it, and was asking himself if Hal knew it. Then the boy from Manitoba took the story and locked it within his heart, sealed his lips above it, and said to his soul, 'Hal Bennington won't know it from me, nor will anyone else. He's made my first day at this school an easy day; the fight won't be half what I thought it would. I owe much to him, and above all I owe him my silence.'

'Coming up, fellows?' asked Hal genially, as Cop Billings stretched his big frame after grind in the evening at recreation hour before going to bed. The word' fellows' embraced him with a look that included Shag.

'Thanks, I guess we will,' said Cop, and the three boys proceeded upstairs to the private room occupied by Hal and one other, a stocky fellow known as 'Shorty' Magee, who was just settling to his letter-writing as the boys entered. He nodded curtly, said 'Hello!' ratlher grumpily, and did not offer to shake hands when Hal introduced Shag Larocque. Shorty always hated to be disturbed at anything, even if it were the irksome weekly letter home. He shoved aside his notepaper, however, and sat with his hands in his trousers pockets, his feet stretched out in front of him, and a tolerant expression on his face.

Hal, always gracious and kindly, seemed more so than ever to-night, evidently trying to make up for his roommate's moroseness by his own geniality. He showed Shag his treasures, his collection of curiosities, his two lynx-skin rugs – animals shot by his father years before – his pet books, and finally came to his photographs.

'This is a splendid one of father,' he said enthusiastically; 'it was taken when he was a young man surveying out West before they put the railroad through. That group of men to the left are axemen. It should interest you, for Professor Warwick told me you came here to study surveying.'

'Yes,' said Shag, 'that is my chosen work.'

'Then,' continued Hal, 'that splendid-looking chap on father's right was his guide and personal cook – the one in the blanket coat and sash. He was part French but mostly Indian, I fancy – Why, what's the matter, Larocque?' for Shag had suddenly made some inarticulate exclamation, and had carried the photograph nearer the light.

'That is my father,' he said quietly. As he spoke the words he was well aware that they might tell against him some time or other. He knew enough of the civilization of the white people to understand that when two boys attend the same school, one with a titled father and the other with a father who had cooked for the titled one, that things are apt to become strained; but never for one second did he hesitate about claiming the Red River trapper as his sire. He would have despised himself far more than any boy in the school could possibly do now, had he failed to say the words, 'That is my father.' The attitude of his three listeners was certainly a study. Cop Billings stood staring at him for a moment, then said, 'Well, if your dad did cook he gets you far better shirts and socks than mine does me.' Shorty Magee uttered the four words, 'Cooked for Sir George!' and with an ugly sneer turned again to his letter-writing.

Hal Bennington had sprung forward, tossing his arms about the Indian's shoulders and exclaiming 'Your father! Is French Pete your father? Oh, I'm so glad! Father will be delighted when I tell him. I have heard him say a hundred times that he would never have lived to be 'Sir' George if it hadn't been for French Pete.'

'Yes, they call my father French Pete because, although he is nearly all Indian, he speaks French so well,' announced Shag.

Then followed a narration of two occasions when Shag's father had saved Sir George's life, once from drowning in the Assiniboine and once from freezing to death on the plains. The recreation interval was all too short for the boys to have their talk out, and when the 'good-nights' came Hal wrung Shag's hand with a sincerity and heartiness that brought a responsive thrill into the fingers of the lonely boy who was spending his first night fifteen hundred miles away from home.

'Well,' snorted Shorty, as the two boys left for the night, 'going to chum around with the son of your father's Cook, are you?'

Hal whirled on his heel, his hand clenched, his knuckles standing out white and bony; then he checked the torrent of words that sprang to his lips and answered quietly, 'Yes, I am.'

'Going to take him to Sir George and Lady Bennington's city residence for the Easter Vac?' sneered Shorty.

The answer came again quietly, 'Yes, I am;' then, after a brief interval, 'if he will pay me the compliment of coming.'

Shorty subsided; he had not expected this, and, truth to tell, he felt at that moment that his sneers had accomplished precisely the opposite effect to what he had intended; but Hal made no comment until just before they got into their beds; then he said evenly:

'Shorty, you and I are room-mates, we have been pals for over a year; we won't discuss Shag Larocque, for I see that we shall never agree about him.'

'I hate a mongrel,' sniffed Shorty; 'this fellow is neither Indian nor white.'

'He's more Indian than white, and better for it, too,' said Hal; 'but, I say, Shorty – what nationality was your father?'

'Irish,' said Shorty, with some pride.

'And your mother?' persisted Hal relentlessly.

'Oh, mother's parents were English; she was born here in Canada,' replied Shorty a little weakly.

'Oh!' was all Hal said, but it held a world of meaning.

'Now, see here, Hal,' began Shorty apologetically, 'I know what you are thinking, but I'm British right through and my skin's white, no matter how you take it. I'm white on both sides of the family; I'm not splashed with tinted blood like this fellow from the North-West that's strayed in here; his skin's almost yellow.'

'Yes,' acquiesced Hal, 'his skin is tinted – it is tinted, not tainted. There's a big difference, Shorty. Do you know, I'd give the world if I had as much of a copper-coloured tint to my skin as Shag has.'

'Rot!' ejaculated Shorty.

'No rot at all,' cut in Hal; 'I love the Indian people. You call this chap a "mongrel," but I tell you he is Indian – anyone can see it, and I know it. His father may have cooked in camp for my father, and did so, but from what my father told me, he, French Pete, was an honest man, and a brave one, too, and his son's good enough for me, and I'm his friend until the last dog's hung.'

That ended things for the time, for the college bells clanged out 'lights out,' and the inmates, both white and Indian, slept.

———•———

'Yes, my dear boy,' wrote Sir George, some weeks later, 'by all means bring young Larocque home for the Easter vacation; I shall welcome the son of my old friend and guide with the greatest delight. I have frequently told you of French Pete's heroism and unselfishness, and if by a little hospitality I can show the son what I think of the father, I shall regard it as a privilege. Your dear mother will write you to-night, and will enclose a little note of invitation from us both to your friend "Shagganappi" – how that good old North-West word brings back my youth! I think I like your friend, even before I see him, just because he has adopted that name.'

So it was all arranged that Shag should spend the Easter vacation at the palatial home of the Benningtons in Montreal. As Hal was so popular, this holiday invitation was always regarded as the greatest compliment by any boy who was fortunate enough to receive it, but never before had Lady Bennington written personally to invite one of Hal's friends. It was such a dear little note, too; Hal never admired his mother quite so much as when Shag handed him the invitation to read. Lady Bennington was famous as one of the few women who always say and do the right thing at the right moment. The note ran:

'Dear Shagganappi, –
Do come with my boy at Eastertide; we want you – come.
Your friend, Hal's mother,
CONSTANCE BENNINGTON.'

So Easter found the boys at Montreal, Shag a little shy at first amidst all the grandeur and wealth of Hal's home, but covering that shyness with a quiet dignity that sat very well on his young shoulders. With a wonderful knack of delicacy, Hal would smooth out any threatened difficulty for the Indian boy – little table entanglements, such as new dishes or unaccustomed foods. But Shag was at times surprisingly outspoken, and the first night at dinner seemingly won Sir George's heart by remarking when the fruit plates and finger-glasses were served, 'Now, Hal, don't be afraid that I won't understand this; fortunately I dined on the dining cars on the way East.' Everyone laughed then, including Shag, and Sir George said, 'Then you are better up in things than I was at your age, my boy. I never saw a finger-glass until I was twenty.' So this little confidence put them all on a kind of family footing; and during the rest of his visit Shag was not afraid to ask and learn any of the usages of wealthy city houses and manners that might puzzle him. When he left he had endeared himself to Hal's parents as no other boy had done before. Lady Bennington especially seemed to have become attached to him. Once when Hal was taking some snapshots of the grounds, she called Shag to her side, and, placing one hand on his shoulder, asked Hal to photograph them together. Shag almost trembled with pleasure, but his delight knew no bounds when a week after their return to school he received a little copy of the photograph framed in silver and inscribed on the back with 'To Shagganappi Larocque, with love from Hal's mother.'

'I don't know why you and your people are so good to me,' he declared to Hal, when they both had duly admired the little picture. Hal stared at him rather oddly, but did not reply, and it was many months before Shag understood what that look meant; but when it was explained the Indian recalled many things that had once perplexed him.

———•———

It was late in May when Sir George and Lady Bennington left on their yearly visit to England, leaving Hal with the enviable holiday ahead of him of playing host at their summer residence in the Thousand Islands. He was privileged to ask what boys he liked; he could have his own canoe and sailboat, any of the servants from the city residence that he wished, and just put in one long, golden summer, swimming, boating, rollicking around, getting tanned and healthy. The only stipulation his parents made was that in addition to the crowd of boys asked he must invite one of the masters. It did not matter which one, so what did Hal do but, 'cheek it up' to the Head, who had no family to summer with, and who usually wandered off to some lonely mountain resort by himself for the entire vacation. Professor Warwick was amazed.

'Why, Bennington,' he exclaimed, 'whatever do you want an old codger like me for? There's young Graham, almost a boy himself, and Lewes, the science man, a funny chap. I always think Mr Lewes is more fun than a cage of cats. I'm a dried-up old fellow that most of the boys are afraid of. You won't enjoy yourself with me around all the time.'

'We're only afraid of you in classes, sir,' laughed Hal; 'no one is afraid of you outside. I've heard the boys josh you on the ball grounds and at the sports no end of times. You've just got to come, Professor!' And the old gentleman did go, to the delight of Hal's parents, who left for England perfectly satisfied that the boys would be well looked after if the Professor was an inmate of their island home.

The party was just about the right size; two of the little boys who lived at the Pacific coast were asked, then Shorty and Cop and little chunky Johnny Miller and Shag Larocque – seven all told, including Hal, and eight, counting the Professor, who, on the first night in camp said, a little gravely, 'Hal, my boy, it is a great privilege to be the son of a wealthy man. I have never cared for money, but I would like to be in a position where I could have the pleasure of entertaining my friends in this delightful way.

'I hope I appreciate it, Professor,' replied the boy. 'Dad is always reminding me of the stacks of people not so well fixed as we are. He frequently tells me of the times when he went hungry – really hungry, without twenty-five cents with which to buy a meal, and he says if ever I forget it and try to put on "side" that he will thrash me within an inch of my life, even after I am twenty-one.'

The Professor roared, a regular boyish shout. 'And he'd do it, too, I believe,' he chuckled. 'That is what makes Sir George so wonderful; with all his wealth he is the same dear old chap he always was. I knew him when he was your age almost – and the only thing about him that has changed is his hair; it is a little thinner now and grey.'

'Yes, dad's a boy yet,' smiled Hal, 'but I won't give him a chance to lick me on the money score; it's too good fun having you all here, and a royal holiday ahead of us without hunting for a trimming from dad because I play the *la-de-da*, or think I'm the whole thing.'

Shag was thinking hard, but he said nothing; yet, little as he knew of the world, he was quite aware how few boys in Hal's position would act as he had done. Had it not been for Sir George's son what would his life at college have been? He knew Locke never liked him, he knew that Shorty positively disliked him, he knew there was a strong element of prejudice in the school against him, and he knew positively that, were it not for Lord Mortimer's influence and recommendation, he would never have been accepted in this exclusive college as a student. What then did he owe to Hal? Everything, as far as making life in the East bearable, as far as being received on an equality with the other boys went. It was a tremendous debt that he owed this handsome boy who was his host for the summer. But before the holiday was ended Shag paid that debt with all his heart, and almost with his life.

It happened one day from the simple cause that the camp had run short of bread, and one of the youngsters from the Pacific coast, Freddy by name, had volunteered to paddle over to the mainland for it. The sailboat being laid up for repairs, Freddy ran out the light little Peterborough, and was just getting away from the island when Hal descried him and shouted to him to wait. 'Think I'd let you go alone in that canoe, kiddie?' he asked. 'There's too much wind to-day; look at her sweep down the north channel. Why, she'd turn you round and round like "Willie waltzing." Hold on, I'm coming with you.' With that he sprang into the canoe and they were away.

It was rather a cold wind for early September, and the two boys were glad to paddle hard to keep their circulation up. Both were in shirt sleeves and both somewhat chilled; but by the time they had reached the mainland they were all tingling with rioting blood and with appetites ready to attack their cargo of bread, even minus the butter. They started back in good shape, although Hal's weather eye observed that the wind was picking up and that they would have to work for it to make the island in good time for supper. All went well for some distance, although sometimes the waves galloped up and slipped over the bow where Freddy knelt, plying his paddle in good form. Out in mid-stream, with both wind and current against him, Hal had considerable difficulty in steering; his strong, muscular arms pulled little Freddy's stroke around, and he bent to the work of 'digging potatoes' with a vengeance. The bow with its light boyish ballast would rise and rise again, slapping down on the surface or taking the waves like a cork. Then came a line of combers, one on top of another. The taut little Peterborough rode the first like a shell, the second she dipped, the third she shipped a whole bucketful of water. As it poured over the deck, little Freddy flung himself backward to escape the drenching, the canoe dipped, Freddy landed full weight on the leeward gunwale – and they were over. For the first instant, Hal was conscious of but one thing, that he was being struck through with the chill of the water on top of being in a heat of perspiration with battling the canoe through the waves. Then he came to the surface to see the canoe, turned turtle, floating bottom up three yards away. Then a limp mass of brown clothes and brown curls cannoned into him, and reaching out, he grasped Freddy.

'Don't get scared, kid,' he gasped, spluttering the water out of his throat; 'keep cool and don't clutch me too tight.' He might as well have spoken to the winds, for little Freddy, chilled through and terror-stricken, was clinging to him like an octopus, impeding his arm and leg action, and almost choking the breath out of his lungs. 'Oh, Hal, we're in mid-stream,' gulped the child; 'we'll be drowned!'

'Not on your life, kiddie!' spluttered Hal. 'I'll get that bally canoe. Only don't hold on around my neck, that's a good kiddie. There, that's better,' as Freddy loosened his fingers from Hal's shirt collar, and the boy struck out with one arm around the child and the other working for all the grit and muscle there was in it. His magnificent stroke, helped by the wind and current, soon overhauled the canoe. By a supreme effort he clutched the immersed gunwale. With one arm around Freddy he could never hope to right the boat, but even bottom up she was a salvation. 'Grip her, kiddie, grip her as I shove you up,' he gasped, 'and don't let go; straddle her and hang on! Promise me you will hang on, – promise me!' he cried.

'I'll promise,' gulped the child. Then Hal's powerful arm flung itself upwards, his two hands 'boosted,' and Freddy landed on the upturned canoe, gripping it with all fours and coughing the water from his mouth.

Hal made an attempt to climb up, his fingers slipped; then two terrible little demons seemed to grasp the calves of his legs; their fingers ripped the muscles out and tied them into knots, knots that extended to his knees, his hips, his stomach; his fingers weakened with the agony of it – Hal Bennington knew he was going down with cramps.

Away off to the right he thought he heard a voice; it was saying, 'Keep up, Hal, keep up, I'm coming!' but he could not answer. With a last effort he literally screamed, 'Hang on, Freddy, hang on!' Then he felt numb, very numb, and all was dark.

Professor Warwick had gone out to furl the awnings against the rising wind. His kindly little eyes were peering through their spectacles at sea and sky when suddenly they rested on a frail canoe that was taking an erratic course toward the island. Instantly he was around at the other side of the cottage. 'Boys, boys,' he shouted frantically, 'Quick, get out the sailboat, Hal's canoe is in danger.'

'Sailboat!' gasped Cop Billings, springing to his feet; 'she's no good; bottom's out, a whole patch of her. She's being repaired.' But while he talked he was running wildly to the boathouse followed by all the others. As they reached the little wharf they were just in time to see the combers strike the canoe, to see Freddy start, then to see it capsize. For a moment they were horror-stricken, speechless, then Cop yelled, 'he's got Freddy. See, he's got him!' It seemed an eternity before they saw Hal grasp the child, then with more horror they saw the upturned canoe floating away, away, away.

'Boys, boys, can nothing be done to help them?' choked the Professor. 'Oh, boys, this is terrible!'

'Who swims?' yelled Shorty, '– swims well, I mean.'

'You do,' jerked Shag at his elbow, with a face bloodless and drawn. 'You're the best swimmer in the school. Will you come with me?'

'Come with you?' yelled Shorty. 'Out there? Why, you know as well as I do that I can't swim that far, not nearly that far; neither can you.'

'I can, and I will,' announced Shag in a strangely quiet voice, while with rapid fingers he stripped off his coat and boots.

'You shan't go alone,' shouted Cop, beginning to undress; 'I'm with you!'

'No, you don't,' said the Indian, gripping him by the wrist. 'You can't swim twenty yards – you know you can't; and if you get played out, Cop, I tell you right here that I can't stop to help you; I'm going to help Hal.'

'Why can't you try it, Shorty?' roared Cop. 'Anything rather than let him go alone!'

But Shorty stood resolute. 'I tell you I can't swim that far and back, and I ain't going to try it only to get drowned,' he snarled; but even as he spoke there flashed past him a lithe, tan-coloured body in skintight silken underwear; there followed a splash, and Shag's clean, dark face rose to the surface as he struck out towards the unfortunates.

The Professor was beside himself with horror. 'Boys, boys!' he cried aloud, 'Hal's going down! Something is wrong; he's sinking!' The words reached Shag's ears and he seemed to leap ahead like a giant fish.

'Heaven help them!' moaned poor Cop. 'Oh, what an idiot I was never to practise more!'

'It's awful!' began Shorty.

'Don't you open your head!' shouted Cop; 'if I could swim like you nothing would keep me ashore.'

'Never mind, boys,' moaned Professor Warwick; 'don't quarrel with this tragedy before us. Look, Shag's simply leaping ahead. There goes Hal again – that's the second time he's gone under! Oh, my boy! – my poor Hal!' and the little old man rushed wildly up to the servants' quarters for the cook and the pantry-boy and ropes – anything, everything that would hold out a hope of rescue.

And on against wind and current Shag battled his way; inch by inch, foot by foot, yard by yard he forged forward, until he saw Hal loose his grip and sink, and then rise and fall to reach the canoe again. It was then that Shag raised his chin and shouted hoarsely, 'Keep up, Hal, keep up! I'm coming!' the words that faintly reached Hal's ears before the silence and the dark came. Then as he rose from the depths, an unconscious, helpless hulk, a strong tan-coloured arm wound around him like a lifebelt, and a well-nigh breathless boy, with almost super-human strength, flung him, limp and nearly lifeless, across the canoe. The impact almost hurled Freddy from his slender hold, but for a few seconds the two boys were safe. Above the slippery bow poor Shag clasped his arms, allowing his body to drift.

With but this frail anchorage, he well knew that the canoe would never float them all. There was but little of her above the water. The waves were beating hard now, any moment weak little Freddy and unconscious Hal might be swept off. Once, as the fear of losing life gripped him, he began to struggle on to the canoe; the he remembered, and slipped back to float, to cling, to slowly – slowly – await the horrors of the unknown.

For five terrible minutes they drifted, minutes that were an eternity to those on shore, and to those fighting for life in mid-stream. Then around the bend of the island came the thin, shrill whistle of a steam launch as it headed directly for the upturned canoe, the skipper signalling to those on the island that he was hot on the way to the rescue.

Old Professor Warwick wept like a woman when he saw it fly past, and the boys gulped back their breath. They dared not even try to cheer; their voices were strangled in their throats.

'Just in time and that's all, captain,' said the engineer as he brought the launch about. 'Better reach for that chap in the water first.'

'No,' Shag managed to say, 'take the kiddie; he's slipping off. I'm good for a minute longer.' So they lifted Freddy into the launch, then poor unconscious Hal, and lastly Shag, exhausted but gritty and game to the last.

Hal had been in his own bed for two hours before he spoke, and the first word he said was 'Freddy?'

'Freddy's here,' trembled Professor Warwick, 'here safe and sound, and you're safe too.'

'I dreamt I heard Shag call, call that he was coming to me,' said Hal feebly.

'It was no dream, Hal,' answered the Professor; 'he did call and went to you, saved you, swam out like the prince he is – saved you, Hal, saved you!' Hal started up, his eyes wild with fear.

'Where is he? Where's Shag?' he demanded.

'Here, Hal,' said the Indian from the opposite side of the room.

Hal stretched out his hand; Shag walked very shakily across and clasped it within his own.

'If you hadn't been here, Shag, I could never have looked dad and mother in the face again,' he sighed.

'But I am here,' smiled Shag, 'and, what is better, you're here and Freddy, too.'

'Yes, but I know the reason that I'm here is that you somehow pulled me out,' said Hal. 'I had an idea once, that Shorty might come, he swims so well; but you came, Shag!' Then he fell asleep; but Shag did not remove his hand, although the boy slept for hours.

———•———

Not long after this college opened for the autumn term, and Professor Warwick and his charges were well settled in residence before the old gentleman was obliged to acknowledge that Hal seemed unable to throw off the shock of the accident, or the chill that seemed to cling to him in spite of all care; but he tucked in bravely at his studies, and only the Professor knew that the boy was not his own self.

But a great event was now absorbing the attention of all the faculty and students. His Excellency Lord Mortimer was to visit the city, and had expressed his wish to spend an hour or two at this famous college for boys, so with much delight at the compliment paid, the entire school began to make preparations. A handsome address was prepared, and a programme of sports – for the Governor dearly loved athletic boys. In fact, gossip at the capital frequently stated that His Lordship would rather witness a good lacrosse match than eat a good dinner. Such a thing as voting as to who should represent the school and read the address was never even thought of. Hal Bennington was the head boy of the whole college, he was the most popular, the best beloved, he had not an enemy in all the scores of boys within its gates, so of course it was a foregone conclusion.

'I hate the idea of it,' asserted Hal. 'I hate these public show-offs, besides, I don't feel well. I wish they would make some other chap do it.' But neither masters nor boys would take no for an answer. Then disaster threatened, for a week before the event Hal fell really ill; a slow fever seemed to grip him, and if Sir George and Lady Bennington had not been already on the sea on their homeward way, Professor Warwick would have felt very much like cabling them. Hal was utterly disgusted when it was mentioned to him. 'Don't you think of it,' he growled. 'You've done as I wished about not telling them about that bally accident, and don't you hurry them home for me.' So the boy was made to stay in bed, and, truth to tell, he was too ill to remonstrate much.

But the night before the viceregal visit Hal knew in his heart that he was too ill to go out and read the address. Late at night he sent for Professor Warwick, told him the truth, and asked him to get a substitute.

'My boy, I am more distressed than I can say,' began the Professor.

'Your illness is worse than any upsetting of arrangements, we are getting a trained nurse for you, and I shall relieve your mind of all worries. We have hardly time now to consult everyone about a substitute, but if I tell the boys you have appointed a deputy, so to speak, I think they will be satisfied.'

'Then let Shag Larocque take my place,' decided Hal instantly.

'Very appropriate, too, I should say,' replied the Professor spontaneously. 'Lord Mortimer has seen Shag and knows him; very appropriate.'

So Hal slept that night contentedly, with never a dream of the storm that would burst on the morrow.

The first indication of the tempest was when Locke burst into his room after breakfast, with, 'Hal, you must be sick! Why, man alive, you are clean batty! Shag read that address – why, it is impossible!'

'And why?' said Hal, glaring at him.

'He can't do it; we won't let him; we won't have that Indian heading the whole school!'

'Who won't?'

'We! we! we! – Do you hear it? We!' yelled Locke.

'You and Shorty and Simpson and about two others, I suppose,' answered Hal. 'Well, he's going to read it; now, get out and shut the door – I feel a draft.'

'Well, he isn't going to read it!' thundered Locke, banging the door after himself as he stormed down the hall to the classrooms, where the boys were collecting to arrange details for the day. Hal shivered back into the bedclothes, listening anxiously to various footsteps trailing past. He could occasionally catch fragments of conversation; everyone seemed to be in a high state of excitement. He could hear his own name, then Shag's, then Shorty's, and sometimes Locke's.

'I've evidently kicked up a hornets' nest,' he smiled weakly to himself, too tired and ill to care whether the hornets stung or not. Presently Locke returned. 'I tell you, Hal, it won't do; that Indian isn't a fit representative of this college.'

'The masters won't do a thing; you've got to appoint someone else. You're disgracing the college,' said Shorty at the door. 'We won't stand for it, Hal; this is no North-West Indian school. We won't have it, I tell you!'

'Shag's going to read that address!' said Hal, sitting up with an odd drawn but determined look around his mouth.

'Well, he isn't!' blurted Shorty. 'There's a big meeting in the classroom, and there's a row on – the biggest row you ever saw.'

'Shag Larocque read that address!' yelled Simpson from the hall; 'not if I know it! He's not a decent sport, even – he won't resent an insult. I called him a Red River halfbreed and he never said a word – just swallowed it!'

'Shut that door!' shouted Hal, the colour surging into his face, 'and shut yourselves on the outside! Go to the classroom, insult him all you like, but you'll be sorry for it – take my word for it!'

Once more they banged the door. No sooner was it closed than Hal sprang out of bed. His legs shook with weakness, his hands trembled with illness, but he began to get into some clothes, and his young face flushed scarlet and white in turn.

Out in the classroom a perfect bedlam reigned. Dozens of voices shouted, 'Shag's the man for us! Hurrah for Shag!' and dozens replied, 'Who will join the anti-Indians? Who will vote for a white man to represent white men? This ain't an Indian school – get out with the Indians!'

Then Shorty took the floor. 'Boys,' he yelled, 'we won't stand for it. No Indian's going to be head of this school, and Shag Larocque isn't even a decent Indian, he's a halfbreed, a French halfbreed, he's –'

The door burst open and Hal Bennington flung himself into the room; his trousers were dragged up over his nightshirt, his feet were in slippers without socks, his hair was unbrushed, his eyes were brilliant with fever, his face was pinched and grey; but his voice rang out powerfully, 'Stop it, boys!' He had taken in the situation instantly – the crowd breaking from all rule, two masters endeavouring to restore order, and Shag, alone, terribly alone, his back to the wall, his face to the tumult, standing like a wild thing driven into a corner, but yet gloriously game. 'Shorty, how dare you speak of Shag Larocque like that?' Hal cried furiously.

'And how dare you support him?' Shorty flung back. 'How dare you ask us to have as our leader a halfbreed North-West Indian, who is the son of your father's cook?'

'Yes, he is the son of my father's cook, and if I ever get the chance I'll cook for him on my knees – cook for him and serve him; he saved my life and nearly lost his own – while you, Shorty, a far better swimmer, would have let me drown like a dog.'

'He's nothing but a North-West halfbreed,' sneered Shorty, hiding his cowardice behind ill words for others.

'So is my mother a North-West halfbreed, and she's the loveliest, the grandest woman in all Canada!' said Hal in a voice that rang clear, sharp, strong as a man's.

There was a dead silence. 'Do you hear me, you fellows?' tormented

Hal's even voice again, 'you who have of your own free will placed me, a quarter-blood, as the leading boy in this school, my mother is a half-breed, if you wish to use that refined term, and my mother is proud of it. Her mother, my grandmother, wore a blanket and leggings and smoked a red stone pipe upon the Red River years ago, and I tell you my mother is proud of it, and so am I. I have never told you fellows this before – what was the use? I felt you would never understand; but you hear me now! Do you quite grasp what I am telling you – that *my mother is a halfbreed?'*

Shorty's hand went blindly to his head; he looked dazed, breathless. 'Lady Bennington a halfbreed!' was all he said.

'Yes, Lady Bennington,' said Hal. 'And now will you let Shag read that address?' But Shag was at his elbow.

'Hal, Hal, oh, why did you tell them?' he cried.

Hal whirled about like one shot. '*Tell them* – what do you mean by tell *them?* Did you know this all along?'

'Yes,' said Shag regretfully, 'I always knew that Lady Bennington was half Indian, but I thought that you didn't, and I promised father that I should never tell when I came down East.' But softly as he spoke the boys nearby heard him. 'Do you mean to say,' said Locke, gripping Shag's shoulders in vice-like fingers, 'that all this time we have been ragging you and running on you, that you knew Hal's mother was a half Indian and you never said a word?'

'Why should I?' asked Shag, raising his eyebrows.

'Boys,' said Locke, facing the room like a man, 'we've been – well, just cads. And right here I propose that Shag Larocque read the address to His Excellency to-day.'

'And I second the motion,' said Shorty – 'second it heartily;' then he walked over to Shag.

'I'm not going to ask you to shake hands with me, Larocque,' he said; 'I've been too much of a cad for that. You must despise me too much to forgive me, despise me for my cowardice in not going with you to help Hal when he was drowning, despise me for my mean prejudices, despise me for – oh, pshaw. I ain't fit to even ask you to forgive me. I ain't fit to even offer you my hand.'

'Hold on! hold on!' smiled Shag. 'There is nothing to despise in a chap who is big enough to offer an apology. Here's my hand, Shorty. Will you take it at last?'

And Shorty took it.

A few hours later, just before Shag stepped out on the platform to read the address to His Excellency, he paid a flying visit to Hal, who, feeling much better, in fact quite on the mend, was sitting up in bed devouring toast and broth.

'Luck to you, old Shag,' he said between mouthfuls.

'Oh, Hal, you've been all the world to me,' was all he could reply.

'And you'll be all the world to my dad and mother when they hear what you have done, fishing me out of the drink and saving my life.' But Shorty shouting up the hall interrupted them.

'Come on, Shag,' he called; then, as he appeared in the doorway, he said bravely, 'I haven't been so happy for years; I've been a sneak and now that I say it I feel better. Shag, there isn't a boy living who I consider better fitted to represent this school than you. Do you believe me?'

'I do believe you, and I thank you, Shorty, old chap,' said Shag happily, and linking arms they left Hal's room together, for cheers outside were announcing the approach of Lord Mortimer – and the feud was ended forever.

THE STINGS OF CIVILIZATION

In her untaught and primitive state one hundred years ago there was no happier woman in all this world than the Red Indian Mother who queened it over her forest home and reared her children in the principles, manners, morals and etiquette that for centuries had been approved and enforced by the men and womenkind of her world-old race.

In other articles published in this magazine I have emphasised the fact that the North American Indian woman, and especially the mother-woman, is most honoured and revered by the younger people and the men of her blood, notwithstanding all that has been said and written to the contrary. That she carries the burdens as well as the babies, that she does the hoeing of corn, drawing of water and chopping of fire wood, is no argument that she is a beast of burden. She is reared by her own mother in the teaching that all this is woman's work, and she accepts it with the cheeriness that the American and English woman in the same walk or strata of life accepts the fact that her birthright of labour is to wash, scrub, split wood, carry coal and rear children while doing it.

I have seen, from railway carriage windows, white women pitching hay and driving harvest machinery right in the State of Ohio. In the Canadian North West I have seen Russian women, flaxen-haired, creamy-skinned, hitched to a plough in bands like horses while the lordly husband, father or relative drove them – a pitiful sight blotting the freedom of God's virgin prairies. And some of these Russian plough-women were mothers!

No Indian man ever asked or permitted his womankind to do such toil, he is exempt also from the vice that prevails amongst the lower orders of white men in the old world cities who from unbridled temper or mere brutality beat their wives if immediate submission is not given them. An Indian man strikes a woman only when the white man's intoxicants have stolen his self-respect and enfeebled or enraged his brain. Thus, we revert to the opening lines of this article – the happiness and content of the Indian mother in her primitive state.

With the onward march of civilization and its accompaniments of Christianity and education in the ways of the alien Whites, all her standards must be changed, standards of childbearing and child rearing that have been upheld for centuries as the acme of excellence in training the coming race. Her entire code of existence must be shattered, and the one that civilization insists must be set up in its place destroys her ideals, berefts her of her mother's traditions and frequently tangles her threads of faith.

It is no easy matter for a mother to turn away from her own mother's teaching, her own mother's God, and hardest of all, her own mother's language and dress, and cradle. The White man's civilization despises this rigid etiquette of her ancestors, stares curiously at the habiliments of a lost century and regards with pity not unmixed with horror the God of her forefathers. These heritages which are her brain and the blood of her heart must be all uprooted, choked, and killed. Civilization does not even allow her to transplant her tree of life to other soil, there to watch it revive and blossom and bear fruit, albeit to her the blossom has no fragrance, the fruit no flavour. Against all her tried and tested practices and principles of years and of her mothers and grandmothers before her, she must rear this child against every sense of right and wrong that she had instilled with her own child and woman soul. She must teach him to go the wrong way according to her own standards, to do the wrong thing, to commit follies, vulgarisms, crimes, everything that she abhors; she must guide him towards being a failure, to bury his pride, to disregard honour, to desert the ways of the very parents who bore him. If she fails to do this she knows her child will fail in the race with civilization with which he is hourly being driven by the press-gang of circumstances; she must endure the heart-ache of watching her child outrage every principle of honour that she believes in and acts up to, and the bitterness of it all lies in the fact that these things which she firmly believes detrimental, lowering, degrading and debasing, she must urge upon him, herself. Was ever a mother's motherhood so filled with anguish?

To illustrate her position, take first of all the most vital force of civilization, that is Christianity – she has been taught that the goodness of the Great Spirit – or God – is free to everybody. The Indian in his native paganism pays nothing to or for his God except tribute of Thanksgiving in the religious dances of his faith. It is against all his principles to pay money for this privilege. The instant he enters a Christian church he is confronted by the collection plate and it horrifies him. The Indian mother is taught that it is an insult to the Great Spirit to speak of, or handle, money in connection with worship of Him. Yet she must teach her child not to omit money from his pocket when he goes to Church, he must offer what she firmly considers an insult to his God. She shudders at it, but civilization demands it. The Great Spirit of her fore-fathers loves the human race, and after death will give them Happy Hunting Grounds for their heritage. Now however, she must teach her child that wrongdoing will estrange him from this all good Great Spirit, that he may be thrust into the horrors of the White man's Hell. In her pagan heart she knows that there is but one world for the Indian's soul, but she must teach her child of a good and bad world to come though her heart will never believe it and she feels she is instructing falsity. Then she has been brought up to believe that to supplicate the Great Spirit for favours and mercies, is an insult to his intelligence, and when she teaches her kneeling child to pray for safe keeping and for guidance, her whole being is crying forth. 'No, no, no, He knows what is good for us all, He'll do as He thinks best.' That is her Pagan faith, and her child's lisping begging prayers sink into her savage heart as positive outrages. Then take the code of honour and morals, of civilization and savagery. She has been reared to think that personal courage and bravery are the first and finest qualities in the character of man. That to meet your enemy, or an enemy of your fathers, or your household, to fight him and slay him in single combat is a matter of untarnished honour, of highest herohood. She must now teach her boy that this thing is not only an evil, but a fearsome thing. Her heart glows with memories of her father's and husband's tales of the glory and honour of scalp-fringed belts, but her son must be taught to lead what she regards as a woman's not a man's life. Civilization demands it, and she must submit to an alien law, though her heart rebels at teaching her child what she regards as frailties and dishonour. Bloodshed in the cause of personal honour, she has always regarded as a prime virtue, it has been for generations instilled with the children of her race. Now she must, contrary to her own convictions teach her child that bloodshed is a horror, not an honour, and in her heart of hearts she feels she is training her boy to be a weakling, a coward, an ignoble off-shoot of his father's house, when she bids him sheath his scalping knife and place the silver chain on his tomahawk.

A peculiar socialism has always obtained amongst the Red Indians. From the cradle-board they are taught that possession of means is nothing short of crime if any known being is without such possessions. Everything a man has is divided with his neighbours and friends should they be less fortunate than himself. Should he kill a deer, those without food are all bidden to share it, he must not keep a shred of it for tomorrow for his own use if there is yet a hungry one to be appeased today. There are consequently no Indian Carnegies or Rockefellers, but impractical as this forest socialism may be, it has been inbred for centuries. Now the mother must teach her boy the Whiteman's thrift, he must not divide all he has amongst his playfellows, must not share with them his clothes, his ammunition, his father's food supplies. In her own estimation she feels she is teaching him a crime and a dishonourable thing, in teaching him self-support only. 'Divide everything' has hitherto been part of her creed. 'Divide what you can spare from your own self support' is what civilization is driving her to tell her child, and she knows that eventually it will all end in his acquiring an avarice, which is a crime unknown to his ancestors.

All these things are essential agencies for developing her ideals of manhood, and her heart resents with bitterness the conditions that necessitate her teaching him against her sense of right. But it is not always the great scars that hurt the most, some of the lesser customs of the Whitemen wound her vitally. Take the seemingly simple matter of having a boy wear short hair – I sometimes think no mother lived who has not suffered pangs, and shed tears when the inevitable scissors clipped the pretty baby curls from her boy's little head and she knows that henceforth he must go about shorn of his beauty and his babyhood – the pangs are none the less severe just because they are of sentiment and the doting mother's wish to keep her boy just as her very own baby, for a little while longer. How then must the Indian mother suffer, when she knows that to compete with White boys, to be educated in the ways of the whiteman's civilization, her boy must never wear long hair, the world-old badge of the Indian's prowess as a warrior and a brave. She remembers her own mother fostering and coaxing her brother's hair with the coveted scalp lock, plaiting and oiling it with bear's fat to help it grow luxuriantly. She can hear her mother's voice saying, 'Ah! Little Arrow, we shall have you wearing a fine long scalp-lock soon. Then when you are big like your sire and grandsire, you can fling the war whoop towards your enemies and defy them to take your hair. Jeer at them, dare them to do it, but remember, if that lock is ever shorn from your head, your honour goes with it. So guard it, treasure it with your life, do not lose your honour while you have life to fight for it.'

But in her musing, the Indian mother of today knows she may never repeat her own mother's words, never see her son defy his enemies to take that scalp-lock. Why she must even teach him that to have enemies at all is not a grand and manly thing; enemies which were the glory and the honour of the ancient Indians' life. Not to have enemies was a disgrace. Must she then teach him to live a life of disgrace?

The position is one that is difficult to define. It matters not whether one agrees or disagrees with her ideas of virtues and honours, and manhood, the fact remains that her position as a mother demands that she instruct her children in things that she does not believe in herself, in customs of which she does not approve, in walks of life which she regards as detrimental to their honour and manhood. That she ignores her own convictions, stifles her own beliefs the better to fit her child to face the world wherein the times and conditions have called him, only proves her to be one of the wisest and most unselfish of that great army that rings the whole world round, the army of mother-women.

Notes

The Chiefswood scrapbook, which includes many poems not collected in *Flint and Feather*, belongs to the collection of books from Johnson's home that is currently in storage at the Woodland Cultural Centre in Brantford. From about 1888 to 1895 Johnson pasted many clippings of her poems and a few other mementos into a commercially produced blank book. Approximately 6″ × 8½″, this well-worn volume is covered in faded black cloth, with a reddish-brown leather spine. In addition to notes and corrections in Johnson's hand there are copious comments by Hector Charlesworth, who was a close friend in the early 1890s.

On the flyleaf appear the following undated epigraphs:

But all the poem was soul of me
Launched out, and wrecked upon a sea
I hoped would float it tenderly
But portless it is toss't.
                    E. Pauline Johnson

And perhaps if I could catch it 'mong the notes
                    that tinkle low
There's a bar of grand sphere-music
                    in the singing 'neath the snow.
                    H.W. Charlesworth

In the following notes, *The White Wampum* (1895) is abbreviated as *WW*, *Canadian Born* (1903) as *CB*, *When George Was King* (1908) as *GK*, and *Flint and Feather* (1912) as *FF*.

The Fourth Act

Copy-text: Douglas Reville, *History of the County of Brant.* Brantford: Hurley Printing, 1920.

Written in Jean Morton's album in 1876, this poem was later expanded and revised as 'The Firs,' published in *The Week*, 1886. Jean Steele Morton (d. 1951), one of Johnson's closest girlhood friends, married Douglas Reville in 1893, after he became editor of the *Brantford Courier.*

'Think of me ...'

Copy-text: album, St Mary's Museum, St Mary's, Ontario.

According to documentation in the St Mary's Museum, this verse, dated 14 Feburary 1878, was written in the autograph album of Kate Askew Howell (Mrs William J. Mills, 1866–1959), who attended school with Johnson in Brantford. Her name is similar to that of Johnson's cousin and lifelong friend, Kathleen (Kate) Victoria Howells (Mrs Washington).

My Jeanie

Copy-text: Jean Waldie, 'The Iroquois Poetess, Pauline Johnson.' *Ontario History* 40 (1948): 65–75.

Written in Jean Morton's album, 17 June 1879.

My Little Jean

Copy-text: Reville, *History of the County of Brant.*

Written to Jean Morton in 1883, this is believed to be Johnson's first published poem. However, reports of its appearance in *Gems of Poetry* in 1883 or 1884 have not been verified.

Rover

Copy-text: *Gems of Poetry,* December 1884, p. 190, amended by Johnson, Johnson fonds, McMaster University.

Johnson's second published work, written in 1883 according to notes in her hand on the copy at McMaster.

The Rift

Copy-text: version in the Chiefswood scrapbook (unidentified clipping), amended by Johnson.

This poem, which appeared in *Gems of Poetry*, August 1884, p. 127, under the pseudonym Margaret Rox, was Johnson's third published work, according to a note in her hand.

The Re-interment of Red Jacket

Copy-text: version in the Chiefswood scrapbook (unidentified clipping), amended by Johnson.

In the fall of 1884 the Buffalo Historical Society invited Pauline Johnson and her sister Evelyn to attend the re-interment of Red Jacket, the influential Seneca orator, in Woodlawn Cemetery, because the original gravesite was endangered by new construction. Johnson's commemorative poem was not recited at the event, but was subsequently published in the society's journal, *Transactions of the Buffalo Historical Society*, and was dated 9 October 1884.

Red Jacket (Otetiani; also Sagoyewatha, 1758?–1830) used his impressive oratorical skills during and after the American Revolution to negotiate on behalf of Iroquois cultural and economic integrity.

The Sea Queen

Copy-text: version in the Chiefswood scrapbook (undated clipping from the *News-Letter*), amended by Johnson.

Other versions apppeared in *The Week*, 16 April 1885, p. 315, and *Gems of Poetry*, June 1885, p. 95.

Iris to Floretta

Copy-text: *Gems of Poetry*, June 1885, p. 90.

A shorter version, titled 'To Florette Maracle' (whose source is not known), appears in Marcus Van Steen's *Pauline Johnson: Her Life and Work* (1965). Floretta Katherine Maracle, a teacher on the Six Nations Reserve and a childhood friend of the Johnson family, married Allen Johnson, Pauline's brother, in June 1908.

A Cry from an Indian Wife

Copy-text: *Flint and Feather*.

First published in *The Week*, 18 June 1885, and revised for *WW*, this was one of Johnson's most effective recital pieces. It was frequently reprinted in newspaper accounts of her performances from 1892 onward. The last four lines originally read:

> O! coward self – I hesitate no more.
> Go forth – and win the glories of the war.
> O! heart o'erfraught – O! nation lying low –
> God, and fair Canada have willed it so.

This poem appeared during the course of the Northwest Rebellion of 1885, between the surrender of Poundmaker on 26 May and the surrender of Big Bear on 2 July. The major confrontation involved Métis and Indians, led by Louis Riel and Gabriel Dumont, who rallied in protest against the land policies of the dominion government. They were opposed by forces assembled under Major-General Frederick Middleton, which included some three thousand volunteers from Eastern Canada who joined another seventeen hundred from the west.

In the Shadows

Copy-text: *Flint and Feather*
    First published in *The Week*, 17 September 1885, p. 664; collected in *WW*. This was one of two poems by Johnson selected by W.D. Lighthall in 1889 for inclusion in his nationalist anthology, *Songs of the Great Dominion*. It was particularly popular in canoeing circles; two hundred copies were printed in 1898 in a souvenir pamphlet to commemorate the nineteenth annual meeting of the American Canoe Association at Stave Island, in the St Lawrence River. An altered version appeared in *The Rudder* in 1895, with six stanzas, each ending with a chorus:

> To and fro, soft and slow
>   I paddle my old canoe,
> To and fro, soft and slow
>   I paddle my bark canoe.

The Firs

Copy-text: *The Week*, 21 January 1886, p. 117.
    An earlier version was written in 1876, as 'The Fourth Act' (see above).

Easter Lilies

Copy-text: *The Week*, 22 April 1886.

The patron saint of girls, St Agnes is celebrated as a young Roman virgin martyr whose refusal to marry led to her execution.

At the Ferry

Copy-text: W.D. Lighthall, *Songs of the Great Dominion* (1889), text amended by Johnson in the Chiefswood scrapbook.

First published in *The Week*, 16 September 1886, this was one of two poems selected by Lighthall for inclusion in his 1889 anthology, *Songs of the Great Dominion*. The Johnson home, Chiefswood, is situated on the eastern bank of the Grand River, which was crossed by a nearby cable ferry before construction of the current bridge. In Greek mythology, Lethe was the river of forgetfulness, tasted by the souls of the dead as they entered the underworld.

'Brant,' A Memorial Ode

Copy-text: souvenir broadside, 8 October 1886, Chiefswood scrapbook.

Composed for the unveiling of a commemorative statue of Joseph Brant on 13 October 1886, this poem was read aloud by W.F. Cockshutt, a prominent Brantford businessman (who later served as a Conservative member of Parliament from 1904 to 1921), while Pauline stood beside him on the platform. It was offered for sale in a copyrighted souvenir broadside in which 'Te-ka-hion-wa-ke' was added to Johnson's name. Originally belonging to her great-grandfather, the name reappeared as 'Tekahionwake' in 1895 on the front cover and title page of *The White Wampum*, after which it was consistently attached to Johnson's signature.

Chief Joseph Brant (Thayendenega, *c.* 1742/43–1807) commanded Iroquois warriors who sided with the British during the American Revolution. After the war he led the Mohawk Loyalists from the Mohawk River in New York State to the Grand River reserve in Ontario, granted to the Six Nations in compensation for their losses across the border. The Six Nations of the Iroquois, an alliance founded by Hiawatha, were the Mohawk, Seneca, Onondaga, Cayuga, Oneida, and Tuscarora.

['alas! how damning praise can be!']

Copy-text: scrapbook, Johnson fonds, McMaster University.

This squib was elicited by the reporter for the Toronto *World*, 14 October 1886, whose coverage of the unveiling of the Brant monument referred to Johnson as 'a pleasant-looking Indian maiden.'

A Request

Copy-text: *The Week*, 18 November 1886, p. 821.

The full title of the organization to whom this poem is addressed is the Women's Auxiliary of the Domestic and Foreign Mission Society of the Church of England in Canada. Organized in 1886, shortly before the appearance of Johnson's poem, it reported a membership of 15,460 in 1900. In addition to supporting Anglican clergy in the Northwest (the men wearing 'robes of snow'), its projects included sending teachers and nurses to Native schools and communities.

Fasting

Copy-text: *Flint and Feather.*

First published as 'The Vigil of St. Basil' in *The Week*, 7 April 1887, p. 301; collected in *WW*. Nepenthe (meaning 'no grief') is an Egyptian drug, mentioned in the *Odyssey*, that drove away care and made people forget their troubles. A censer is a vessel in which incense is burned, during a religious ceremony.

Life

Copy-text: *The Musical Journal*, 15 July 1887, p. 108–9.

This song was set to music by Arthur E. Fisher (1848–1912), a musician and composer active in Toronto during the 1880s and 1890s.

My English Letter

Copy-text: *Flint and Feather.*

First published in *Saturday Night*, 17 March 1888, p. 6; collected in *WW*.

Easter

Copy-text: *Flint and Feather.*

First published as 'Easter, 1888' in *Saturday Night*, 31 March 1888, p. 6; collected in *WW*. In 1888, Easter Sunday occurred on 1 April, thus marking the end of the sacrificial period of Lent with the beginning of a new month.

Joe

Copy-text: *Flint and Feather.*
   First published as 'Joe (A Sketch from Memory)' in *The Week*, 24 May 1888, p. 413; collected in *WW.*

Unguessed

Copy-text: *Saturday Night*, 16 June 1888, p. 6.
   In the Chiefswood scrapbook, a hand other than Johnson's comments that 'blonde' in the third stanza is 'not a poetic word,' and strikes out the fifth stanza.

Our Brotherhood

Copy-text: *The Week*, 26 July 1888, p. 449.

The Death-Cry

Copy-text: *Saturday Night*, 1 September 1888, p. 6.

Keepsakes

Copy-text: *Saturday Night*, 29 September, 1888, p. 6, amended by Johnson in the Chiefswood scrapbook.

The Flight of the Crows

Copy-text: *Flint and Feather.*
   First published in *Saturday Night*, 13 October 1888, p. 6; collected in *WW.* Te Deum: from Te Deum Laudamus (We praise thee, O God), the opening words of an ancient Latin hymn of praise or thanksgiving. In English translation it is sung regularly at Morning Prayer in the Church of England.

Under Canvas

Copy-text: *Flint and Feather.*
   First published in *Saturday Night*, 17 November 1888, p. 6; collected in *WW.* Lake Rosseau is one of three large interconnected lakes in the Muskoka region, east of Georgian Bay, a popular recreation area where Johnson enjoyed several canoeing vacations.

Workworn

Copy-text: *Flint and Feather.*
First published in *Saturday Night*, 8 December 1888, p. 7; collected in *WW.*

The Lumberman's Christmas

Copy-text: *Saturday Night*, Christmas Number, 1888, p. 12, amended by Johnson in the Chiefswood scrapbook.
Titled 'A Backwoods Christmas ' before Johnson changed the title and trimmed the ending. As 'The Lumberman's Christmas,' it frequently appeared on her concert programs.

The Happy Hunting Grounds

Copy-text: *Flint and Feather.*
First published in *Saturday Night*, 12 January 1889, p. 6; reprinted 'by request,' *Saturday Night*, 5 September 1891, p. 6; collected in *WW.* In Greek mythology, Lethe was the river of forgetfulness, tasted by the souls of the dead as they entered the underworld.

Close By

Copy-text: *Flint and Feather.*
First published in *Saturday Night*, 2 February 1889, p. 6; collected in *WW.*

Overlooked

Copy-text: *Flint and Feather.*
First published as 'Ungranted' in *Saturday Night*, 27 April 1889, p. 6; collected in *WW.*

Erie Waters

Copy-text: *Flint and Feather.*
First published as 'Old Erie' in *Saturday Night*, 25 May 1889, p. 6, with an additional final stanza; collected in *WW.*

Shadow River

Copy-text: *Flint and Feather.*

First published in *Saturday Night*, 20 July 1889, p. 6; collected in *WW*. The rivers and lakes of the Muskoka region, east of Georgian Bay, were popular with canoeists and campers.

Nocturne

Copy-text: *Flint and Feather.*

First published in *The Week*, 26 July 1889, p. 534; collected in *WW*. The 'peace that passes human understanding' paraphrases 'the peace of God, which passes all understanding,' Philippians: IV. 7. Johnson may have remembered it from the blessing for Holy Communion in the *Book of Common Prayer* used in the Church of England. In a note to the clipping in the Chiefswood scrapbook, Johnson identifies the golden cross in the fifth stanza as '"Old Trinity" spire, New York City.'

Bass Lake (Muskoka)

Copy-text: *Saturday Night*, 2 August 1889, p. 6.

Bass Lake, now the site of a provincial park, is several miles west of Orillia, Ontario.

Temptation

Copy-text: *Saturday Night*, 24 August 1889, p. 6, amended by Johnson in the Chiefswood scrapbook.

Misguided

Copy-text: undated typescript, Brant County Museum

This poem exists in two versions, both included in this edition. As 'Temptation,' a third-person version was published in *Saturday Night*. A rather different first-person version, titled 'Misguided,' survives in the Brant County Museum as an undated typescript, whose source is described as 'manuscript.' A pencilled note adds, 'given to Mrs Revelle.'

Fortune's Favours

Copy-text: *Saturday Night*, 14 September 1889, p. 6.

Rondeau

Copy-text: *Saturday Night*, 16 November 1889, p. 6.

Christmastide

Copy-text: *Flint and Feather.*
  First published in *Saturday Night,* 21 December 1889, p. 4; collected in *WW.*

Evergreens

Copy-text: *Christmas Globe,* 1889, p. 6.

What the Soldier Said

Copy-text: undated clipping, 'For the Brant Churchman,' Chiefswood scrapbook.
  Published in the 'Brant Churchman,' a serial that seems to have vanished without a trace, this poem likely appeared in 1889, the date of the other poems on the same page of the Chiefswood scrapbook.
  In his account of the battle of Balaclava (1854) in the Crimean War, journalist William Howard Russell described the British troops as a 'thin red line' resisting Russian attack (*The British Expedition to the Crimea,* 1877). One of Johnson's first pieces of journalism admiringly recounts her impressions of a veteran of the Crimean War, whom she met unexpectedly on a Muskoka pier; see 'Charming Word Pictures. Etchings by a Muskoka Idler,' *Brantford Courier,* 23 August 1890.
  'For Valour' is the citation on the Victoria Cross, instituted in 1856 by Queen Victoria as the Empire's highest award for bravery. This poem may refer to Alexander Roberts Dunn (1833–68), the first Canadian to receive the Victoria Cross. The 'cross upon my brow' refers to the practice in the Anglican Church of making the sign of the cross – Father, Son, and Holy Ghost – during communion.

'Comrades, we are serving ...'

Copy-text: undated clipping, Chiefswood scrapbook.
  These verses were sung by children at the laying of the cornerstone for the rebuilding of Central School, which Johnson had attended. Sheila Johnston, in *Buckskin & Broadcloth* (1997, p. 92), dates the event as 1890.

Beyond the Blue

Copy-text: *Flint and Feather.*
  First published as 'We Three' in *Saturday Night,* 12 April 1890, p. 6; collected in *CB.*

In April

Copy-text: *Saturday Night*, 26 April 1890, p. 6.

For Queen and Country. May 24th

Copy-text: *Saturday Night*, 24 May 1890, p. 6.
Queen Victoria's birthday, the 24th of May, was a national holiday. After the death of her husband in 1861, Victoria always wore black when she appeared in public.

The Idlers

Copy-text: *Flint and Feather.*
First published in *Saturday Night*, 1 July 1890, p. 18; collected in *WW*. Johnson revised the ending of this poem for *WW*, removing the penultimate stanza. The version in the Chiefswood scrapbook concludes:

Has destiny a bliss,
A counterpart of this
Wild flame your kiss has left upon my palm?
Does heat respond to heat?
Does fire with fervor meet?
Or does a storm tempestuous but image empty calm?

Ah! no, the falling day
Confirms our will to stay
Then die with [passion crossed out, and not replaced] in its afterglow
And hearts will pay the cost,
For you and I have lost
More than the homeward blowing winds that died an hour ago.

Depths

Copy-text: *Saturday Night*, 19 July 1890, p. 6.

Day Dawn

Copy-text: *Flint and Feather.*
First published in *Saturday Night*, 9 August 1890, p. 6; collected in *FF.*

'Held by the Enemy'

Copy-text: *Saturday Night*, 23 August 1890, p. 6, amended by Johnson in the Chiefswood scrapbook.

In the Chiefswood scrapbook, Johnson has written 'J.H.R.' beside the title. Below the poem she pasted the following unidentified newspaper clipping: 'The poem republished above from Saturday Night is so entirely foreign to the author's well-known style that it is unique and betokens a versatility that her own best friends believed her unpossessed of.'

To Peggy

Copy-text: Peggy Webling, *Peggy: The Story of One Score Years and Ten* (London: Hutchinson, 1924), pp. 148–9.

Peggy Webling, member of a troupe of performing sisters based in London, England, spent the summer of 1890 visiting relatives in Brantford. Lucy, the youngest child of the family, was later to marry Johnson's stage partner, Walter McRaye. Peggy Webling's memoir recounts receiving this poem from Johnson, inscribed on a strip of birchbark.

Two Women

Copy-text: *Saturday Night*, 20 September 1890, p. 6.

October in Canada

Copy-text: *Massey's Illustrated*, 6 October 1895.

First published as 'In October,' *Saturday Night*, 11 October 1890; reprinted frequently as 'October in Canada' (*Public Opinion*, 28 September 1894; *Living Age*, 23 February 1895; *Massey's Illustrated*, October 1895).

'Through Time and Bitter Distance'

Copy-text: *Flint and Feather.*

First published as 'Thro' Time and Bitter Distance' in *Saturday Night*, 13 December 1890, p. 6; collected in *CB*. The title is taken from Charles G.D. Roberts's sonnet 'Rain,' first published in 1886 and subsequently included in several collections of his poems.

As Red Men Die

Copy-text: *Flint and Feather.*

First published in *Saturday Night*, Christmas Number 1890, p. 32; collected in *WW.*

In the seventeenth century, the Huron group of Iroquoian tribes occupied the area that became Simcoe County, along the shore of Lake Simcoe. The Mohawks lived farther south, in present-day New York State, along the shores of the Genesee and Mohawk rivers. The two were long-standing rivals in the fur trade, the Hurons as allies of the French, and the Mohawk as allies of the English.

In line 10, 'stoops not to be to any man a slave' echoes the claim in 'Rule Britannia' that Britons 'never, never, never shall be slaves.'

According to Johnson's friend, Isabel Ecclestone MacKay, her Mohawk grandfather, John Smoke Johnson, frequently recounted 'the stirring tale of his great uncle who died a "Warrior's death" when taken captive by the Hurons. It seems that, when Indians on the warpath were to make a new raid, the captives were given a choice. They might be left behind with the women and old men (eternal disgrace) or they might "walk the coals" and die gloriously. For this ceremony a long pine tree was felled and reduced to red hot coals. Back and forth on this glowing bed walked the warrior, chanting his death song, defiant to the end.' (PABC, MS-2367, Isabel Ecclestone MacKay, 'Pauline Johnson: A Memory and an Appreciation,' typescript, pp. 8–9).

The Last Page

Copy-text: *Saturday Night*, 3 January 1891, p. 6.

The Snowshoer

Copy-text: *Saturday Night*, 7 February 1891, p.6, amended by Johnson in the Chiefswood scrapbook.

Outlooking

Copy-text: *Saturday Night*, 28 February 1891, p. 6.

The Seventh Day

Copy-text: *Saturday Night*, 21 March 1891, p. 6.

Star Lake (Muskoka)

Copy-text: *The Young Canadian*, 22 April 1891, p. 198, amended by Johnson in the Chiefswood scrapbook.

The Muskoka region, popular with canoeists and campers, abounds in small lakes.

Vulcan, the Roman god of fire and patron of workers in metal, was thought to forge thunderbolts.

The Vagabonds

Copy-text: *Flint and Feather.*

First published in *Saturday Night*, 9 May 1891, p. 6; collected in *WW*.

Re-Voyage

Copy-text: *Flint and Feather.*

First published in *The Independent* (New York), 2 July 1891, p. 1; reprinted in the *Brantford Expositor*, 18 July 1891; collected in *WW*.

In Days to Come

Copy-text: *Saturday Night*, 25 July 1891, p. 6.

An undated typescript of a briefer version lacking the second stanza, titled 'If I Could Only Know,' survives in the Frank Yeigh papers, MG 30 D58, NA.

The Camper

Copy-text: *Flint and Feather.*

First published in *Outing Magazine* (New York), September 1891, p. 480; collected in *WW*.

At Husking Time

Copy-text: *Flint and Feather.*

First published in *The Independent* (New York), 24 September 1891, p. 30; reprinted in *Saturday Night*, 31 October 1891, p. 6; collected in *WW*.

The Pilot of the Plains

Copy-text: *Flint and Feather.*

First published in *Saturday Night*, Christmas Number, 1891, p. 36; collected in *WW.*

Rondeau: The Skater

Copy-text: *Saturday Night*, 23 January 1892, p. 6.
The messenger god, known as Hermes to the Greeks and Mercury to the Romans, was represented wearing a winged hat and winged sandals.

The Song My Paddle Sings

Copy-text: *Flint and Feather.*
First published in *Saturday Night*, 27 February 1892, p. 7, and reprinted many times; collected in *WW.* Several verses appeared under the title 'Outlook,' *OAC [Ontario Agricultural College] Review* 24, no. 10 (July 1912): 544.
A lateen is a triangular sail. In her recreation articles, Johnson frequently describes hoisting such a sail on her canoe, to take advantage of lake winds.

At Sunset

Copy-text: *Flint and Feather.*
First published in *Saturday Night*, 7 May 1892, p. 6; collected in *WW.*

Rainfall

Copy-text: *Flint and Feather.*
First published as 'Rain-fall' in *Saturday Night*, 6 August 1892, p. 6; collected in *WW.*

Penseroso

Copy-text: *Flint and Feather.*
First published in the *Lake Magazine* (Toronto), August 1892, p. 16; collected in *WW.* Three verses, without title, appeared in the *OAC [Ontario Agricultural College] Review* 18, no. 7 (April 1906): 308.
'Penseroso,' is the Italian word for 'thoughtful' or 'pensive,' and recalls the title of 'Il Penseroso,' John Milton's famous invocation to melancholy, published in 1645.

Wave-Won

Copy-text: *Flint and Feather.*
 First published in *Belford's Magazine* (Chicago), August 1892, 415–16; collected in *WW.*

The Avenger

Copy-text: *Saturday Night*, Christmas Number 1892, p. 15.
 The Cherokee, who formed a powerful southern Native confederacy, were traditional rivals of the Iroquois, but like them, were often allies of the British during the American Revolutionary War. In 1892 they were forced to leave Georgia, Tennessee, and North Carolina to resettle on a reservation in Oklahoma. This painful expulsion became known as the 'Trail of Tears.'

The Birds' Lullaby

Copy-text: *Flint and Feather.*
 First published in the *Canadian Magazine*, March 1893, p. 72; collected in *WW.*

The Portage

Copy-text: Mrs W. Garland Foster, *The Mohawk Princess* (Vancouver: Lion's Gate 1931) p. 61.
 It has not been possible to verify Foster's claim that this poem was first published in the *American Canoe Club Yearbook*, 1893.

The Mariner

Copy-text: *Flint and Feather.*
 First published in *Saturday Night*, 25 March 1893, p. 12; collected in *CB.*
 The epigraph comes from Swinburne's poem 'Felise' (*Poems and Ballads*, 1866), which tells the story of a failed romance.

Brier

Copy-text: *Flint and Feather.*
 First published in *Saturday Night*, 1 April 1893, p. 8; collected in *WW.*

Wolverine

Copy-text: *Flint and Feather.*
　First published in *Saturday Night*, Christmas Number 1893, p. 24; collected in
WW.

In Grey Days

Copy-text: *Flint and Feather.*
　First published in the *Ladies' Journal*, February 1894, p. 7; collected in *FF.*

In Freshet Time

Copy-text: fair copy in the Chiefswood scrapbook
　Published in *Acta Victoriana*, February 1894, p. 148.
　A freshet is the overflowing of a river. Teasel is a bienniel herb, native to
Europe, West Asia, and North Africa, formerly cultivated for its flowers, which
were used to tease fabric in order to raise a nap.

Thistle-Down

Copy-text: *Flint and Feather.*
　An illustrated version, created by Robert Holmes in 1894 for an art calendar,
was reproduced in 'A Pictorial Poem and a Picture,' in the *Canadian Courier*,
21 December 1912; collected in *CB.*

Moonset

Copy-text: *Flint and Feather.*
　First published as 'Moon-Set' in *Outing Magazine*, October 1894, p. 43;
collected in *WW.* The final stanza has been substantially altered from the
original:

> O! music of the night, your minstrelsy
> 　Is tender as the tone
> Of some dear voice outcalling unto me
> 　Responsive to my own.
> Your harp-strings throb beneath an unseen hand,
> And sing the moon to sleep in shadow land.

The Cattle Thief

Copy-text: *Flint and Feather.*
    First published in *The Week*, 7 December 1894, p. 34; collected in *WW.*
    The dramatic decline in the buffalo herds after the 1850s, in combination with federal policy after 1871 to concentrate the prairie tribes on limited reserves without adequate provisions or support, led to widespread starvation. See 'Silhouette' for the similar fate of the Blackfoot.

At Crow's Nest Pass

Copy-text. *Flint and Feather.*
    First published as 'Rondeau: Crow's Nest Pass,' *Globe* 15 December 1894, p. 4; collected in *CB.*
    This and the subsequent twelve poems appeared in a light-hearted travel article which describes Johnson's first trip to the West coast. Titled 'There and Back,' it was co-authored by 'Miss Poetry (E. Pauline Johnson) and Mr Prose (Owen A. Smily).'

Benedictus

Copy-text: *Globe*, 15 December 1894, p. 3.
    After Johnson's death, this poem appeared in the *Canadian Magazine* (July 1913, p. 278) with the erroneous note: 'Here published for the first time.'

Fire Flowers

Copy-text: *Flint and Feather.*
    First published as 'The Fire Flowers' in the *Globe*, 15 December 1894, p. 3; collected in *CB.* In the *Globe*, Johnson comments that the plant is commonly known as fire-weed.

The Gopher

Copy-text: *Globe*, 15 December 1894, p. 4.

Harvest Time

Copy-text: *Flint and Feather.*
    First published as 'Summer,' *Globe* 15 December 1894, p. 4; collected in *CB.*

His Majesty, the West Wind

Copy-text: *Globe*, 15 December 1894, p. 4.
The poem refers to the opening lines of 'The Song My Paddle Sings.'

Kicking-Horse River

Copy-text: *Globe*, 15 December 1894, p.4.
The Kicking Horse River flows westward into British Columbia from Kicking Horse Pass, on the continental divide between Alberta and British Columbia. The name derives from an 1858 incident when Sir James Hector, exploring the pass with the Palliser expedition, was kicked in the chest by a packhorse.

Little Vancouver

Copy-text: *Globe*, 15 December 1894, p. 4.
The small wooden settlement that began as Gastown burned to the ground in June 1886, two months after its incorporation as the city of Vancouver. Nonetheless, it rapidly grew to overtake New Westminster, known as the Queen City and the official capital of British Columbia, due to the extension of the CPR's main line to the Vancouver harbour.

The Prairie

Copy-text: *Globe*, 15 December 1894, p. 4.

Silhouette

Copy-text: *Flint and Feather.*
First published as 'Silhouetted,' *Globe* 15 December 1894, p. 4; collected in *CB.*
See the note on 'The Cattle Thief' regarding the similar fate of the Cree.

Where Leaps the Ste Marie

Copy-text: *Flint and Feather.*
First published as 'The Leap of the Ste Marie,' *Globe*, 15 December 1894, p. 3; collected in *CB.* The Ste Marie River rapids give their name to the town of Sault Ste Marie.

The Wolf

Copy-text: *Flint and Feather.*
    First published in the *Globe*, 15 December 1894, p. 4; collected in the second edition of *FF* (1916).

Curtain

Copy-text: *Globe*, 15 December 1894, p. 4.
    This poem concludes 'There and Back.'

Marshlands

Copy-text: *Flint and Feather.*
    First published as 'Marsh-Lands' in *The Varsity* (Toronto), 17 December 1894, p. 96; collected in *WW.*
    Sedges are perennial herbacious grasslike plants growing throughout the world, mainly in swampy places.

Sou'wester

Copy-text: *The Rudder,* January 1895, p. 5.

Boots and Saddles

Copy-text: *Globe* 1 June 1895, p. 11.
    This and the four subsequent poems appeared in 'The Races in Prose and Verse,' the second piece of light-hearted journalism by Miss Poetry (Johnson) and Mr Prose (Owen Smily).

The Favourite

Copy-text: *Globe*, 1 June 1895, p. 11.
    Mammon, from the early Greek version of the New Testament, refers to people who worship wealth.

In the Boxes

Copy-text: *Globe*, 1 June 1895, p. 11.

The Last Hurdle

Copy-text: *Globe*, 1 June 1895, p. 11.

Perspective

Copy-text: *Globe*, 1 June 1895, p. 11.

The White and the Green

Copy-text: undated clipping from the *Year Book*, in the Chiefswood scrapbook.
    In her letter of 9 June 1895 to Arthur Henry O'Brien (Archives of Ontario), Johnson says that she encloses a copy of 'The White & the Green' (no longer in the collection) which she considers 'one of my best recent efforts.'
    The plover is a common bird that inhabits open regions and shorelines.

Dawendine

Copy-text: *Flint and Feather.*
    There is no record of this poem's publication before its appearance in *WW* in July 1895.

Ojistoh

Copy-text: *Flint and Feather.*
    There is no record of this poem's publication before its appearance in *WW* in July 1895.

Becalmed

Copy-text: *The Rudder*, October 1895, p. 242.

The Lifting of the Mist

Copy-text: *Flint and Feather.*
    First published in *Black and White* (London), 28 December 1895, p. 839; collected in *FF.*

The Songster

Copy-text: *Flint and Feather.*

First published in *Massey's Magazine*, May 1896, p. 296; collected in *CB*. In the sixth edition of *FF*, and all subsequent editions and impressions, the first line erroneously appears as the sixth.

The Good Old N. P.

Copy-text: *Daily Mail and Empire*, 4 June 1896, p. 6.

The 'N. P.' refers to the National Policy implemented by Sir John A. Macdonald in 1879, which erected tariff barriers to protect Canadian manufacturing. The term remained a rallying cry for the Conservative party, even after the death of Macdonald in 1891. Johnson's poem, dated 26 May 1896, was written during the campaign which would see Laurier lead the the Liberals to victory over Sir Charles Tupper in the election held on 23 June.

Accompanying the poem is a note that 'Miss E. Pauline Johnson has been awarded the first prize of the three offered by the Industrial League for the best campaign song.'

Lullaby of the Iroquois

Copy-text: *Flint and Feather.*

First published in *Harper's Weekly*, 11 July 1896, p. 686; collected in *CB*. Johnson later used this poem to open her article 'Outdoor Occupations of the Indian Mother and Her Children,' published in *Mother's Magazine* in July 1908. Her ensuing sentence suggests that this is a traditional song: 'So croons the Mohawk mother when the early evening shadows fall across her forest home ...'

The Corn Husker

Copy-text: *Flint and Feather.*

First published in *Harper's Weekly*, 5 September 1896, p. 868; collected in *CB*.

Low Tide at St Andrews

Copy-text: *Flint and Feather.*

First published as 'Low Tide at St Andrews, New Brunswick,' *Black and White*, 5 September 1896, p. 298; collected in *CB*. St Andrews is a town on the Bay of Fundy, which is noted for its extreme tides.

The Quill Worker

Copy-text: *Flint and Feather.*

First published in *Black and White* (London), 31 October 1896, p. 558; collected in *CB* and *GK.*

The Cypress Hills in southeastern Alberta and southwestern Saskatchewan are now two provincial parks, one in each province. They were the site of illicit whisky trading in the 1860s, and in 1873 of the massacre of thirty-six Assiniboine by a gang of Canadian and American wolf hunters.

During the eighteenth and early nineteenth centuries, many Dakota (Sioux) moved south, into American territory. However, after the battle of Little Big Horn in 1876, Sitting Bull (*c.* 1834–93) and his band entered Saskatchewan as political refugees. Despite their pledges of loyalty to Queen Victoria, Sitting Bull and the Dakota were barely tolerated by Ottawa, and returned to the United States under a general amnesty in 1881. The Sioux leader was killed during renewed hostilities in 1893.

His Sister's Son

Copy-text: 'Johnson-Smily Entertainment,' *Fort Wayne Indiana Gazette,* 25 November 1896, clipping, McMaster University.

Although frequently recited, this poem remained unpublished except for these lines recorded by a journalist, who commented: 'in her reading of "His Sister's Son," showing the tragic results of the present unhappy system of civilizing the Indians, her nationality bespoke her love for her native land and people, and scorn for those who would take her parentage from her.' The same lines also appear in an undated clipping from the *Terre Haute Gazette,* which describes their context as a

> most effective recitation ... of an Indian girl who has been taken from her parents by the missionaries, educated, taught of a heaven and – a hell.
> When she wanted to return to her kinsfolk after completing her education, she was urged to remain and never more look upon her heathen parents.
> The tragic attributes of her nature assert themselves when her white lover is persuaded to give her up and wed a fair haired maiden. She poisoned him so that the golden haired girl cannot have him.

This description tells us that the poem is an early version of Johnson's 1899 story 'As It Was in the Beginning,' which contains the phrase 'his sister's son' in reference to the white lover, who is the nephew of the clergyman responsible for the tragedy.

Traverse Bay

Copy-text: undated clipping, Johnson fonds, McMaster University.

Occasioned by a performance in Traverse City, Michigan, possibly on the itinerary that included Grand Rapids late in 1896. As Johnson returned to Michigan in 1903 and 1907, this poem might have been composed later.

The Mouse's Message

Copy-text: undated holograph manuscript, reproduced with the permission of John Wilkes.

Written around 1896 to Gerald Wilkes (b. 1891), young son of Johnson's canoeing friend, Florence Wilkes. Many years later, Mr Wilkes recalled, 'Miss Johnson had begun her travels and the poem was sent to me from Vancouver or Victoria, and was enclosed with two small toy mice which I kept for many years. I was about five years old at the time.' (Gerald Wilkes to Art Solomon, 23 September 1966, copy at Chiefswood historical site.)

The Indian Corn Planter

Copy-text: *Flint and Feather.*
First published in *Massey's Magazine,* June 1897, p. 397; collected in *FF.*

Canadian Born

Copy-text: *Flint and Feather.*
This poem joined Johnson's recital repertoire late in 1897, and was first published in the *Halifax Herald* and other Nova Scotia newspapers, 15 June 1900; collected in *CB* and *GK.*

The Legend of Qu'Appelle Valley

Copy-text: *Flint and Feather.*
First published as 'The Indian Legend of the Qu' Appelle Valley' in *Town Topics* (Winnipeg), 1 October 1898; collected in *CB* and *GK.*

The Qu'Appelle River, of southern Saskatchewan, is believed to have received its name from a story like the one recounted in this poem. 'Qu'Appelle' ('Qui appelle') translates as 'Who calls?'

'Give Us Barabbas'

Copy-text: *Flint and Feather.*
First published in the *Free Press Home Journal* (Winnipeg), 28 September 1899 and the *Manitoba Morning Free Press,* 30 September 1899; collected in *CB.*

In the Bible, at the crucifixion of Jesus Christ, Barabbas is the criminal saved by the mob who called for his release while demanding the death of Jesus; see Luke 23:18 and John 18:40. In 1894 Alfred Dreyfus (1859–1935), a Jewish officer in the French army, was convicted of selling military secrets and sentenced to life imprisonment on Devil's Island. A lengthy campaign by his defenders culminated in his pardon in September 1899. In *FF*, Johnson added an explanatory note: 'Written after Dreyfus was exiled.'

Winnipeg – At Sunset

Copy-text: undated clipping, *Winnipeg Pree Press*, Johnson fonds, McMaster University.

This poem probably appeared in the late 1890s, when Johnson was planning to settle permanently in Winnipeg.

'H.M.S.'

Copy-text: *Christmas Globe* (Toronto), December 1899.

H.M.S. (Her or His Majesty's Ship) designates ships belonging to the Royal Navy. The original version includes the note: 'Written after a visit aboard H.M.S. "Crescent," in Halifax Harbour, N.S.'

The Riders of the Plains

Copy-text: *Flint and Feather.*

First recited in 1899, this poem does not seem to have been published before its appearance in *Canadian Born* in June 1903. All editions include Johnson's note to the title:

> The above is the Territorial pet name for the North-West Mounted Police, and is in general usage throughout Assiniboia, Saskatchewan and Alberta. At a dinner party in Boston the writer was asked, 'Who are the North-West Mounted Police?' and when told that they were the pride of Canada's fighting men the questioner sneered and replied, 'Ah! Then they are only some of your British Lion's whelps, *We are not afraid of them.*' His companions applauded the remark.

The North-West Mounted Police were created in 1873 to secure the Northwest for Canadian and European settlement and to control the Native tribes. They received their current name, the Royal Canadian Mounted Police, in 1920.

Rondeau: Morrow-Land

Copy-text: holograph manuscript, dated Holy Saturday, 1901, Johnson fonds, McMaster University.

It is believed that this poem was written to Charles H. Wuerz, Johnson's manager for about a year, from 1900 to 1901. In the corner is a note: 'E.P.J./ To [Toronto] / "Mine, – to Amuse."' Easter Sunday is the last day of Passion Week.

To C.H.W.

Copy-text: undated holograph manuscript, Johnson fonds, McMaster University.

Believed to date from the same period as 'Morrow-Land,' this poem is also addressed to Charles H. Wuerz, who came from Heidelberg. Published as 'In Heidelberg' in the *Canadian Magazine* 42 (November 1913), 53, with one line omitted and other errors. Foster cites another version: see below.

Heidleburgh

Copy-text: Mrs W. Garland Foster, *The Mohawk Princess* (Vancouver: Lion's Gate 1931), p. 104

A different version of 'To. C.H.W.,' its source remains unknown.

His Majesty the King

Copy-text: undated broadside, Johnson fonds, McMaster University.

This poem celebrates Edward VII's accession to the British throne, after the death of Queen Victoria in 1901.

A Prodigal

Copy-text: *Flint and Feather.*

First published as 'The Prodigal' in *The Smart Set*, April 1902, p. 149; collected in *CB* and *GK.*

Made in Canada

Copy-text: *Saturday Night*, 28 February 1903, p. 3.

Written for a manufacturers' banquet in Brantford, where it was read aloud by W.F. Cockshutt, the same man who had earlier read Johnson's poem 'Brant.'

The Art of Alma-Tadema

Copy-text: *Flint and Feather.*
There is no record of this poem's publication before its appearance in *Canadian Born* in June 1903.
On her 1894 visit to London, Johnson met Laurence Alma-Tadema (1836–1912), a popular painter best known for his scenes from antiquity.

At Half-Mast

Copy-text: *Flint and Feather.*
There is no record of this poem's publication before its appearance in *Canadian Born* in June 1903.

The City and the Sea

Copy-text: *Flint and Feather.*
There is no record of this poem's publication before its appearance in *Canadian Born* in June 1903.
Of Aramaic origin, 'Mammon' signifies riches, often personified, as in Matthew 6:24.

Golden – of the Selkirks

Copy-text: *Flint and Feather.*
There is no record of this poem's publication before its appearance in *Canadian Born* in June 1903.
Situated on the CPR line in eastern British Columbia, the town of Golden was a regular stopping point on Johnson's cross-Canada tours.

Goodbye

Copy-text: *Flint and Feather.*
There is no record of this poem's publication before its appearance in *Canadian Born* in June 1903.

Guard of the Eastern Gate

Copy-text: *Flint and Feather.*
There is no record of this poem's publication before its appearance in *Cana-*

dian Born in June 1903. It may have been written in 1900, when Johnson first performed in Halifax. Also known as 'Warden of the North,' Halifax was the last North American city with a British garrison, which departed in 1906.

Lady Icicle

Copy-text: *Flint and Feather.*
   An undated clipping in the Johnson fonds at McMaster University indicates that this poem appeared as 'My Lady Icycle' in an unidentified newspaper, which in turn cites its source as the New York *Independent,* presumably some time before its appearance in *Canadian Born* in June 1903.

Lady Lorgnette

Copy-text: *Flint and Feather.*
   There is no record of this poem's publication before its appearance in *Canadian Born* in June 1903; collected in *GK.*

Prairie Greyhounds

Copy-text: *Flint and Feather.*
   There is no record of this poem's publication before its appearance in *Canadian Born* in June 1903. The first section appeared under the title 'C.P.R. Westbound' in the *O.A.C. [Ontario Agricultural College] Review* 17, no. 8 (May 1905), p. 460.

The Sleeping Giant

Copy-text: *Flint and Feather.*
   There is no record of this poem's publication before its appearance in *Canadian Born* in June 1903.

A Toast

Copy-text: *Flint and Feather.*
   There is no record of this poem's publication before its appearance in *Canadian Born* in June 1903.

Your Mirror Frame

Copy-text: *Flint and Feather.*

There is no record of this poem's publication before its appearance in *Canadian Born* in June 1903.

The Train Dogs

Copy-text: *Flint and Feather.*
    First published in *Rod and Gun,* December 1904; collected in *GK* and *FF.* In March 1908 this poem appeared in *Outing Magazine* (New York), attributed to Owen E. McGillicuddy. This apparent case of plagiarism has since been revealed to have been an elaborate prank; see Betty Keller, *Pauline: A Life of Pauline Johnson* (Vancouver: Douglas and McIntyre, 1981), p. 205.

When George Was King

Copy-text: *Flint and Feather.*
    First published in *Black and White* (London), Christmas Number 1906, p. 15; collected in *GK* and *FF.*

The Cattle Country

Copy-text: *Flint and Feather.*
    First published in the *Canadian Magazine,* January 1907, p. 240, and *Saturday Night,* 26 January 1907, p. 20; reprinted as 'The Foothill Country,' *Saturday Night* 2 May 1908, p. 9; collected in *GK* and *FF.*

The Trail to Lillooet

Copy-text: *Flint and Feather.*
    First published in the *Canadian Magazine,* June 1907, p. 128; collected in *FF.*
    Lillooet, a village in the Fraser canyon in British Columbia, was a stopping place on the route to the Cariboo, where Johnson toured in 1904. The poem was written during her visit to England in 1906.

The Man in Chrysanthemum Land

Copy-text: *Flint and Feather.*
    This poem was composed after the end of the Russo-Japanese War (1904–5), considered especially significant for marking the first major defeat of a European country by an Asian power. However, it does not seem to have been published in full until its inclusion in the 1916 edition of *FF,* with the note 'Written

for "The Spectator."' The first stanza appeared on the front page of the *Calgary Daily News*, 18 June 1907, in an article covering the visit of Prince Fushimi of Japan. A fair copy in the Johnson fonds at McMaster University bears the crossed-out heading: 'For Competition in "Topical" Verse.'

Canada

Copy-text: *Flint and Feather.*
    First published in the *Brantford Daily Expositor,* 22 February 1908; collected in *FF.* This verse won a prize of five pounds from the *Referee,* an English journal, for the best acrostic on Canada.

Autumn's Orchestra

Copy-text: *Flint and Feather.*
    First published in *When George Was King and Other Poems* by E. Pauline Johnson (Brockville: Brockville Times 1908). The copy of this pamphlet in the Johnson Papers at Trent University is inscribed: 'Ev. With love from Paul. Easter 1908.' Printed on the cover is a variant of the first stanza of 'Autumn's Orchestra':

> Foreword
> Know by the thread of Music woven through
> This fragile web of cadences I bring,
> That song is soul, and soul is song, if you
> Re-echo in your hearts – the songs I sing.
>   – E. Pauline Johnson.

The Homing Bee

Copy-text: *Flint and Feather.*
    First published in the *Canadian Magazine,* January 1910, p. 272; collected in *FF.*

The Lost Lagoon

Copy-text: *Flint and Feather.*
    First published in the *Vancouver Daily Province Magazine,* 22 October 1910, p. 6; collected in *FF.*
    Lost Lagoon, a small body of water in Vancouver's Stanley Park, was known as Coal Harbour until renamed by Johnson. The poem opens her story, 'The True

Legend of Deadman's Island,' later collected in *Legends of Vancouver* as 'Deadman's Island.'

La Crosse

Copy-text: *Vancouver Daily Province*, 10 June 1911, p. 10.
    The poem is preceded by a note by Johnson, dated 30 May 1911: 'This is to certify that the Acrostic Poem entitled "La Crosse" I have written exclusively for Mr Bror Florman for his lacrosse tour of 1912. I give to Mr Florman the exclusive rights of the use of the poem.'

The Archers

Copy-text: *Flint and Feather.*
    There is no record of this poem's publication before its appearance in *FF* in 1912.

Brandon

Copy-text: *Flint and Feather.*
    There is no record of this poem's publication before its appearance in *FF* in 1912.

The King's Consort

Copy-text: *Flint and Feather.*
    There is no record of this poem's publication before its appearance in *FF* in 1912; a clipping in the Johnson fonds at McMaster University remains unidentified.

Calgary of the Plains

Copy-text: *Flint and Feather.*
    First published in the *Calgary Herald*, 19 April 1913; collected in the second edition of *FF* in 1916.

The Ballad of Yaada

Copy-text: *Flint and Feather.*
    First published in *Saturday Night*, 23 August 1913, p. 29; collected in the

second edition of *Flint and Feather*. According to the accompanying article in *Saturday Night*, this poem, believed to be Johnson's last completed work, 'was originally intended for a Christmas number of *Saturday Night*, but plans for that publication were altered.' Johnson also recounted the story of Yaada in 'The Grey Archway: A Legend of the Charlotte Islands,' published in *Mother's Magazine* (June 1910) and the *Daily Province Magazine* (January 1911), and included in *Legends of Vancouver*.

Lulu Island, at the mouth of the Fraser River between its North and South Arms, now mostly belongs to the city of Richmond, south of Vancouver. The Capilano River flows into the Burrard Inlet, north of Vancouver.

Song

Copy-text: *Canadian Magazine* 41 (October 1913), p. 548.

Betty Keller (*Pauline* 1981, p. 158) suggests this poem may have been written *c.* 1900–1, during Johnson's relationship with Charles Wuerz.

'And He Said, Fight On'

Copy-text: souvenir program (based on holograph).

First published 20 November 1913 in a souvenir program issued by Musson to accompany their release of the second, more lavish edition of *FF,* and included in the fourth and subsequent editions. It is believed that Johnson wrote this poem shortly after her doctors informed her that her illness would be fatal.

In 'The Revenge' (1878), Tennyson commemorated the valour of Sir Richard Grenville, commander of *The Revenge,* who died in September 1591 while resisting the more powerful Spanish fleet. The tenth stanza of Tennyson's poem concludes: 'And he said, "Fight on! fight on."'

Aftermath

Copy-text: *Canadian Magazine* 42 (December 1913), p. 183.

The dyked landscape of 'Aftermath' and 'Reclaimed Lands' suggests the Bay of Fundy region, where Johnson visited Charles G.D. Roberts in the late 1890s.

Reclaimed Lands

Copy-text: *Canadian Magazine* 42 (January 1914), p. 254.

To Walter McRaye

Copy-text: Walter McRaye, *Town Hall Tonight* (Toronto: Ryerson 1929), p. 62.
McRaye claims that this is 'the last poem written by Pauline Johnson.'

The Ballad of Laloo

Copy-text: Walter McRaye, *Pauline Johnson and Her Friends* (Toronto: Ryerson 1947), 131–32.
According to McRaye, these are the surviving stanzas of a poem that Johnson left unfinished. They correspond to a page of notes in Johnson's hand in the Queen's University Archives, in which the hero is named Leloo. A few more lines about Leloo survive on half a page of rough draft in the Johnson fonds at McMaster University:

and it was known to women & to a ...
that Leloo would wed with Ollienn
And great rejoicings all their kinsmen gave
In honour of The Beauty & The Brave
Dances & feasts & fires a long month through
to pledge sweet Ollienn to young Leloo.

Both Sides

Copy-text: clipping from *N.Y. Life*, Chiefswood scrapbook; in Johnson's hand, dated 1888.
If Johnson was not the author of these anonymous verses, she may have kept them because they refer to a flirtation between a young woman and a youth five years her junior, much like her relationship with Hector Charlesworth, with whom she exchanged verses on the flyleaf of the scrapbook. A description of Johnson by Harriet Converse, which appeared in the *Twentieth Century Review* in 1890, notes that 'her muse has a veiled humor, in such lines as she occasionally offers to various comic papers, including Life of New York.' The scrapbook also contains an undated clipping of the second stanza, titled 'Disillusioned,' identified as 'From *Judge*.' In a handwriting that does not seem to be Johnson's, the word 'fair' has been replaced by 'dark.'

In the Shadows: My Version

Copy-text: undated clipping, Johnson fonds, McMaster University, amended by Johnson.

This is the only poem associated with Johnson to appear under the pseudonym, 'The Pasha,' a title borne by high-ranking Turkish officers. If she was not its author, she was suffiently amused to keep a copy.

Lent

Copy-text: undated clipping, Chiefswood scrapbook.

This is the only poem associated with Johnson to appear under the pseudonym 'Woeful Jack.'

A Turned Down Page

Copy-text: holograph manuscript, Trent University Archives, Pauline Johnson Papers, 89-013, folder 5; verso, dated Brantford, 25 January 1884.

The Johnson papers at Trent University, which originally belonged to Evelyn Johnson, contain an empty envelope with a note in Evelyn's hand: 'Piece of E. P. Johnson's Dress and some original poetry never published, Keep.' Also included in the collection is a sheet of paper with two poems, both in a script that looks more like Evelyn's than Pauline's. 'A Turned Down Page' is written in black pencil; on the verso, in purple pencil appear the following untitled verses. At the very bottom, in black pencil in a hand that could be Pauline's, is the comment 'What about Man!'

> Oh! woman! if by simple will
>   Thy soul has strayed from honour's track
> 'Tis mercy only can beguile
>   By gentle ways the wanderer back.
>
> The stain that on they virtue lies
>   Washed by thy tears may yet decay,
> As clouds that sully morning skies
>   May all be wept in showers away.
>
> Go go – be innocent and live –
>   The tongues of man may wound thee sore;
> But Heaven in pity can forgive,
>   And bids thee 'go, and sin no more.'

Outdoor Pastimes for Women

Copy-text: *Outing Magazine* (New York), Monthly Record, February 1892, p. 77.

This was the first of Johnson's thirteen columns titled 'Outdoor Pastimes for Women' that appeared in *Outing's* 'Monthly Record' supplement in 1892 and 1893. In the first paragraph the parenthetical question marks after 'beauty' and 'refined' are Johnson's.

Page 175: Mrs Grundy, who became a well-known mythical representative of social propriety, first appeared in Tom Morton's play *Speed the Plough* (1798), where a character continually asks, 'What will Mrs Grundy say?'

'la grace' refers to 'the graces,' 'a game played with hoops and slender rods' [OED].

'Tambour work' refers to embroidery done on cloth held tightly in a hooped frame known as a tambour frame.

Page 176: Diana, ancient Roman goddess of the moon, was often depicted as a huntress with bow and arrow.

Johnson's quotation, 'And now abideth these three – skating, tobogganing, and snowshoeing' parodies 1 Corinthians 13: 'And now abideth these three, faith, hope, and charity, and the greatest of these is charity.'

Hiawatha, historical founder of the Iroquois League of Five Nations, is given enchanted moccasins in Henry Wadsworth Longfellow's long narrative poem, *The Song of Hiawatha* (1855).

A Strong Race Opinion: On the Indian Girl in Modern Fiction

Copy-text: *Toronto Sunday Globe*, 22 May 1892, p. 1; this title may have been created by the *Globe* staff, rather than by Johnson.

Page 178: The 'Mic Macs of Gaspé' are now known as the Mi'kmaw, and are the major Native group in Atlantic Canada. The 'Kwaw-Kewlths of British Columbia' are now known as the Kwakiutl or the Kwagulth.

Pages 179–83: The name 'Winona' likely derives from 'Wenona,' a name commonly given by Sioux families to their first-born daughters. In an example apparently unknown to Johnson, Canadian poet Isabella Valancy Crawford (1850–87) wrote a novel, serialized in *The Favorite* (Montreal) in 1873, titled 'Winona: or, the Foster-Sisters.'

Charles Mair (1838–1927), a good friend of Johnson's, published his poetic drama, *Tecumseh*, in 1886. *Ramona* (1884), a popular novel by American author Helen Hunt Jackson (1831–85), called attention to the plight of the displaced Natives of the American Southwest. In 1832, John Richardson (1796–1852) published *Wacousta; or, The Prophecy*, a novel set during the 1763 conflict between the British army, commanded by the fictional Colonel de Haldimar, and the Native resistance led by Pontiac (1720?–69), chief of the Ottawa. *An Algonquin Maiden*, by Graeme Mercer Adam (1839–1912) and Ethelwyn Wetherald (1857–1940), was published in 1886. American writer Bret Harte (1836–1902) published *M'liss: An Idyll of Red Mountain* in 1873. Jessie M. Freeland's story, 'Winona's Tryst,' appeared in *The Week* (Toronto; 6 February 1891, pp. 155–7). *Lalla Rookh* (1817), by Irish Romantic poety Thomas Moore (1779–1852), was a popular volume of pseudo-Oriental poems.

Page 183: Lake Simcoe, originally known as Lac aux Claies, was the site of the Jesuit Mission destroyed by the Iroquois in 1648. At the battle of Cut Knife Creek (2 May 1885), during the Northwest Rebellion, war chief Fine Day successfully led a small group of Cree and Assinboine warriors against three hundred soldiers under Lieutenant-Colonel William Otter.

'Bright Eyes' was Susette La Flesche (1854–1903), Omaha public speaker and Native advocate.

Forty-Five Miles on the Grand

Copy-text: *Brantford Expositor,* Christmas Number, December 1892, p. 17, 20.

Page 185: Johnson's 'Peterboro' refers to a type of all-wooden canoe designed and built in Peterborough, Ontario, for many years a centre of Canadian canoe production.

Page 186: The Tutela, better known as the Tutelo, were a small Siouan tribe which sided with the English during the American Revolution and subsequently merged with the Cayuga on the Six Nations Reserve.

Horatio Hale (1817–96), American anthropologist and linguist who specialized in studying the Iroquois of the Six Nations, was a friend of the Johnson family.

Page 187: Born in Scotland, inventor Alexander Graham Bell (1847–1922) emigrated to Canada in 1870 with his parents. The family settled in Brantford, where Bell regularly visited during the summers. The Bell family homestead at Tutela Heights is now an historic site.

Page 188: Bow Park farm, outside of Brantford, was developed by George Brown (1818–80), Reform (Liberal) political leader and founder of the Toronto *Globe*, as a large-scale cattle-breeding enterprise.

A Red Girl's Reasoning

Copy-text: *The Moccasin Maker.*

First published in the *Dominion Illustrated* (Montreal), February 1893, 19–28; and as 'A Sweet Wild Flower' in the *Evening Star* (Toronto) 18 February 1893.

Page 190: The 'white man's disease,' tuberculosis, killed vast numbers of Native North Americans.

Page 191: M.P. stands for member of Parliament: the local representative elected to the federal parliament in Ottawa, Ontario.

Page 192: The lieutenant-governor is appointed at the provincial level by the governor general, to represent the monarch in government functions.

Page 196: In 1886 Canadian courts denied the legality of marriages contracted according to 'the custom of the country.'

Page 197: The 'most holy marriage known to humanity' refers to the mystic union of the Holy Ghost and the Virgin Mary.

Page 202: The Biblical 'land of Canaan' was the area along the Mediterranean coast, west of the Dead Sea and the Jordan River. Metaphorically the phrase refers to the 'Promised Land' to which the Jewish people were led by Moses, after their escape from Egypt. He was known as the 'Law Giver' because he conveyed to the Jews the Ten Commandments received from their god, Jehovah.

The Iroquois Women of Canada

Copy-text: National Council of Women, *Women of Canada* (1900), pp. 440–2.
   First published the *Halifax Herald* (1 October 1895) and the *Brantford Expositor* (8 October 1895).

Page 203: American historian Francis Parkman (1823–93) wrote many dramatic accounts of the history of New France, which shaped the predominant view of the early history of North America.

   The National Council of Women of Canada, founded in 1893 by Lady Ishbel Gordon, Marchioness of Aberdeen and Temair, was a member of the International Council of Women, established in 1888. A federation of women's organizations, it was Canada's largest women's group. Although many suffragists were members, it did not publicly endorse woman's suffrage until 1910. Officially non-partisan and non-sectarian, the NCWC was also overwhelmingly White in membership in the years before the First World War.

As It Was in the Beginning

Copy-text: *The Moccasin Maker.*
First published in *Saturday Night*, Christmas number, 1899, pp. 15–18. The title is taken from the Anglican creed: 'As it was in the beginning, is now, and ever shall be.'

Page 206: While the term 'Blackrobe' was often applied to Catholic priests, Johnson points out that Father Paul, described in this story as a 'Blackcoat,' is Protestant. St Paul was the author of the major Epistles of the New Testament. Esther, in the Old Testament's Book of Esther, heroically saved the Jews from destruction by the Persians. Laurence's name invokes the great St Lawrence

River (named in honour of the early Roman martyr) which carried the first Europeans into North America.

A Pagan in St Paul's Cathedral

Copy-text: *The Moccasin Maker.*
First published in the London *Daily Express,* 3 August 1906, p. 4, as 'A Pagan in St Paul's ... by Tekahionwake,' with the note: 'The visit of the three Red Indian chiefs to London gives the following article by Tekahionwake, the Iroquois poetess, an additional topical interest.' Chiefs Joe Capilano, Charlie Silpaymitt, and Basil Bonaparte met with Edward VII to explain their grievances.
Page 213: The Saskatchewan river system drains much of western prairie region comprising the provinces of Saskatchewan and Alberta. The Sault Ste Marie rapids are on the St Mary's River, between Lake Huron and Lake Superior.
Page 215: The white dog sacrifice of the Onondaga, which Johnson witnessed as a child on the Six Nations Reserve, appears several times in her writing. See 'We-hro's Sacrifice,' also in this volume.

The Lodge of the Law-makers

Copy-text: London *Daily Express,* 14 August 1906, p. 4.
Page 216: The Parliament Buildings in London, England, are on the north bank of the River Thames. This article appeared during the English suffragettes' militant campaigns spearheaded by the Women's Social and Political Union led by Emmeline Pankhurst, who was also a prominent visitor to Canada in the years before the First World War.

We-hro's Sacrifice

Copy-text: *The Shagganappi.*
First published in *Boys' World* as 'We-eho's Sacrifice,' 19 January 1907, pp. 1, 7.
Page 218: Before Johnson's birth, her father destroyed a wooden idol belonging to the Delaware, a small tribe allied to the Iroquoian Six Nations. See her story 'The Delaware Idol,' *Boys' World,* 1 May 1909, pp. 1–2, reprinted in *The Shagganappi.* The Onondaga were the leading traditionalists of the Six Nations.

Mothers of a Great Red Race

Copy-text: *Mother's Magazine,* January 1908, p. 4, 14.
Page 226: The mothers of Sparta, a city in ancient Greece famous for its mili-

tary strength, were known for their willingness to sacrifice their sons for the good of their city-state.

Mother of the Motherless

Copy-text: *Mother's Magazine*, November 1908, pp. 13, 50.
   Page 228: A drummer is a commercial traveller.

The Legend of the Two Sisters

Copy-text: *Mother's Magazine*, January 1909, pp. 12, 13.
   In the original version of this story, reprinted here, the teller of the first of the many Squamish legends that Johnson was to recount was Líxwelut, known as Mary Agnes Capilano. In the later version published in the *Daily Province Magazine* (16 April 1910) as 'The True Legend of Vancouver's Lions' and collected in *Legends of Vancouver* as 'The Two Sisters,' the story is attributed to her husband, Chief Joe Capilano (Su-á-po-luck).

The Silver Craft of the Mohawks: The Protective Totem

Copy-text: *Boys' World*, 2 April 1910, p. 3.
   This is the first of six articles on Mohawk silver work that Johnson contributed to *Boys' World* in 1910. The four drawings were likely her own illustrations.

From the Child's Viewpoint

Copy-text: *Mother's Magazine*, May 1910, pp. 30–1; June 1910, pp. 60–2.
   Page 240: Max O'Rell was the pseudonym of French writer Paul Blouet (1848–1903), author of amusing books about English-speaking countries.

The Siwash Rock

Copy-text: *Legends of Vancouver.*
   First published in the *Daily Province Magazine*, 16 July 1910, p. 4, as 'A True Legend of Siwash Rock: a Monument to Clean Fatherhood.'
   Page 246: Tillicum is the Chinook word for friend.

The Potlatch

Copy-text: *The Shagganappi.*
   First published in *Boys' World*, 8 October 1910, pp. 1–3.

The potlatch, an important cultural ceremony for the coastal tribes of British Columbia, was banned by the Canadian federal government from 1884 until 1951.

Hoolool of the Totem Poles

Copy-text: *The Shagganappi.*
　　First published in *Mother's Magazine*, February 1911, pp. 12–13, 71.
　　Page 257: The Klondike gold rush occurred in 1897–8, after gold was discovered along the Klondike River, near present-day Dawson in Yukon.
　　This portrayal of avaricious collectors of Native artifacts reflects Johnson's observation of the West coast at the time when Franz Boas and other anthropologists were active, as well as her own family's experiences at Six Nations.

The Shagganappi

Copy-text: *The Shagganappi.*
　　Perhaps because of its length, this story seems not to have been published before its inclusion in *The Shagannappi*, which appeared shortly after Johnson's death.
　　Page 262: The Red River valley in Manitoba is the geographical origin of the Métis, the Mixed-blood people who arose from the encounter of European and French-Canadian men with Native women.
　　Page 267: American poet John Greenleaf Whittier (1807–92), who wrote Johnson an appreciative letter in 1891, published the poem 'The Red River Voyageur' in 1859, from which three verses are quoted.
　　Johnson's fictional governor general, Lord Mortimer, while clearly idealized, draws on her own acquaintance and that of her family with the British viceroys, notably the Marquess of Dufferin (1872–8), the Marquess of Lorne (1878–83), and the Earl of Aberdeen (1893–8). The Métis Lady Bennington recalls Isabella Hardisty, the Mixed-race wife of Donald Smith (Lord Strathcona), principal shareholder of the Hudson's Bay Company and the C.P.R., and also Johnson's occasional patron.

The Stings of Civilization

Copy-text: manuscript, City of Vancouver Archives, Vancouver Museum and Planetarium Association fonds, Add. MSS.336, 547-B-7.
　　Intended for the *Mother's Magazine*, this article is published here for the first time.

Selected Bibliography

Books by Pauline Johnson

The White Wampum. London: John Lane; Toronto: Copp Clark; Boston: Lamson, Wolffe, 1895.

Canadian Born. Toronto: Morang, 1903.

'When George Was King' and Other Poems. Brockville, ON: Brockville Times, 1908.

Legends of Vancouver. Vancouver, privately printed, 1911. Many subsequent editions.

Flint and Feather. Toronto: Musson, 1912. Many subsequent editions.

The Moccasin Maker. Toronto: Briggs, 1913; reprinted 1927. Several subsequent editions.

The Shagganappi. Toronto: Briggs, 1913; reprinted 1927.

For a complete list of Johnson's publications in newspapers and magazines, see the appendix to *Paddling Her Own Canoe.*

Selected Works about Pauline Johnson

Brant, Beth. 'The Good Red Road: Journeys of Homecoming in Native Women's Writing.' *Writing as Witness: Essays and Talk.* Toronto: Women's Press, 1994.

Calbeck, Scott. 'Pauline.' Videotape produced for '"The Canadians,' History Channel, 1999.

Collett, Anne. 'Pauline Tekahionwake Johnson: Her Choice of Form.' *Kunapipi* 19, no. 1 (1997): 59–66.

Crate, Joan. *Pale as Real Ladies: Poems for Pauline Johnson.* Iderton, ON: Brick Books, 1989.

Foster, Mrs W. Garland. *The Mohawk Princess: Being Some Account of the Life of Teka-hionwake (E. Pauline Johnson)*. Vancouver: Lion's Gate Publishing, 1931.

Gerson, Carole. '"The Most Canadian of all Canadian Poets": Pauline Johnson and the Construction of a National Literature.' *Canadian Literature* 158 (Autumn 1998): 90–107.

Johnston, Sheila M.F. *Buckskin and Broadcloth: A Celebration of E. Pauline Johnson – Tekahionwake 1861–1913*. Toronto: Natural Heritage Books, 1997.

Keller, Betty. *Pauline: A Biography of Pauline Johnson*. Vancouver: Douglas & McIntyre, 1981.

Leighton, Mary Elizabeth. '"Performing" Pauline Johnson: Representations of the "Indian Poetess" in the Periodical Press, 1892–95.' *Essays on Canadian Writing* 65 (Fall 1998): 141–64.

Lyon, George W. 'Pauline Johnson: A Reconsideration.' *Studies in Canadian Literature* 15, no. 2 (1990): 136–59.

McRaye, Walter. *Pauline Johnson and Her Friends*. Toronto: Ryerson, 1946.

– 'East and West With Pauline Johnson.' *Town Hall Tonight*. Toronto: Ryerson, 1929.

Rose, Marilyn. 'Pauline Johnson: New World Poet.' *British Journal of Canadian Studies* 12, no. 2 (1997): 298–307.

Ruoff, A. LaVonne Brown. 'Justice for Indians and Women: The Protest Fiction of Alice Callahan and Pauline Johnson.' *World Literature Today* 66, no. 2 (1992): 249–55.

– Introduction. *The Moccasin Maker*, by E. Pauline Johnson. Norman: University of Oklahoma Press, 1998.

Ruffo, Armand Garnet. 'Out of the Silence – The Legacy of E. Pauline Johnson: An Enquiry into the Lost and Found Work of Dawendine – Bernice Loft Winslow' in Christl Verduyn, ed., *Literary Pluralities*. Broadview Press/*Journal of Canadian Studies*, 1998.

Strong-Boag, Veronica. '"A Red Girl's Reasoning": E. Pauline Johnson Con-structs the New Nation.' Veronica Strong-Boag, Sherrill Grace, Avigail Eisen-berg, and Joan Anderson, eds., *Painting the Maple: Essays on Race, Gender, and the Construction of Canada*. Vancouver: UBC Press, 1998.

Strong-Boag, Veronica, and Carole Gerson. *Paddling Her Own Canoe: The Times and Texts of E. Pauline Johnson (Tekahionwake)*. Toronto: University of Toronto Press, 2000.

Van Steen, Marcus. *Pauline Johnson: Her Life and Work*. Toronto: Hodder and Stoughton, 1965.

Willmott, Glenn, 'Paddled by Pauline.' *Canadian Poetry* 46 (2000), 43–68.

Illustration Credits

Index of Titles

Index of First Lines